Challenges for European Management in a Global Context

Challenges for European Management in a Global Context – Experiences from Britain and Germany

Edited by

Mike Geppert, Dirk Matten and Karen Williams

First published 2002 by
PALGRAVE MACMILLAN
Houndmills, Basingstoke, Hampshire RG21 6XS and
175 Fifth Avenue, New York, N. Y. 10010
Companies and representatives throughout the world

PALGRAVE MACMILLAN is the global academic imprint of the Palgrave Macmillan division of St. Martin's Press, LLC and of Palgrave Macmillan Ltd. Macmillan® is a registered trademark in the United States, United Kingdom and other countries. Palgrave is a registered trademark in the European Union and other countries.

ISBN 0–333–98711–X hardback

This book is printed on paper suitable for recycling and made from fully managed and sustained forest sources.

A catalogue record for this book is available from the British Library.

Library of Congress Cataloging-in-Publication Data

Challenges for European management in a global context : experiences from Britain and Germany / Mike Geppert, Dirk Matten, Karen Williams (eds.).
   p. cm.
   Includes bibliogaphical references and index.
   ISBN 0–333–98711–X (cloth)
      1. International business enterprises–Great Britain–Management.
2. International business enterprises–Germany–Management. 3. Corporate culture–Great Britain. 4. Corporate culture–Germany. 5. Globalization.
I. Geppert, Mike. II. Matten, Dirk. III. Williams, Karen.

HD2845 .C43 2002
338.8'8941–dc21   2002072122

10   9   8   7   6   5   4   3   2   1
11   10   09   08   07   06   05   04   03   02

Printed and bound in Great Britain by
Antony Rowe Ltd, Chippenham and Eastbourne

Contents

Preface

The idea for this book came about in spring 2000 when we were about to set up a new comparative research project on multinational companies in Britain and Germany. The WSYS Project, as we called it, is a joint effort between our British research team in Swansea (the editors of this book) and a German research group from Humboldt University in Berlin (Karin Lohr, Florian Becker-Ritterspach, Knut Lange). The project examines the influence of globalization forces, on the one hand, and national business systems, on the other, on the design of work systems. As the project progressed and produced the first results, we invited several colleagues in the field to Swansea in order to exchange ideas and critically discuss the project. The result of these talks was the Research Colloquium Series in the European Business Management School (EBMS), Swansea in early 2001. This proved to be a success and the calibre of the papers given by colleagues was such that we decided that they deserved to be published in a single volume to reflect an important contribution to the current debate in this particular area of research. As the WSYS project went on, we also organized a research conference with the title 'Management of Change in Multinational Companies: Global Challenges and National Effects' in Berlin in November 2001 and we are happy to include two of the papers given there in this volume as well.

We gratefully acknowledge the support of the EBMS at the University of Wales Swansea for supporting the empirical work of the WSYS project as well as for funding the Research Colloquium Series. We owe special thanks to the heads of department, most notably Professor Eberhard Bischoff, for their constant encouragement, support and help in the early stages of the project. Furthermore, we are indebted to the Anglo-German Foundation for the Study of Industrial Society (AGF), represented by Dr Ray Cunningham, for funding the research conference in Berlin in November 2001.

Mike Geppert
Dirk Matten
Karen Williams
Swansea, March 2002

Abbreviations

A level	Advanced Level
APEC	Asia Pacific Economic Cooperation
BA	British Airways
BAES	British Aerospace Systems
BBC	British Broadcasting Corporation
BT	British Telecom
CCAS	Socialist Hotel and Restaurant Workers Union (Belgium)
CCVD	Christian Hotel and Restaurant Workers Union (Belgium)
CEO	Chief Executive Officer
CFDT	French Democratic Confederation of Labour
CSE	Certificate of Secondary Education
DQP	Diversified Quality Production
EEA	European Economic Area
EH&S	Environment, Health and Safety
EIRO	European Industrial Relations Observatory (used in reference)
EU	European Union
FDI	Foreign Direct Investment
FECOHT	(Socialist) Hotel and Restaurant Workers Union (Spain)
FNV	Confederation of Dutch trade unions
GAAP	Generally Accepted Accounting Principles
GATT	General Agreement on Trade and Tariffs
GDP	Gross domestic product
GMB	General Municipal and Boilermakers Union (UK)
HCN	Host Country National
HGPD	Hotel and Restaurant Workers Union (Austria)
HNC	Higher National Certificate
HND	Higher National Diploma
HORE CABOND	Hotel and Restaurant Workers Union (Netherlands)
HQ	Headquarters
HRAF	Hotel and Restaurant Workers Union (Norway)
HRF	Hotel and Restaurant Workers Union (Sweden)

HRM	Human Resource Management
ILO	International Labour Office
IMF	International Monetary Fund
ISO	International Standards Organisation
ITGWU	Irish Transport and General Workers Union (became SIPTU in 1990)
MNC	Multinational Company
NAFTA	North American Free Trade Agreement
NGG	Food, Hotel and Restaurant Workers Union (Germany)
NUM	National Union of Mineworkers
O level	Ordinary Level
ONC	Ordinary National Certificate
OND	Ordinary National Diploma
PCN	Parent Country National
QCPC	Quality Control Process Charts
R&D	Research and Development
RBF	Hotel and Restaurant Workers Union (Denmark)
SIPTU	Services, Industrial, Professional and Technical Union (Ireland)
SME	Small and Medium-sized Enterprise
TGWU	Transport and General Workers Union (UK)
TPM	Total Productivity Maintenance
US	United States
UK	United Kingdom
USDAW	Union of Shop Distributive and Allied Workers (UK)
WB	World Bank
WTO	World Trade Organisation

Contributors

Florian Becker-Ritterspach   Research Assistant, PhD-Fellow
and Lecturer,
Faculty of Management and
Organization,
University of Groningen, Landleven 5,
9700 AV Groningen, The Netherlands

Dr Martin Brussig   Senior Research Fellow,
Zentrum für Sozialforschung
Halle e.V., Martin-Luther-
Universität Halle, Emil-
Abderhalden-Strasse 6,
06108 Halle/Saale, Germany

Professor Hans-Dieter Ganter   Professor of International Management,
Director of Studies European
Tourism Management,
Fachhochschule Heilbronn,
Max-Planck-Straße 39, 74081
Heilbronn, Germany

Dr Mike Geppert   Lecturer in Organizational Behaviour,
European Business Management
School, University of Wales,
Swansea, Singleton Park, Swansea
SA2 8PP, United Kingdom

Lutz Gerlach   Lecturer in Management Studies,
Lehrstuhl für BWL VI – Personal
und Führung, Fakultät für
Wirtschaftswissenschaften,
Technische Universität Chemnitz,
09107 Chemnitz, Germany

Dr Anne-Wil Harzing — Senior Lecturer in International Management, Department of Management, Faculty of Economics & Commerce, Parkville campus, University of Melbourne, Melbourne, Victoria 3010, Australia

Professor Ian M. Taplin — Professor of Sociology, Management and International Studies, Department of Sociology, Box 7808, Wake Forest University, Winston-Salem, NC 27109-7808, USA

Jean J. Boggis — Lecturer in Human Resource Management, European Business Management School, University of Wales, Swansea, Singleton Park, Swansea SA2 8PP, United Kingdom

Knut Lange — Research Assistant, Max-Planck-Institut für Gesellschaftsforschung, Paulstrasse 3, 50676 Köln, Germany

PD Dr Karin Lohr — Reader in Industrial Sociology, Institut für Sozialwissenschaften, Humboldt Universtiät zu Berlin, Universitätsstrasse 3b, 10099 Berlin, Germany

Anna Lorbiecki — Director of MA/MRes in Management Learning, The Department of Management Learning, Lancaster University Management School, Bailrigg, Lancaster LA1 4YX, United Kingdom

Dr Dirk Matten

DAAD Fachlektor,
European Business Management
  School, University of Wales,
  Swansea, Singleton Park, Swansea
  SA2 8PP, United Kingdom

Dr Michael Mayer

Senior Lecturer in Management,
Department of Business and
  Management, University of
  Glasgow, West Quadrangle, Gilbert
  Scott Building, Glasgow G12 8QQ,
  United Kingdom

Professor Jan Paauwe

Professor of Organization Studies,
  Department of Business and
  Organization, Faculty of Economics,
Erasmus University Rotterdam, Burg
  Oudlaan 50, 3062 PA Rotterdam,
  The Netherlands

Dr Tony Royle

Reader in International and Comparative
  Industrial Relations,
Department of Human Resource
  Management, Nottingham Business
  School, The Nottingham Trent
  University, Burton Street,
  Nottingham NG1 4BU,
  United Kingdom

Professor Gert Schmidt

Professor of Industrial and
  Organizational Sociology,
Institut für Soziologie,
Philosophische Fakultät I, Friedrich-
  Alexander-Universität Erlangen-
  Nürnberg, Kochstrasse 4, 91054
  Nürnberg, Germany

Professor Arndt Sorge

Professor of Organization Studies,
Faculty of Management and
Organization, University of
Groningen, PO Box 800, 9700AV
Groningen, The Netherlands

Dr Anne Tempel

Senior Lecturer in Organization
Theory and Management,
Lehrstuhl für Organisationslehre
und Organisationspraxis,
Staatswissenschaftliche Fakultät,
Universität Erfurt, Nordhäuser
Straße 63, 99006 Erfurt, Germany

Professor Peter Walgenbach

Professor of Organization
Theory and Management,
Lehrstuhl für Organisationslehre
und Organisationspraxis,
Staatswissenschaftliche Fakultät,
Universität Erfurt, Nordhäuser
Straße 63, 99006 Erfurt, Germany

Dr Richard Whittington

Reader in Strategy,
Saïd Business School and New
College, University of Oxford,
Oxford OX1 3BN, United Kingdom

Dr Karen Williams

Lecturer in Industrial Relations,
European Business Management
School, University of Wales,
Swansea, Singleton Park, Swansea
SA2 8PP, United Kingdom

Introduction: Challenges for European Management in a Global Context – Introduction, Approaches and Directions of Future Research

Mike Geppert, Dirk Matten and Karen Williams

Research into multinational organizations has been heavily character-ized – if not flawed – by two major and mutually determining elements. Firstly, for a long time there has been a dominant bias on evolutionary concepts (Westney and Zaheer, 2001) and secondly, the North American perspective has been an overwhelming influence on the field. An example of this is the *Oxford Handbook of International Business*, in which nearly all the authors of this state-of-the-art work are based at, or completed the major part of their work in, American business faculties.

Although the work in the field so far is undoubtedly of value, this orientation has naturally resulted in a certain selectiveness, which this book and its contributions seek to counter. In the first place, empirical investigation of multinational corporations, particularly those whose home country is not in North America, provides us with a considerable spectrum of different patterns of internationalization and this book focuses especially on the influence of different nation-specific cultural and institutional contexts on the multinational company (MNC). Secondly, Europe, rather than North America, with its broader variety in terms of distinct national cultures, its different historical legacies and its still fairly distinct intellectual traditions provides an empirical background for research on multinational enterprises, which is still somewhat underresearched. Europe and the European Union, with their recent discontinuities and rapid ongoing changes taking place in the political framework, require a more refined approach or, to use the words of well-known authors on managerial strategies: 'we are no longer in a world where strategy can be a US export industry' only (Whittington et al., 2002: 486). This volume is part of a growing stream of literature investigating the effects of national business systems on MNCs (recent examples include Whitley and Kristensen, 1997; Quack et al., 1999; Morgan et al., 2001b).

This book focuses on the MNC as an organization exposed to two major forces. On the one hand, there are the forces of globalization, which work towards global markets and globally convergent rationales of conducting business. On the other hand, there are specific national backgrounds, which influence organizational processes, structures and actors in distinct ways. This tension has consequences for research in this field and was alluded to by James March in a recent interview (Dobak and Balaton, 2002: 48):

> We should always strive to have a global theory, but we'll never succeed. The tension between idiosyncratic institutional, historical and cultural factors and our desire to have an overall, overarching theory is a good tension.

Rather than seeking to eliminate this tension by veering towards one extreme or the other, the chapters in this volume reflect different aspects, approaches and stages in the process of identifying the complex interplay of converging and diverging forces influencing the multinational corporation.

Research in international management: low- and high-context perspectives

In a recent chapter, John Child has given an overview of the state of the art in international business research (Child, 2000) which is helpful in positioning the research presented in this volume. The various approaches can be characterized according to the criterion of 'their sensitivity to nations or regions as analytically significant contexts' (Child, 2000: 30). Consequently, one can identify research that pays considerable attention to national contexts (so-called 'high-context' perspectives) and those that emphasize universal rationales and are insensitive to specific national contexts ('low-context' perspectives). Low-context perspectives see corporations as structured by their environment, which, in most cases, is dominated by the market. Examples of the latter approach include Chandler and Hikino (1997) and authors such as Bartlett and Ghoshal (1989) among others (see Dunning, 2001 for an overview), who have conceptualized the 'multiunit business enterprise' as the dominating, transnationally homogeneous pattern of organizing. Alongside economic factors, low-context perspectives also stress the role of technology, especially information technology, in the creation of global organizations, which are becoming increasingly homogeneous. Finally, Child identifies the common assumption that all human beings are similar in their needs and motivational structures as a powerful third pillar of these low-context approaches. High-context perspectives, on the other hand, see organizations as institutionally deeply enrooted and socially embedded in their respective national contexts. National cultures and national institutions, therefore, significantly influence organizations. MNCs operating in different national contexts and the massive opening up of the Eastern European and Asian economies have given considerable impetus to these high-context research perspectives.

From the perspective of this volume, the interesting point about Child's analysis is the need to integrate both perspectives when doing research in transnational organizations. Globalization, on the one hand, strengthens the arguments of the low-context perspectives as it leads to an increasing worldwide convergence and standardization of market conditions, technologies, HRM practices and decision-making processes in corporations. On the other hand, globalization also makes the differences in national cultures and institutions even more visible as it brings these, often diverse, contexts closer together. 'The question, therefore, arises as to how and where, within an overall trend toward globalization, national cultures and institutions will continue to shape organizational forms and behavior' (Child, 2000: 54–5).

Globalization is undeniably a vital force shaping organizations in the twenty-first century and, consequently, this book deliberately takes into account low-context perspectives. The trend towards convergence and worldwide standardization of organizational structures and practices is clearly visible. Mayer and Whittington, for example, argue in this book that even in Europe, despite the variety of national differences, the American Chandlerian multiunit business enterprise model is increasingly becoming the standard organizational form for corporations. Similarly, the chapters by Royle and Boggis focus on the pressures of global competition and the globally standardized approaches of MNCs on the European fabric of industrial relations. At the same time, these chapters link both high- and low-context perspectives, as they show the role of national business systems in either amplifying or mitigating these global influences.

Having stressed the necessity of low-context approaches, however, it must be pointed out that these perspectives tend to focus too much on particular structural configurations of MNCs rather than on processes, key actors and their strategic choices (see Geppert et al., in this volume). There is a growing stream of research in international business on the role of the subsidiaries of MNCs, which is, however, still heavily influenced by the idea of transnationals as differentiated networks (Bartlett and Ghoshal, 1989; Nohria and Ghoshal, 1997). More current work on the role of subsidiary initiatives and change management in subsidiaries to develop new markets and product innovation indicates the emergence of a growing independence of subsidiaries from HQ decision-making processes (Birkinshaw and Fry, 1998; Birkinshaw and Hood, 2001). However, from a high-context perspective, the picture looks rather more differentiated. In this volume, the work of Harzing et al. and Becker-Ritterspach et al. indicates that there is a variety in the forms of control and coordination used by the headquarters in different MNCs.

This volume seeks in particular to highlight the relevancy of these high-context perspectives. The major stream of research on which this volume draws is the national business systems approach associated with the names of Whitley (1992), Lane (1992) and Sorge (1995). This approach not only helps to explain the influence of national business systems on the whole multinational group but also the influence of the respective business systems in the host countries on the MNCs' subsidiaries. The chapters by Lorbiecki and Schmidt explore this perspective in our two main countries of concern in this volume, whereas Ganter and Walgenbach offer a comparative analysis of middle managers' roles in both national business systems. Furthermore, Taplin stresses the persistence of national, especially governmental institutions in the globalization process, in contrast to the low-context perspectives, which identify markets and MNCs as the most powerful forces in the global economic framework.

A particular focus within the national business systems approach is the investigation of the effect of the MNC's country of origin on its operations in different national environments. MNCs' strategies are strongly influenced by the cultural and institutional context of their home country, as is evident, for instance, in Japanese MNCs with operations in Europe (Morgan et al., 2001a). Various chapters in this volume shed specific light on these effects, not only for MNCs (for example Geppert et al., Harzing et al. and Tempel), but also for globalizing SMEs (Brussig and Gerlach).

Beyond global universalism and cultural idiosyncrasy: integrative perspectives

In the following section we will ponder some ideas which seek to integrate so-called global effects and national business system influences. Firstly, we refer back to Child's framework and its attempt to bridge the gap between low-context and high-context theories in international management research and assess its usefulness in developing new directions for further research. Secondly, we discuss the idea that organizational arrangements in and between MNCs can be seen as 'transnational social spaces'. These two approaches can be seen as alternatives to the dominant economic and structuralist frameworks in international management research and important steps towards a more interactionist approach to understanding the impact of globalization on established organizational arrangements.

Various arguments expounded in recent critiques of globalization and converging organizational and institutional patterns across societies were historically foreshadowed in earlier research, which questioned the culture-free arguments of contingency theory. More than 20 years ago, Child and Kieser suggested, in their empirically based revision of common contingency approaches, that 'both contingencies and cultural factors are likely to assist in the shaping of organisation structure and roles' (Child and Kieser, 1979: 268). Child's more recent considerations about the implications of globalization for cross-national organizational analysis continue the earlier focus on both technological and economic contingencies and institutional components (Child, 2000: 59–61). However, organizational arrangements of MNCs are not seen as determined by technological contingencies or international and national institutional systems, but as the product of conscious and intentional actions or strategic choices of key managers and dominant coalitions. By underlining the role of key actors in understanding change in MNCs, Child's framework offers not just an attempt to integrate the opposing streams of discourse, but also avoids contextual determinism where either institutional isomorphism or technological and market rationalities are seen as driving forces towards convergence. Managerial choices and environmental constraints are seen as interdependent and point to the need for future cross-national research in intra- and interorganizational relationships, such as authority, interpersonal ties and trust.

The idea of 'transitional social space' takes a similar direction by focusing on social networks in and between multinational enterprises (Morgan, 2001a, 2001b). This research agenda calls for more ethnographically 'thick' studies into the social nature of emerging 'transnational communities' in order to understand the influence of globalization practices in business and management. The idea of transnational social space is also an attempt to break away from the fruitless polarizing debates of 'hyperglobalists', who stress trends towards homogenization of business systems worldwide, and 'sceptics', who stress its continued differentiation. The emergence of transnational communities is discussed in three particular areas of international economic development: the development of MNCs, the development of international regulatory bodies and the development of international cognitive and normative frameworks driven by management education and consultancy (Morgan, 2001a). In relation to MNCs, the approach suggests the need to study the emergence of shared interests and social spaces within and between 'global firms'. Social relationships within social spaces can hardly be seen as congruent, but must instead be understood as differing and fluctuating. Future research in the field must examine how far transnational practices, routines, norms and values from within these spaces differ, are transferable, adaptable or resistant to change. The key question in this approach is: 'how boundaries of these transnational communities are structured, managed, redefined, and negotiated' (Morgan, 2001a: 11).

Thus, future research on globalization, MNCs and distinct national effects needs to move away from the either-or logic of common approaches and focus instead on the degree and scope for strategic choices in MNCs, the particular roles and politics of relevant social actors, and whether and how they actually create new social space across national boundaries.

Comparative management research in Britain and Germany: Is the distinctiveness disappearing?

The majority of the chapters in this volume contribute to a well-established European tradition in cross-national management research, which focuses on a comparison of Britain and Germany. The overall conclusions from these comparisons, no matter what their theoretical angle, is that management and organization practices in British and German companies are distinctive.

Culturalist approaches, such as Hofstede (1994), locate the national differences in management style and organizational arrangements in societal value systems acquired through individual socialization in a particular national context. His research found significant differences between the national cultures in Germany and the UK, especially along the dimensions of uncertainty avoidance and individualism – collectivism. The largest difference was found in the first named dimension, where German managers are seen as less willing or prepared to develop 'tolerance of the unpredictable' (Hofstede, 1994: 110). Strong uncertainty avoidance is reflected in certain organizational and managerial practices such as conflict avoidance, precise instructions and rules, detailed job descriptions and clear subordination rules. Institutionalist comparisons also view the business systems in Britain and Germany as 'polar opposites in all fundamental components' (for example Lane, 1992: 92). It is argued that the higher degree of institutional embeddedness of German firms gives them advantages in terms of capital, human resources, technical know-how and productivity in comparison to their British counterparts. Comparative societal analysis (for example Sorge, 1995) has also shown that differences in both countries' training and education systems provides the opportunity for different strategic choices in terms of market segment and production strategy. Compared to British firms, companies in Germany are seen as much better suited to differentiated quality production (Sorge, 1995: 291–2) due to their organization and qualifications structures and skilled labour. As discussed earlier, even Anglo-German comparisons made by contingency theorists found differences in management style and organizational structure, which were not just the outcome of variations in task environment; a far cry from the arguments of the common culture-free thesis. A recent study explains the strengths and weaknesses of British and German parent company approaches to the management of subsidiaries in both countries in relation to the contrasting structural and cultural environmental characteristics (for example Ebster-Grosz and Pugh, 1996). The work of Ganter and Walgenbach, Geppert et al., Harzing et al. and Tempel in this volume also shows clearly the enduring institutional and cultural distinctiveness of managerial and organizational patterns in British and German companies, even in their MNCs, which are seen by many as the principal driving force behind the globalization process.

However, there are a few cross-national studies, which depart from the well-established distinctiveness thesis. Studies by Lane (2000) and Mueller and Loveridge (1997) question whether national effects, especially those in Germany, will continue to be influential in shaping what are increasingly internationalized business activities. Lane sees the German business system, in particular, as under increasing pressure and discusses local disadvantages that are becoming more visible, such as the difficulties of achieving low-cost production in the 'German high-cost environment', or the transfer abroad of the R&D capacities of German chemical companies because of a less permissive German legal system for sensitive research in biotechnology (Lane, 2000: 205). Research on MNCs in the chemical industry, presented in this volume, also indicates the dissatisfaction of a British MNC with the institutional constraints of German industrial relations, which led to the diversion of FDI to other European countries (Tempel in this volume). In addition, Schmidt's chapter as well as Mayer and Whittington's (in this volume) suggest that the distinct national patterns of the German model are fading. The first author sees evidence of a radical restructuring of the 'German model' in particular industrial sectors, such as the software industry, and the other two authors' study points to a substantial diffusion of the Anglo-Saxon multidivisional diversified organization across national and sector barriers, not just in Britain but also in Germany and France.

Although it is possible to group the research presented in this book into those chapters that show a continuing societal distinctiveness and those pointing to the emergence of more universal organizational arrangements and the decline of distinct business systems in both countries, we want to suggest that future research projects go beyond such a dualistic approach and have discussed some promising approaches towards such a research agenda in the previous section. However, empirical research in German and British subsidiaries carried out by Geppert et al. (in this volume) shows that deliberate change management strategies related to the globalization rationalities do not necessarily lead to an abrupt shift in the social logic of historically entrenched national business systems. New management ideas, prerogatives and actions positing greater convergence are 'in sharp contrast to the lessons learned by the science of industrial organization from the debate which made it clear, Fordism was only one of many possible work systems' (Kristensen, 1997: 4). Future cross-national research, especially if it is undertaken in Britain and Germany, has, therefore, to consider distinct national trajectories and the emergence of new transnational social spaces and that the logic of the different actors involved might lead to tension and conflict rather than global harmonization. In this sense, the relationship between national and global effects is not linear but dialectical, since the appearance of global or transnational rationalities does not automatically eliminate distinct national institutional and cultural patterns.

The contributions in this book

Part I of the book looks at the divergence–convergence dichotomy in cross-national organization in Europe. The chapters examine low-context and high-context perspectives from various conceptual angles and, using a diversity of empirical data and research methods, investigate the impact of the internationalization strategies of MNCs in a variety of national institutional contexts.

Mayer and Whittington trace the proliferation of the diversified multi-divisional corporation model in Europe, providing empirical data to support the convergent effects of globalization. Their research shows the proximity of 'globalization' and 'Americanization', since the diversified multidivisional corporation clearly was, and still is, an American 'export' into post-war Europe. However, their research also unveils considerable differences in the actual adaptation of this American organizational structure in the different countries in Europe, particularly in Britain and Germany. Therefore, they emphasize the necessity of differentiating between the notion of 'convergence vs. divergence' and 'homogeneity vs. diversity'. Using their research dimensions of time, territory and practical depth, they develop the notion of a bounded and adapted approach to cross-national research, leading to the identification of a converging, but at the same time, diverse proliferation of the organizational pattern of the American multidivisional corporation in Europe.

Unlike the preceding chapter, the work of *Geppert, Matten and Williams* focuses specifically on the aspect of divergence and diversity. They look at MNCs in the heavy engineering sector and analyse both their globalization strategies and the actual implementation of these global policies within the work systems of their subsidiaries in Britain and Germany. Although all the MNCs in their sample are exposed to the same global economic and technological constraints, the MNCs' perception of globalization and their strategic approach to it differ substantially. Furthermore, even within the same MNC, a group-wide global change management policy is implemented in strikingly different ways in the two host country subsidiaries. The authors explain these differences by highlighting the crucial role of national business systems in the implementation global change management policies, a role which seems to have even gained in importance within an industrial sector where globalization rationalities are increasingly significant.

The chapter by *Becker-Ritterspach, Lange and Lohr* explores the influence of the control mechanisms used by MNCs on the development of reorganization patterns. Referring to the same empirical database as the chapter of Geppert et al., the authors show that specific forms of control, classified as indirect/direct and personal/impersonal, influence the distribution of resources and the power relations between the key actors involved in the reorganization process. The comparison of the three MNCs clearly illustrates that the dominance of certain control mechanisms increases or decreases authority and resource allocation in the host subsidiaries. High levels of centralized personal control, for example, decreased the local power resources of the subsidiaries, whereas strong impersonal bureaucratic control strategies led to a more prescribed and structured reorganization approach. Another interesting finding is that output control, where it is linked to strong internal competition, undermines optimal cross-unit communication and reduces the organization's slack resources. Last but not least, the authors raise doubts about whether a shared organizational culture throughout the MNC can be deliberately created and controlled, as has been suggested in the debate about the 'transnational'.

The study by *Harzing, Sorge and Paauwe* focuses on the differences in HQ–subsidiary relationships in German and British MNCs and contrasts these findings with data collected in Japan and the USA and in a variety of industrial sectors. Their results make an important, empirically based, contribution to the debate in the globalization literature about convergence versus divergence. The cross-national comparison illustrates clear differences in nearly all aspects of HQ–subsidiary relationships between Britain and Germany, except in the area of control mechanisms. Compared to the German companies, British subsidiaries have a lower level of expatriate presence, lower interdependence with the HQs, higher interdependence with other subsidiaries and a higher local responsiveness. Contrary to one of the key assumptions of the globalization debate, which foresees the decline of national distinctiveness and the emergence of the MNC as a 'global enterprise', the authors describe the MNCs they studied as 'national firms with international operations'.

All the chapters in this section focus on large MNCs. However, in Germany, but also to a lesser degree in other European countries, the most important organizational form in the economy (in terms of employment, turnover and profits), are small and medium-sized enterprises (SMEs). Their internationalization strategies differ significantly from those of large companies. *Brussig and Gerlach* analyse these companies and discuss patterns of internationalization by presenting a typical example for the internationalization trajectories of German SMEs.

One of the areas where Europe differs most substantially from North America or Asia is in the longstanding legacy of their industrial relations systems and, consequently, their human resource management practices. The chapters in **Part II** focus on these aspects and open up a variety of perspectives on diversity as well as homogeneity, which have been induced by globalization pressures in the European context.

The chapter by Tempel is based on research in the chemical and pharmaceutical industry. She compares two British and two German MNCs, in terms of their pay determination and employee representation practices, as part of a larger Anglo-German research project on industrial relations and HRM practices. Her comparison shows that German MNCs, compared to the British, are more strongly influenced by their country of origin institutional context and are, therefore, less transnational in their structures and processes than their British counterparts. However, German MNCs seem to be less keen to play by the rules of its home country system when operating in a business system with weak trade unions and labour laws, preferring to sack employees in Britain rather than at home, where dismissals would cause legal problems and higher costs. She concludes that there is a threat that countries with 'thicker' national institutions such as Germany will be increasingly less attractive to FDI. This was shown in the example of the British MNCs who were shifting investment from Germany to countries 'with less restrictive industrial relations'.

The study by *Ganter and Walgenbach* follows the tradition of cross-national research on Britain and Germany introduced earlier in this chapter. However, the authors take a new angle by focusing their research on managerial jobs and the behaviour of middle managers in three different industrial sectors. The study clearly illustrates that management practices in both countries are still distinct across different sectors, despite globalization and an increasing standardization of management language. Thus, differences in the managerial behaviour of middle managers are explained in terms of their embeddedness in distinct national business systems. The authors' comparison shows that middle managers, who are expected to implement decisions taken by others, develop significant national-specific approaches to this task. Whereas British middle managers are more concerned about motivation and the human problems of their subordinates, their better-qualified German counterparts are more involved in detailed technical decision-making problems.

However, if we take the example of McDonald's as discussed by *Royle*, we see a different picture. Countries with well-established industrial relations systems, such as the Scandinavian countries, Austria and Germany, are included in the multinational's investment policy. The research is based on an ongoing comparative case study about McDonald's and its European labour relations strategies. The focus of this chapter is McDonald's global HRM policy and its labour relations in Europe and it shows clearly that national institutions do still matter. The multinational's non-union policy is related to the system of industrial relations in its country of origin, the USA. Moreover, the chapter discusses different national approaches of trade unionists and works council to McDonald's and differences in McDonald's willingness to recognise trade unions and adhere to collective agreements. Successful arrangements with the MNC cannot just be explained by different levels of union density in each European country, but also by the specific contingencies of the fast-food sector such as age and qualifications of the workforce and the use of franchising.

The contribution of *Boggis* to this book lies in her detailed discussion of industrial relations in the Welsh manufacturing sector. The author discusses globalization policies in the mostly foreign-owned Welsh industry and their influence on established employment relations between local management and workplace union representatives. The detailed case study-based research shows how key components of the British business system, such as training and education as well as the weakness of the industrial relations system and labour law provisions, contrary to the received wisdom, actually endanger the competitiveness of Welsh subsidiaries and make them increasingly vulnerable to closure. Examples are given of where manufacturing has already been transferred to so-called 'low wage countries' in, for example, Eastern Europe. Moreover, local managers use the employees' 'fear of unemployment' to strengthen their own power base and further undermine the influence of trade unions.

This book has a specific focus on the importance of national institutional frameworks for international business activities. **Part III** looks at global challenges to established 'models' of capitalism in Germany and the UK, and examines both how they are currently being shaped and, particularly, how they will be shaped in the future by the ongoing globalization process.

One of the main theses about national institutions, especially in a business context, is that globalization will ultimately result in a substantial weakening and disempowerment of national governments and the institutional fabric which is dependent on governmental functions. *Taplin*, however, presents a political science perspective in favour of the persistent, if not growing, importance of national governments. The chapter skilfully shows the threat globalization poses to the notion of a sovereign state, especially in the areas of financial and capital markets, transnational business activities and technological change. At the same time, the chapter shows the crucial role of governments in providing and maintaining the institutional framework which enables globalization to take place and be successful. This leads to the conclusion that globalization, rather than threatening the state, is dependent on strong states to secure the conditions necessary for well-functioning markets.

However, globalization not only influences MNCs, but also shapes the institutional framework of nation states. *Lorbiecki* argues in her chapter that the notion of 'Britishness', which has been an important concept in much of Britain's cross-national business activity, has been faced with substantial pressures recently. Globalization not only changes the definition and the connotations of what a national character constitutes, but also gives a new bias to the concept of a 'British' company. The notion of what makes a company British has been enriched and at the same time weakened by the considerable influx of multiple cultures into post-war Britain. Its colonial legacy has also been increasingly challenged; companies, whose very name reflects their home country, have found being British an ambivalent, if not a disadvantageous market position in recent years.

Schmidt's chapter offers a concluding commentary to the book and discusses some of its key findings against the background of the impact of MNCs' globalizing strategies on the German welfare state. On the one hand, he shows that the consensus model of German industrial relations has been weakened and that, to some extent, 'the ideology of the market has cleared the market of ideologies' in the new Germany. On the other hand, he refers to empirical research which questions the convergence of the 'German model' towards Anglo-Saxon capitalism. Leading German managers still see the advantages of strong unions and are aware of the pitfalls of giving up the welfare state; they are also loathe to lose the advantages of having one of the lowest rates of industrial action in Europe. The author develops three scenarios for the future development of the 'German model': 'conservative remodelling', 'aggressive remodelling' and 'radical remodelling'.

Conclusion

The aim of this book is not to argue the case for either the low- or high-context perspective in international business research. The various chapters should be read as contributions to the ongoing debate, which seek to integrate and enrich the research in the field by taking a multifaceted approach along the lines of James March's comment (Dobak and Balaton, 2002: 48):

> So whenever people start having global theories we need to say: 'Well, you have to worry about institutions, history.' And whenever people emphasize historical and institutional idiosyncrasies, we need to say: 'Let's make it more general.'

The majority of the chapters in this volume, and indeed the general message of the book, is that national 'idiosyncrasies' continue to be significant for international business. We stress these factors because we think they have so far been neglected in favour of other approaches. Perhaps we are also particularly sensitive to the peculiarities of national institutions for another reason: comparing the institutional fabric in the UK and Germany in the area of our own profession, the differences and, indeed, the idiosyncrasies of the academic world are still remarkably persistent in both countries. Although we are witnessing strong political moves to change the German system, in particular, in line with international (that is, Anglo-American) standards, developments so far seem to confirm much of the research in this volume that: 'the rules of the game are usually longer lived and more deeply entrenched than are the specific policies...which they govern' (Whitley, 1997: 257). Thus, politically enforced measures, such as the introduction of Anglo-Saxonized Master or Bachelor degrees and even the introduction of so-called 'junior professorships' in German universities, have so far not led to radical change in the deeply entrenched social relationships within the rather hierarchical framework of German academic life, despite the enthusiasm of politicians and the apprehensions of their critics. Hence, although globalization rationalities strongly shape the agenda of organizations and governments nowadays, and every sound international research agenda must assume this, the success and thus ultimately the impact of these policies are crucially shaped and influenced by national institutions. This book aims to elucidate exactly this latter aspect of the globalization processes in the world of international business.

References

Bartlett, C. and Ghoshal, S. (1989) *Managing across borders: The transnational solution* (2nd edn), Boston: Harvard Business School Press.

Birkinshaw, J. and Fry, N. (1998) 'Subsidiary to develop new markets', *Sloan Management Review*: pp. 51–61.

Birkinshaw, J. and Hood, N. (2001) 'Unleash innovation in foreign subsidiaries', *Harvard Business Review* (3): pp. 131–7.

Chandler, A. D. and Hikino, T. (1997) 'The large industrial enterprise and the dynamics of modern industrial growth', in Amatori, F., Hikino, T. and Chandler, A. D. (eds), *Big business and the wealth of nations*, Cambridge: Cambridge University Press, pp. 24–57.

Child, J. (2000) 'Theorizing about organizations cross-nationally', in Cheng, J. L. C. and Peterson, R. B. (eds), *Advances in international comparative management, Volume 13*, Stamford, CN: JAI Press, pp. 27–75.

Child, J. and Kieser, A. (1979) 'Organization and managerial roles in British and West German companies: An examination of the culture-free thesis', in Lammers, C. J. and Hickson, D. J. (eds), *Organizations alike and unlike: International and inter-institutional studies in the sociology of organizations*, London: Routledge, pp. 251–71.

Dobak, M. and Balaton, K. (2002) 'Interview with James G. March', *Journal for East European Management Studies*, 1: pp. 47–54.

Dunning, J. H. (2001) 'The key literature on IB activities: 1960–2000', in Rugman, A. M. and Brewer, T. (eds), *The Oxford handbook of international business*, Oxford: Oxford University Press, pp. 36–68.

Ebster-Grosz, D. and Pugh, D. (1996) 'Management problems of Anglo-German business collaboration', *Anglo-German Foundation Report*, London.

Hofstede, G. (1994) *Cultures and organizations. Software of the mind*, London: HarperCollins.

Kristensen, P. H. (1997) 'National systems of governance and managerial prerogatives in the evolution of work systems: England, Germany and Denmark compared', in Whitley, R. and Kristensen, P. H. (eds), *Governance at work: The social regulation of economic relations*, Oxford: Oxford University Press, pp. 3–46.

Lane, C. (1992) 'European business systems: Britain and Germany compared', in Whitley, R. (ed.), *European business systems*, London: Sage, pp. 64–97.

Lane, C. (2000) 'Understanding the globalization strategies of German and British multinational companies', in Maurice, M. and Sorge, A. (eds), *Embedding organizations: Societal analysis of actors, organizations, and socioeconomic content*, Amsterdam/Philadelphia: John Benjamins, pp. 188–208.

Morgan, G. (2001a) 'The multinational firm: Organizing across institutional and national divides', in Morgen, G., Kristensen, P. H. and Whitley, R. (eds), *The multinational firm*, Oxford: Oxford University Press, pp. 1–24.

Morgan, G. (2001b) 'Transnational communities and business systems', *Global Networks*, 1(2): pp. 113–30.

Morgan, G., Kelly, B., Sharpe, D. and Whitley, R. (2001a) 'Multinationals as organisations', *ESRC Transnational Communities Programme Conference.* Warwick.

Morgan, G., Kristensen, P. H. and Whitley, R. (eds) (2001b) *The multinational firm*, Oxford: Oxford University Press.

Mueller, F. and Loveridge, R. (1997) 'Institutional, sectoral, and corporate dynamics in the creation of global supply chains', in Kristensen, P. H. (ed.), *Governance at work*, Oxford: Oxford University Press, pp. 139–57.

Nohria, N. and Ghoshal, S. (1997) *The differentiated network. Organizing multinational corporations for value creation*, San Francisco: Jossey-Bass.

Quack, S., Morgan, G. and Whitley, R. (1999) *National capitalisms, global competition, and economic performance*, Amsterdam/Philadelphia: John Benjamins.

Sorge, A. (1995) 'Cross-national differences in personnel and organization', in Harzing, A.-W. and van Ruysseveldt, J. (eds), *International human resource management. An integrated approach*, London: Sage, pp. 99–123.

Westney, D. E. and Zaheer, S. (2001) 'The multinational enterprise as an organization', in Brewer, T. (ed.), *The Oxford handbook of international business*, Oxford: Oxford University Press, pp. 349–79.

Whitley, R. (ed.) (1992) *European business systems*, London: Sage.

Whitley, R. (1997) 'The social regulation of work systems: Institutions, interest groups, and varieties of work organization in capitalist societies', in Quack, S., Morgan, G. and Whitley, R. (eds), *National capitalisms, global competition, and economic performance*, Amsterdam/Philadelphia: John Benjamins, pp. 227–60.

Whitley, R. and Kristensen, P. H. (eds) (1997) *Governance at work*, Oxford: Oxford University Press.

Whittington, R., Pettigrew, A. and Thomas, H. (2002) 'Conclusion: doing more in strategy research', in Pettigrew, A., Thomas, H. and Whittington, R. (eds), *Handbook of strategy and management*, London: Sage, pp. 475–88.

Part I

Cross-national Organizations in Europe: Between Convergence and Divergence

1

For Boundedness in the Study of Comparative and International Business: The Case of the Diversified Multidivisional Corporation

Michael Mayer and Richard Whittington

Introduction

The fate of national approaches to management in the global economy is contested (Whitley, 1999; Geppert et al. in this volume). As we shall see, the arguments are complex, the stakes high. Nevertheless, the key question may, initially at least, be put quite simply: are previously diverse national forms of business organization and management practice converging on common patterns and processes? For a long line of commentators (Rostow, 1960; Ohmae, 1990, 1995; Yip, 1992; Reich, 1993) the answer is a clear yes. They believe that economic processes will ultimately lead to the erosion of any notable national distinctiveness, a 'wilting away of the idea of a cohesive and sequestered national economy and society' (Amin and Thrift, 1994: 1). For advocates of the convergence thesis there is, ultimately, one best way of organizing, one best way of managing, which firms must adopt if they wish to succeed in the global economy. Such views have been strongly opposed by those who suggest that national cultures and unique societal and institutional structures will continue to support different, yet sustainable, patterns of economic organization and management practice (Whitley, 1994; Zysman, 1994; Hollingsworth and Boyer, 1997; Thomas and Waring, 1999).

The debate, then, remains polarized. This polarization is not restricted to the question of convergence itself but extends to underlying assumptions about the nature of management knowledge. Convergence in managerial practices would justify the universalist aspirations of the positivist tradition, which has shaped much of management theorizing (Camerer, 1984; McKelvey, 1997). Convergence, particularly convergence on an essentially American approach to management, would also help to vindicate at least some of the teleological expectations of American post-war social science (Kerr et al., 1960; Rostow, 1960; Parsons, 1964) which played a central role in the early formation of organization and management theory (for example Chandler, 1962).

In the wake of the postmodern critique (for example Bauman, 1991), such universalist aspirations have been facing growing criticism for some time now (Toulmin, 1990). As already suggested, there are strong arguments for the territorial limits to specific approaches to management and organization (Hollingsworth and Boyer, 1997; Ganter and Walgenbach in this volume); there are equally strong arguments for their temporal precariousness (Locke, 1996). The growing contextualism within contemporary organization theory (Lorbiecki in this volume) is thus questioning the possibility of universal, and hence generalizable, managerial and organizational knowledge.

In this chapter we engage with the twin challenges of convergence and generalization. We will draw upon an unusual combination of existing and new data to provide statistical trends on the evolving corporate practices that are comparable over more than forty years and across the world's leading economies in Europe, Asia and America (Chandler, 1962; Suzuki, 1991; Fligstein, 1990; Whittington and Mayer, 2000). Our empirical focus is on the adoption of the multidivisional organization by large industrial firms not only in the United Kingdom and Germany but also in France. The multidivisional organization is a touchstone of longstanding debates in organization theory and comparative business (Channon, 1973; Williamson, 1975; Dyas and Thanheiser, 1976; Fligstein, 1990; Kogut and Parkinson, 1998). Evidence of its apparent international diffusion up to the early 1970s has been used to support a positivist management science offering valid prescriptions across international borders and over time (Chandler, 1990; Donaldson, 1996), exactly the sort of issues considered here. Given such historical and theoretical associations, the multidivisional organization provides us with an excellent opportunity to examine both processes of convergence and possibilities for generalization.

With France, we include a country whose approach to business organization has been characterized by Albert (1991) as being pulled between the German and UK approaches. Together, these countries provide us with an ideal testing ground for examining managerial responses to global competitive processes. They are linked through numerous economic and institutional relationships, yet remain characterized by significant differences in their institutional structures and managerial practices (Lane, 1995). Consequently, any findings concerning these countries are not only of interest in and of themselves, but can help to illuminate the more fundamental challenges facing comparative studies of business organization.

Our argument unfolds as follows: after setting out the orthodox characterizations of the multidivisional, the territorial contexualizations of the national institutionalists and the temporal qualifications of the international institutionalists, we employ our data to comment on the question of convergence in patterns of corporate organization. We will suggest that the relative success of the multidivisional organization in contemporary Europe licences what we shall call a 'bounded management science'. Such an approach acknowledges the validity of generalizations, but emphasises that typical universalist claims need to be enriched with contextual sensitivity to offer substantial practical help. We then use our own study to illustrate some observations about key methodological issues in comparative research. Specifically, we will suggest that comparative studies can be differentiated along three dimensions: territorial coverage, temporal scope and practical depth. Differences in the coverage of these three dimensions in empirical studies not only determine the 'reach' of any possible generalizations and circumscribe the boundedness of their validity but can lead to different positions with regard to convergence and generalizability.

The multidivisional structure in orthodoxy

In the account of Alfred Chandler (1962), the multidivisional structure originated in such great American corporations as DuPont and General Motors in the 1920s. For these large and increasingly diversified corporations, the advantage of the multidivisional was its separation of strategy from operations. Unlike in the highly centralized functional organization, or in the highly decentralized holding form of organization, it became possible to differentiate strategic and operational control. Corporate strategy – the allocation of resources across the portfolio and the monitoring of their use – could be centralized in the hands of top management and staff at headquarters; responsibility for the operations of the business units could be decentralized to middle managers out in the divisions.

Chandler (1962: 309) was clear about the importance for the multidivisional of this separation of responsibilities: 'The basic reason for its [the multidivisional's] success was simply that it clearly removed the executives responsible for the destiny of the entire enterprise from the more routine operational activities and so gave them the time, the information, and even the psychological commitment for long-term planning and appraisal'.

This distinction between the multidivisional structure and the other key structural types in the Chandlerian tradition is summarised in Figure 1.1. In the functional structure, top managers retain responsibility for key operating functions such as production or marketing, while at the same time trying to exercise strategic control from the centre. The holding structure, on the other hand, does allow a great deal of autonomy to its operating businesses, but exercises relaxed central control over strategy because of its small headquarters functions, partially integrated business units and incomplete ownership of the subsidiaries. Finally there is the functional-holding structure, something of a hybrid. Here, the centre is dominated by the functional directors of its core business, but surrounded by a periphery of smaller subsidiaries that operate on a holding company basis. According to economic theory, each of these structural alternatives suffer from deficiencies by comparison with the multidivisional (Williamson, 1975). The functional structure, although reasonable for small and simple businesses, overwhelms its functional top managers with the complexity of large-scale and diversified operations, at the same time as denying headquarters the clear and comparable performance metrics required

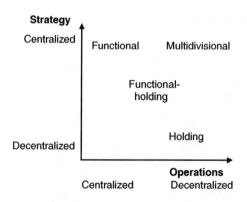

Figure 1.1   The Harvard types of organizational structure.

for effective capital allocation between different business units. In the loosely decentralized holding company structure, operations miss opportunities for corporate synergies, while the centre lacks the power and information to carry out portfolio management and performance appraisal for the corporate whole. The functional holding might be able to run its centralized core business adequately, but tends to neglect its peripheral subsidiaries and is unable to appraise their performance commensurately with the functional core. The multidivisional's trick of centralizing strategy while decentralizing operations gives it an advantage over them all.

From this perspective, it was not surprising that multidivisional structures spread rapidly through American business, driven by increasing scale and widening diversification over the course of the twentieth century. By 1969, 77 per cent of large American industrial firms were multidivisional (Rumelt, 1974); by 1979, the proportion was 84 per cent (Fligstein, 1990). It was also a reasonable expectation that large, diversified corporations in other advanced economies would also adopt this apparently superior form of organization. Up to 1970, however, the evidence for multidivisional adoption in the three major economies of Western Europe was patchy and uneven. According to Harvard researchers Channon (1973) and Dyas and Thanheiser (1976), by 1970 British firms were quite substantially divisionalized, with 74 per cent of the largest industrial firms adopting the multidivisional structure. However, in France, the proportion was only 42 per cent, and in Germany just 40 per cent.

For the Harvard researchers, these figures were enough to predict a continued European movement in the American direction: 'As long as the impetus continues to be given by technological innovation and competition, and as long as there are market-sensitive, profit-oriented managements to provide the catalyst, the divisional, diversified corporation will increase in importance' (Dyas and Thanheiser, 1976: 299). But the evidence up to 1970 does leave room for doubt. The majority of Continental European firms were still resisting the multidivisional long after its discovery in the United States. In the United Kingdom, divisionalization had been achieved in a surge during the 1960s, leaving Channon (1973) to observe that many of the British multidivisionals were still incomplete, particularly in regard to the use of performance-related pay and centralized strategic planning. Until recently, with the evidence available, it has been possible to argue either the case for considerable national barriers to the diffusion of the multidivisional, an argument from territory, or that the early

1970s represented a high point for the multidivisional, which was then most probably followed by a retreat in line with the American decline, an argument from time. It is these two lines of argument to which we now turn.

The multidivisional structure in territory and time

The role of territory: the national institutionalists

The neo-institutionalist tradition has highlighted how organizational forms may be influenced by normative, mimetic or coercive pressures within their immediate organizational fields (Meyer and Rowan, 1977; DiMaggio and Powell, 1983). Several multi-perspective studies of structural choice have tested for these kinds of institutional effects within sectoral fields (Fligstein, 1985; Palmer et al., 1987, 1993). Relatively neglected, as Scott (1995: 148) and Gooderham et al. (1999) point out, is the consideration of different nations as organizational fields. This is an important point, as theorists of national institutions suggest that the specific institutional arrangements of particular countries can shift the balance of advantage between organizational forms, whether for reasons of local economics or local legitimacy (Hamilton and Biggart, 1988; Whitley, 1994; Boissot and Child, 1996; Khanna and Palepu, 1999; Guillén, 1994).

Germany and the United Kingdom, in particular, are often contrasted as near opposites (Lane, 1995; Whitley, 1994). For example, Michel Albert (1991) describes two main capitalist models in Europe. On the one hand, there is the 'Rhenish' capitalism of the Germanic countries, the Netherlands and Scandinavia; this is characterized by consensual and long-term management styles, underpinned by close relationships between companies and their banks. On the other hand, there is the 'Anglo-Saxon' model, of which the United Kingdom was the chief representative on one side of the Atlantic, the United States on the other. Anglo-Saxon capitalism is characterized as highly competitive and financially short term, driven by reliance on external capital markets. Vis-à-vis its two large neighbours, Albert (1991) places France somewhere in between, neither Rhenish nor Anglo-Saxon. By the beginning of the 1990s, however, he feared that international pressures were forcing France to veer in the Anglo-Saxon direction.

These different models of capitalism may have implications for prevailing forms of organization on an international basis. As in business systems theory, institutional differences across nations define the types of economic organization that are feasible and successful in specific contexts (Whitley, 1994). Fligstein (1990: 312) insists that there is no one international standard of organization and that the multidivisional was a specific creation of its institutional birthplace in twentieth-century America. Prima facie, there would be good reason to expect the Anglo-Saxon British economy to be most receptive to the multidivisional (cf. Chandler, 1990). On the other hand, Germany, together with France, is singled out by Fligstein (1990) as particularly unlikely to be amenable to the 'finance conception of control' embodied in the multidivisional. These countries have different kinds of managerial resources available for running their firms. In Germany and France, technical backgrounds and skills are more prevalent among senior managers. In the United Kingdom, accounting and finance skills dominate, both of which are well suited to the remote management style of the multidivisional (Lane, 1995; Whittington and Mayer, 2000). These countries also have different needs with regard to their sources of finance. In Germany, the close and long-term relationships enjoyed by firms with their banks, typically holding significant equity stakes, may provide a familiarity that reduces the need for the type of transparent structures provided by the multidivisional (Cable and Dirrheimer, 1983).

In the United Kingdom, on the other hand, where ownership is highly dispersed and firms depend upon short-term and detached relationships in the capital markets, adoption of the multidivisional structure may be important to attract and reassure their sources of finance. France is a slightly different case. There, firms may favour centralized and integrated structures in response to the pervasive power of the state as owner and customer, thus inhibiting the kind of decentralization embodied in the multidivisional (Zysman, 1994; Whitley, 1994). According to the argument in a business system approach, these institutional differences in prevailing sources of finance, managerial labour markets and market contracts do not simply have a direct effect on firms, but can shift the whole balance of advantage within a particular country. Effectiveness is institutionally constructed on the basis of local conditions, so that what is efficient and legitimate is defined according to the dominant characteristics of the national business system (Whitley, 1994: 155). Whitley (1997: 55) concludes that '...diversified, multidivisional firms are more likely to be developed in Anglo-Saxon economies than in most continental European ones...'. In other words, cultural heritage and enduring institutional differences raise barriers against the even diffusion of the multidivisional across the various economies of Western Europe. France and Germany will resist conver-gence on the Anglo-Saxon model of the United States and the United Kingdom.

The role of time: the international institutionalists

Compared to national institutionalists, the international institutional-ists offer a stronger sense of change by relating national developments to shifting socioeconomic, political and ideological patterns, which characterize the international political economy. From an international institutionalist perspective, even the limited divisionalization achieved in France and Germany by 1970 was a somewhat artificial construc-tion. It was an expression of the spread of the American model of man-agement, grounded not only in the technical efficiency of American business practices but at least as much in the ideological and economic hegemony of the United States (Guillén, 1994). According to Djelic (1998: 273), the American Marshall Plan had introduced new models of management to Europe in advance of the conditions in which they would, theoretically, be appropriate: '...a large-scale process of struc-tural transformation had already been in progress in the 1950s in Western Europe, well before the economic and technological environ-ment had started to change in that part of the world'.

In the post-war period, the influence of American organizational models on the transformation of European industry was initially closely linked to the 'European Recovery Programme', or 'Marshall Plan', which not only involved the transfer of financial aid but also extensive tech-nical advice. For Djelic (1998: 114), the ultimate objective of the Marshall planners was to bring about a radical structural transformation of European economies and industries and to redefine trade patterns on the old continent using the American economic space as the model of reference'. By the 1960s, the main channel of American influence had switched from Marshall planners to the leading consulting firms. Of these, McKinsey appeared to be the arch divisionalizer. Its client list included Shell, ICI, Dunlop, Pechiney, Rhône-Poulenc, Air France, Volkswagen, Deutsche Bank and BASF (McKenna, 1997). By 1970, McKinsey had introduced the multidivisional structure to no less than 22 of the top 100 industrial corporations in the United Kindgom; in Germany, the figure was at least 12 (Channon, 1973; Dyas and Thanheiser, 1976). McKenna (1997: 228) quotes the German academic Fiedler-Winter on the trend towards multidivisionalization: 'the main driving force in Germany, as elsewhere, has been provided by the American consultants McKinsey'.

However, for the international institutionalists, the hegemony of the American model of management in Europe was short-lived. Djelic (1998: 271) observes that: '... the fate of the peculiar American system of industrial production was closely linked, throughout the twentieth century, to the fate of the USA as a country'. Political, economic and, above all, managerial influence peaked in the 1960s. European post-war recovery and Japanese success in industrial markets combined to dislodge the pre-eminence of the American model. The decline of American prestige is captured in the proportion of articles published on Japan in the American general management journal, the *California Management Review*. Between 1978 and 1982, there was only 1 article on Japanese management; in 1982–83 there were 3; in 1983–84 there were 8; by 1984–85, 18 out of the total 45 published articles were on Japan (Locke, 1996: 172). By the 1980s, the world had seen what Locke (1996) calls 'the collapse of the American mystique'.

To summarize: national institutionalists are sceptical of the multidivisonal's relevance to Continental Europe, whilst international institutionalists doubt its staying power with the decline of American prestige. We can map these two sets of expectations along the lines of Figure 1.2.

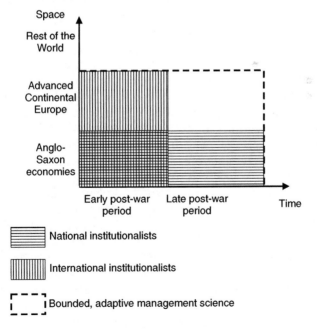

Figure 1.2 Contrasting scopes for corporate generalization.

The expectations of the national institutionalists are represented by the long, narrow area marked by diagonal lines: the multidivisional would be limited to advanced Anglo-Saxon economies, such as the United Kingdom, although it would endure throughout the whole post-war period, even after America's relative decline. The expectations of the international institutionalists are almost the opposite: pushed by hegemonic agencies such as the Marshall Plan and McKinsey & Co, the multidivisional would spread across the whole Western European space in which the Americans held sway. As indicated by the area in vertical lines, however, this adhesion to the multidivisional idea would be short-lived, ending sometime in the 1970s. The dotted lines anticipate our findings: the success of the multidivisional suggests more robust patterns of corporate convergence.

Studying the multidivisional

Our empirical material draws upon a larger study of strategy, structure, ownership and top management of large industrial corporations in France, Germany and the United Kingdom in the post-war period (Mayer and Whittington, 1999; Whittington and Mayer, 2000). Here we extend the original Harvard studies of corporate strategy and structure in Britain, France and Germany between 1950 and 1970 (Channon, 1973; Dyas and Thanheiser, 1976) to the early 1990s. In this chapter, we shall just focus on corporate structure and look primarily at the decentralization and control of business units within these large corporations.

Consistency with the Harvard studies is a central principle of our research. By extending the Harvard studies to 1993, we stretch the static or short-term perspectives of many comparative studies (Hollingsworth and Boyer, 1997: 35) to a period of more than four decades. By using the same measures as the Harvard studies, we achieve comparability not only between the three European countries but also between Europe and the United States, where Rumelt (1974) and Markides (1995) have carried out equivalent studies. The Harvard concepts have been widely used internationally (Suzuki, 1980; Cable and Dirrheimer, 1983; Capon et al., 1987; Armstrong et al., 1998) and their data is frequently cited in institutionalist commentary on European business (Gospel, 1992; Guillén, 1994; Lane, 1995; Jong, 1997; Djelic, 1998). The Harvard measures have also been used by both American institutionalists to counter economistic accounts (for example Fligstein, 1990), as well as by contingency theorists such as Donaldson (1996) who argue for universalism. Moreover, the strategic and structural variables central to the Harvard approach have been seen as critical to both the success of individual firms (Rumelt, 1974; Armour and Teece, 1978) and the economic performance of whole nations (Servan-Schreiber, 1969; Chandler, 1990; Lazonick, 1991; Guillén, 1994). Thus Harvard gives us a robust, significant and comparable measure of corporate change over four countries and during, more or less, the whole post-war period.

We also focus on the same populations as the original Harvard studies – the top 100 industrial firms in each country. Large firms are dominant actors in advanced economies, with the top 100 industrial firms accounting directly for between 35 and 40 per cent of net industrial output in France, Germany and the UK (Hannah, 1995). More broadly, large firms are seen as drivers of technological advance (Chandler and Hikino, 1997) and 'key carriers of modernity' (Clark and Mueller, 1996: 25). Due to our interest in national institutional effects, we shall focus in each country on just the domestically owned top 100 industrial firms (by sales), as did the original Harvard European studies (Channon, 1973; Dyas and Thanheiser, 1976). Our sources are the annual lists published in the *Times 1000, L'Expansion* and the *Schmacke Directory*. In line with Harvard, we have compared countries at ten-yearly intervals and included non-public companies. In Britain, there were 75 domestically owned firms in the 1983 Top 100 and 67 in 1993, reflecting the increasing internationalization of British industry over this period (Channon, 1973, had 84 British-owned firms in 1970). The number of French domestically owned top 100 firms in 1983 was 74 and 66 in 1993. In Germany, there were 60 domestically owned firms in 1983, and 63 in 1993. The overlap between the lists of the top 100 domestically owned industrials for 1970 and 1993 were 43 per cent in France, 45 per cent in Britain and 51 per cent in Germany.

All firms were classified according to the four structural categories used in the Harvard studies and in many other studies since: functional, functional-holding, holding and divisional (for example Fligstein, 1990; Armstrong et al., 1998). The categories focus on formal corporate structure, especially the control of operating and strategic activities. Indicators include organizational charts, director responsibilities, accounting procedures, the legal status of the units and levels of shareholding. Data sources included annual reports, published case studies, press articles, business histories and interviews. These interviews were generally tape-recorded and covered both strategy and structure with senior managers (including chief executives, but, more typically, directors of finance, planning or personnel or their direct reports). In France, managers in 28 firms were interviewed; in Germany and the UK, 25 each, equivalent proportions to the original Harvard studies. We believe that interviewing in just a subset of firms did not introduce significant biases into the classification (Channon, 1973, changed one of his diversification classifications and none of his organizational classifications after interviewing), and certainly increased our understanding of strategic and structural categories in practice. We will return to this point later in our discussion.

While formal structure and informal structure may sometimes become semi-detached (Meyer and Rowan, 1977), these structural indicators do set significant limits on what can and cannot be done within firms (Williamson, 1975). We can review the meaning of the structural categories and the limits associated with each of them by introducing some typical examples from amongst our sample. Firstly, the 'functional' firm is centralised around key operating functions, such as manufacturing and marketing, and, therefore, has limited capacity to decentralize profit responsibility. By 1993, there were very few functional companies, but an example is the undiversified Dairy Crest, where distribution and dairy management functions were represented on the main board. The 'functional-holding' is a company with a functionally centralized core and a substantial periphery of free-standing businesses: Suedzucker's sugar business was centralized, for instance, while its cream, frozen foods, milling, baking and agricultural activities operated through its subsidiaries. This hybrid form, with profit accountability mainly at the fringes, is unable to allocate capital and monitor its usage consistently across its portfolio. The 'holding' is highly decentralized, lacking administrative control over its activities. Legal and managerial restrictions prevent the centre from maximizing the profitability of the corporate whole. Thus, Financière Agache was legally constrained by its many minority stakeholders and quoted subsidiaries and managerially confused by its overlapping businesses. The 'multidivisional' combines decentralization of operations into clear divisions with centralized HQ control over strategy and investment, which are enforced through majority ownership and systematic accounting. Here, the centre can monitor operating profits and reallocate resources across the portfolio according to consistent criteria. We followed the Harvard researchers in interpreting the multidivisional more broadly than the ideal type found in Williamson (1975) and Channon (1973).

We classified structures by using two researchers as independent judges, with a third helping to resolve disagreements. The level of initial agreement was 97.3 per cent. This high level of agreement is attributable to the prevalence of multidivisional firms and, amongst holding companies, the very clear evidence of incomplete administrative control in the substantial asset values of their minority shareholdings. The shift from a holding to a divisional structure would typically require large expenditures on equity, boardroom change, alterations in legal status and consolidation of subsidiary companies.

Mapping the multidivisional in post-war Europe

The original Harvard studies left the European multidivisional structure in a somewhat precarious, niche position at the beginning of the 1970s. The multidivisional was still in a clear minority in France and Germany; only in Britain had it achieved equal numbers to the United States, and even this had been achieved in a great rush over a single decade, leaving doubts about its substance in practice. In our research, we are now in a position to check how the multidivisional has fared since the collapse of the American mystique and beyond the borders of Anglo-Saxon rationality.

As Figure 1.3 indicates, the multidivisional has done rather well. Our measures of strategy also indicate parallel movements towards similar levels of diversification over the same period, although French companies are marginally the least diversified on average (Mayer and Whittington, 1999). There is little evidence here for substantial national barriers to the diffusion of the multidivisional. There are, of course, differences, with British firms being the most divisionalised at

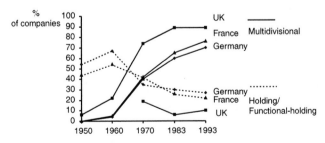

Multidivisional: centralized strategically, decentralized operationally
Holding: lacks central strategic control; Functional-holding: hybrid

Figure 1.3 Organisational structure in post-war France, Germany and the United Kingdom.
Sources: 1950–70, Dyas and Thanheiser (1976) and Channon (1973) (no separate holding figures available for UK before 1970); 1983–93, Mayer and Whittington (1999).

89 per cent by the 1990s. But by 1993, even France and Germany were at or approaching the three-quarters level of divisionalization that American business reached in 1969 (Rumelt, 1974). The progress of the Continental countries towards the Anglo-Saxon organizational model may have been slow, but it has been sure: in each decade, divisionalization has increased markedly. Striking too is the universal collapse of the centralized functional organization, even in statist France. French big business transformed itself from over half of companies being functionally organized in 1950, to just two per cent in 1993. France, Germany and the UK now all follow the Harvard model discovered by Chandler (1962) and Rumelt (1974) in the United States of two or three decades ago.

The multidivisional is not just successful in terms of penetration; it also appears to be the most robust form of organization. Table 1.1 compares the proportions of firms that have retained the same structure over the two time periods, 1970 to 1983, 1983 to 1993, while remaining within their national top 100 firms. As can be seen, the multidivisional structure is clearly the most stable structure over time in all three countries and in both time periods. Over the two

Table 1.1   Structural stability of domestic top 100 survivors

	Functional	**Functional-holding**	**Divisional**	**Holding**
France				
% same structure, 1970–83	0	11.1	31.4	16.7
% same structure, 1983–93	25.0	33.3	56.9	15.4
Germany				
% same structure, 1970–83	9.5	40.0	64.5	45.5
% same structure, 1983–93	33.3	28.6	79.4	66.7
United Kingdom				
% same structure, 1970–83	14.3	0	65.6	0
% same structure, 1983–93	33.3	0	62.7	25.0

Source: 1970 Classifications based upon Channon (1973) and Dyas and Thanheiser (1976).

time periods and three countries, only two companies switched back to a functional structure, notwithstanding many strategic shifts to more narrowly focused strategies, and only 15 multidivisionals dissolved into holding forms of organization (for further analysis see Whittington and Mayer, 2000). Returning to Table 1.1, it is striking that the multidivisional's structural stability actually increased over time in both France and Germany, even in a period when American influence was in decline. The fate of the multidivisional in Europe does not seem to be dependent upon American power and has, in this sense, a wider temporal significance. Large corporations in Western Europe appear to be converging on the common model of the multi-divisional firm.

Generalization and the mapping of comparative research

In our introduction, we saw the fate of the multidivisional organization as a test case for the possibility of generalization in manage-ment and organization theory. The success of the multidivisional suggests that we can be optimistic. Generalizations across time and countries, such as those by Chandler (1990) and Donaldson (1996), are possible – within limits. Some ideas will have greater geograph-ical scope, some greater temporal scope, but they will generally have sufficient legs to make it worthwhile mapping how far they go. Nevertheless, spatial and temporal limitations must be taken seriously. Our data only relates to a particular combination of time and space – albeit, an economically diverse and important region and a period of more than forty years. We must, therefore, map the boundaries of relevance and convergence quite tentatively. We take a position close to Mouzelis (1995) for the social sciences in general and seek a sphere for bounded and provisional generalization. Such a bounded management science would set out limits for the multidivisional within the sphere indicated by the dotted lines in Figure 1.2. This encompasses both the longer time period allowed by the national institutionalists and the wider relevance claimed by the international institutionalists. We mark out this sphere in dotted lines to acknowledge the possibility of a wider and longer term relevance for which, at this point, we still lack the evidence.

By acknowledging the time dependence of our findings, we are making a further conceptual point. The notions of convergence and generalizability can be separated from the teleological heritage of American post-war social science. We need not imagine some specific point in time at which countries will have converged on common organizational models. Rather, national or local business practices will pass through periods of greater convergence or divergence as managerial models disseminate internationally and new organizational innovations emerge out of local practices. Convergence, then, is a dynamic and time-dependent construct. Consequently, we must distinguish between the notions of convergence and divergence and the more temporally specific constructs of homogeneity and diversity. Diversity at a given point in time, therefore, does not necessarily deny the existence of convergence. Indeed, as can be seen in Figure 1.3, at any given point in time the levels of multidivisionalization in the three countries may be similar, but they are not identical. Countries can both exhibit diversity in their patterns of management and business organization *and* follow convergent trends. Alongside such simultaneity of convergence and diversity, the findings from our study suggest that convergence will only become 'visible' if a longitudinal perspective is adopted. To draw on an everyday image: at any given point in time it would be difficult to judge if the glass of water (read: convergence) is half full or half empty. Only by following changes over time are we able to demonstrate that the glass is becoming fuller.

Having mapped our findings along the dimensions of territory and time, we can now introduce Figure 1.4 which adds the third of the dimensions set out in the introduction: practical depth. This dimension relates to the lived, everyday reality of managerial practice

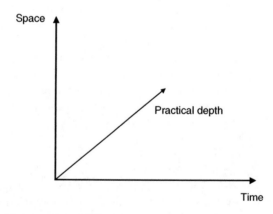

Figure 1.4 Mapping the empirical scope of comparative research.

(Whittington, 2002). It captures the way abstract managerial principles are expressed in concrete local situations and contexts and the ways in which they are modified, transformed, or even negated. Research method becomes important here (note the methodological comments by Becker-Rittersbach et al. in this volume). As described earlier, the present study centres on the classification of companies into the various categories of organizational structure. In each case, a firm is assigned to its respective category following an assessment of the fit between company characteristics (for example the proportion of assets associated with joint ventures) and the essential characteristics of the respective organizational forms (for example the ability to exert systematic control in a multidivisional organization). Through this procedure, we are effectively abstracting from the concrete expressions of the multidivisional form by extracting a set of common principles from a variety of locally 'lived' managerial practices. To use the terminology of Lyotard (1984), we are extracting the savoir from the savoir-faire. The classification process, therefore, can be seen as a reversal of the process of translation (Czarniawska, 1997) and contextualization, which managers effect in their daily work practices when they draw consciously or subconsciously on existing models of management and organization.

This approach has the advantage of yielding constructs and measures, which are comparable, both over time and across countries. It enables us to track the spread of specific managerial and organizational models and ideas. At the same time, however, this approach sidelines variations within each of the various categories. In the first instance, this extends to variations between individual firms, even in the same country, such as the German multidivisionals, Siemens and Bertelsmann (Whittington and Mayer, 2000). More importantly for our present concerns is the fact that the categorizations are less sensitive to changes in the way particular forms are enacted over time, as well as to possible systematic differences in the way particular managerial models are played out in different countries. The changes in the way a particular form becomes realized can be readily seen in the ways in which individual firms change their corporate organization over time, whilst retaining the key characteristics of the multidivisional. One only need consider here the various transformations of long-established multidivisional concerns such as Siemens in Germany and Unilever in the United Kingdom (Whittington and Mayer, 2000): the essential organizing principles of the multidivisional firm have remained intact over time, but have been assembled in different ways in line with changing business environments and technological possibilities (Whittington and Mayer, 1997, 2000).

Just as the expression of particular organizational forms changes over time, so too may their implementation differ from country to country. Evidence from our interviews suggests, for instance, that UK companies were often more consistent in the way the multidivisional principles were implemented throughout the organization. German and French managers, in contrast, highlighted more frequently the cases where local practices or arrangements lead to greater variation (Whittington and Mayer, 2000: 178). As can be visualized by comparing Figure 1.2 with Figure 1.4, generalizations across time and territory based on abstract principles and ideas, but not capturing the realities of lived practice, remain flat. Put differently, a manager competent in one multidivisional is not necessarily equally competent in another, just because they share the same structure. Nevertheless, although UK and German multidivisionals may be different in many ways from each other and from American multidivisionals of the 1960s, they do share important common organizing principles. Managerial behaviour and organizational realities can only be fully understood if we capture both the locally specific characteristics and those which are stable across countries and over time. We not only can track abstract principles and ideas, we must. Generalizations, therefore, can be of practical value under two conditions: firstly, that managers and researchers should be aware of their real temporal and spatial boundaries and secondly, that managers, particularly those seeking to transfer practices across borders, also need to have the institutional and cultural understanding that allows them to apply abstract principles with contextual sensitivity.

For the conduct of research itself, one can conclude that a research strategy such as the one reported here provides a good means of capturing the spread of ideas and models of management over time and across territory but are less sensitive to nuance and variance. The converse is true for the more 'fine grained' studies. This may further help to explain some of the polarization in the debates about the fate of distinct national approaches to business and management, which we highlighted at the beginning of this chapter. Studies focusing on abstract organizational models and managerial ideas, such as the multidivisional organization, will be more likely to capture aspects of managerial practice that suggest convergence, whereas studies focusing on more concrete or micro-level phenomena will be more sensitive to variation and diversity. We need both perspectives in order to develop a rounded picture of the complexity and possible simultaneity of convergence and divergence, of homogeneity and diversity.

Concluding comments

As reflected in various contributions to this volume (for example Becker-Rittersbach et al. and Geppert et al.), the notion of convergence is central to any debate about the relationship between processes of globalization and the development of national approaches to business and management. Processes of convergence are not only significant as empirical phenomena but also for what they can tell us about the possibility of generalizable managerial and organizational knowledge. Unfortunately, much of the debate has remained polarized, with the universalist and contextualist traditions remaining largely unconnected alongside each other. We suggest that this opposition is a false one. Just as managers combine global best practice with local procedures, just as they translate abstract principles into locally lived practice, research needs to transcend the tensions between universalist positivism and contextual relativism that still divides the field.

The notion of bounded and adaptive generalization mapped along the dimensions of time, territory and practical depth can be of help here, both in conceptual and practical terms. The programmatic implications of our findings are twofold. Firstly, the quest for generalizable managerial knowledge should not be abandoned. Rather, the provisional boundaries of possible generalizations should be explicated and explored. Generalized principles should be related carefully and systematically to a contextual understanding of business practice. Secondly, comparative research needs to develop an agenda which allows research findings to be related systematically to each other. Only in this way can we develop a rounded and cohesive articulation of the generalizable *and* the locally specific. Given the wealth of studies that are now appearing, as demonstrated in this volume, there is an opportunity to map, and ultimately combine and synthesize, what we know about the relationship between the global competitive context and national business practice. In any case, we are hopeful that research is moving towards a phase in which a more systematic and balanced understanding of the fate of national approaches to business and management in the global economy can be developed.

References

Albert, M. (1991) *Capitalisme contre capitalisme*, Paris: Le Seuil.

Amin, A. and Thrift, N. (1994) 'In the Global' in Amin, A. and Thrift, N. (eds) *Globalization, Institutions and Regional Development*, Oxford: Oxford University Press, pp. 1–22.

Armour, H. O. and Teece, D. J. (1978) 'Organizational Structure and Economic Performance: A Test of the Multidivisional Hypothesis', *Bell Journal of Economics*, 9, pp. 106–22.

Armstrong, P., Marginson, P., Edwards, P. and Purcell, J. (1998) 'Divisionalization in the UK: Diversity, Size and the Devolution of Bargaining', *Organization Studies*, 19/1, pp. 1–22.

Barley, S. and Kunda, G. (1992) 'Design and Devotion: Surges of Rational and Normative Ideologies of Control in Managerial Discourse', *Administrative Science Quarterly*, 37/3, p. 363.

Bauman, Z. (1991) *Modernity and Ambivalence*, Cambridge: Polity Press.

Boissot, M. and Child, J. (1996) 'From Fiefs to Clans and Network Capitalism: Explaining China's Emerging Economic Order', *Administrative Science Quarterly*, 41, pp. 600–29.

Cable, J. and Dirrheimer, M. J. (1983) 'Hierarchies and Markets: an Empirical Test of the Multidivisional Hypothesis in West Germany', *International Journal of Industrial Organization*, 1, pp. 43–62.

Camerer, C. (1984) 'Redirecting Research in Business Policy and Strategy', *Strategic Management Journal*, 6, pp. 1–16.

Capon, N., Christodolou, C. and Hubert, J. F. (1987) 'A Comparative Analysis of the Strategy and Structure of United States and Australian Corporations', *Journal of International Business Studies*, 18, pp. 51–74.

Cassis, Y. (1997) *Big Business: the European Experience in the Twentieth Century*, Oxford: Oxford University Press.

Chandler, A. D. (1962) *Strategy and Structure: Chapters in the History of the American Industrial Enterprise*, Cambridge, MA: The MIT Press.

Chandler, A. D. (1990) *Scale and Scope: the Dynamics of Industrial Capitalism*, Cambridge, MA: Harvard University Press.

Chandler, A. D. and Hikino, T. (1997) 'The Large Industrial Enterprise and the Dynamics of Modern Industrial Growth' in Amatori F., Hikino, T. and Chandler, A. D. (eds), *Big Business and the Wealth of Nations*, Cambridge: Cambridge University Press, pp. 24–57.

Channon, D. (1973) *The Strategy and Structure of British Enterprise*, Cambridge, MA: Harvard University Press.

Clark, P. and Mueller, F. (1996) 'Organizations and Nations: From Universalism to Institutionalism', *British Journal of Management*, 7/2, 125–40.

Czarniawska, B. (1997) 'Learning Organizing in a Changing Institutional Order', *Management Learning*, 28/4, pp. 475–95.

DiMaggio, P. and Powell, W. (1983) 'The Iron Cage Revisited: Institutional Isomorphism and Collective Rationality in Organizational Fields', *American Sociological Review*, 59, pp. 547–70.

Djelic, M.-L. (1998) *Exporting the American Model: the Postwar Tranformation of European Business*, Oxford: Oxford University Press.

Donaldson, L. (1996) *For Postitivist Organization Theory*, London: Sage.

Dyas, G. P. and Thanheiser, H. T. (1976) *The Emerging European Enterprise*, London: Macmillan.

Fligstein, N. (1985) 'The Spread of the Multidivisional Form Among Large Firms', *American Sociological Review*, 52, pp. 44–58.

Fligstein, N. (1990) *The Transformation of Corporate Control*, Cambridge, MA: Harvard University Press.

Gooderham, P. N., Nordhaug, O. and Ringdal, K. (1999) 'Institutional and Rational Determinants of Organizational Practices: Human Resource Management in European Firms', *Administrative Science Quarterly*, 44, pp. 507–31.

Gospel, H. F. (1992) *Markets, Firms and Management of Labour in Modern Britain*, Cambridge: Cambridge University Press.

Guillén, M. F. (1994) *Models of Management: Work, Authority and Organization in a Comparative Perspective*, Chicago: University of Chicago Press.

Hamilton, G. C. and Biggart, N. W. (1988) 'Market, Cultures and Authority: A Comparative Analysis of Management and Organisation in the Far East', *American Journal of Sociology*, 94, supplement, pp. 52–94.

Hannah, L. (1995) 'The Joint Stock Company, Concentration and the State: 1894–1994' in Allan, A. (ed.) *Proceedings of the Annual Conference*, London: Business Archives Council.

Hollingsworth, J. R. and Boyer, R. (1997) 'The Coordination of Economic Actors and Social Systems of Production' in Hollingsworth, J. R. and Boyer, R. (eds) *Contemporary Capitalism: the Embeddedness of Institutions*, London: Cambridge University Press, pp. 1–54.

Jong, H. W. de (1997) 'The Corporate Triangle: the Structure and Performance of Corporate Systems in a Global Economy, in Lazonik, W. (ed.) *The Corporate Triangle: the Structure and Performance of Corporate Systems in a Global Economy*, Oxford: Blackwell, pp. 34–61.

Kerr, C., Dunlop, J. T., Harbison, F. H. and Myers, C. A. (1960) *Industrialization and Industrial Man*, Boston, MA: Harvard University Press.

Khanna, T. and Palepu, K. (1999) 'Policy Shocks, Market Intermediaries and Corporate Strategy: the Evolution of Business Groups in Chile and India', *Journal of Economics and Management Strategy*, 8, pp. 271–310.

Kipping, M. (1999) 'American Management Consulting Companies in Western Europe, 1920 to 1990s: Products, Reputation and Relationships', *Business History Review*, 73, pp. 190–220.

Kogut, B. and Parkinson, D. (1998) 'Adoption of the Multidivisional Structure: Analyzing History from the Start', *Industrial and Corporate Change*, 7/2, pp. 249–73.

Lane, C. (1995) *Industry and Society in Europe: Stability and Change in Britain, Germany and France*, Aldershot: Edward Elgar.

Lazonick, W. (1991) *Business Organisation and the Myth of the Market Economy*, Cambridge: Cambridge University Press.

Locke, R. (1996) *The Collapse of the American Management Mystique*, Oxford, Oxford University Press.

Lyotard, J.-F. (1984) *The Postmodern Condition: a Report on Knowledge*, Manchester: Manchester University Press.

Markides, C. C. (1995) *Diversification, Refocusing, and Economic Performance*, Cambridge, MA: The MIT Press.

McKelvey, B. (1997) 'Quasi-Natural Organization Science', *Organization Science*, 8/4, pp. 352–80.

McKenna, C. (1997) 'The American Challenge: McKinsey & Co.'s Role in the Transfer of Decentralization to Europe, 1957–1975', *Academy of Management Best Papers Proceedings*, pp. 226–31.

Mayer, M. C. J. (1997), Large Industrial Firms in Western Europe: Strategy, Structure and Performance in Social Context, unpublished PhD thesis, University of Warwick.

Mayer, M. and Whittington, R. (1999) 'Strategy, Structure and Systemness: National Institutions and Corporate Change in France, Germany and the UK, 1950–1993', *Organization Studies*, 20/6, pp. 933–60.

Meyer, J. W. and Rowan, B. (1977) 'Institutionalised Organisations: Formal Structure As Myth and Ceremony', *American Journal of Sociology*, 83/2, pp. 340–63.

Mouzelis, N. (1995) *Sociological Theory: What Went Wrong?*, London: Routledge.

Ohmae, K. (1990) *The Borderless World*, London: Collins.

Ohmae, K. (1995) 'Putting Global Logic First', in Ohmae, K. (ed.) *The Evolving Global Economy: Making Sense of the New World Order*, Boston: Harvard Business Review.

Palmer, D. A., Friedland, R., Devereaux Jennings, P. and Powers, M. (1987) 'The Economics and Politics of Structure, The Multidivisional Form and the Large U.S. Corporation', *Administrative Science Quarterly*, 32, pp. 25–48.

Palmer, D. A., Deverearux Jennings, P. and Zhou, X. (1993) 'Late Adoption of the Mulitidivisional Form by Large U.S. Corporations: Institutional, Political, and Economic Accounts', *Administrative Science Quarterly*, 38, pp. 100–31.

Parsons, T. (1964) 'Evolutionary Universals in Society'. *American Sociological Review*, 29, pp. 339–57.

Reich, R. (1993) *The Work of Nations: Preparing Ourselves for 21st Century Capitalism*, New York: Vintage Books.

Rostow, W. W. (1960) *Stages of Economic Growth: a Non Communist Manifesto*, Cambridge: Cambridge University Press.

Rumelt, R. (1974) *Strategy Structure and Economics Performance*, Boston: Harvard Business School Press.

Scott, R. (1995) *Institutions and Organizations*, Thousand Oaks: Sage.

Servan-Schreiber, J.-J. (1969) *The American Challenge*, London: Penguin.

Suzuki, Y. (1980) 'The Strategy and Structure of Top 100 Japanese Industrial Enterprises, 1950–1970'. *Strategic Management Journal*, 1/3, pp. 265–91.

Suzuki, Y. (1991) 'Japanese Management structures, 1920–1980 Basingstoke: Macmillan.

Thomas III, L. G., and Waring, G. (1999) 'Competing Capitalisms: Capital Investment in American, German, and Japanese Firms', *Strategic Management Journal*, 20, pp. 729–48.

Toulmin, S. (1990) *Cosmopolis: The Hidden Agenda of Modernity*, Chicago: Chicago University Press.

Whitley, R. (1994) 'Dominant Forms of Economic Organization in Market Economies', *Organization Studies*, 15/2, pp. 153–82.

Whitley, R. (1997) 'The Social Construction of Economic Actors' in Whitley, R. and Kristensen, P. H. (eds) *The Changing European Firm*, London: Routledge.

Whitley, R. (1999) *Divergent Capitalisms*, Oxford: Oxford University Press.

Whittington, R. (2002) 'Corporate Structure: From Policy to Practice', in Pettigrew, A., Thomas, H. and Whittington, R. (eds) *The Handbook of Strategy and Management*, London: Sage, pp. 113–38.

Whittington, R. and Mayer, M. (1997) 'Beyond or Behind the M-Form? The Structures of European Business, in Thomas, H., O'Neil, D. and Ghertman, M. (eds) *Strategy, Structure and Style*, Chichester: John Wiley, pp. 241–58.

Whittington, R. and Mayer, M. (2000) *The European Corporation: Strategy, Structure and Social Science* Oxford: Oxford University Press.

Whittington, R., Mayer, M. and Curto, F. (1999) 'Chandlerism in Post-War Europe: Strategic and Structural Change in Post-War Europe', *Industrial and Corporate Change*, 8/3, pp. 519–50.

Williamson, O. E. (1975) *Markets and Hierarchies: Analysis and Anti-Trust Implications*, New York: Free Press.

Yip, G. (1992) *Total Global Strategy*, Englewood Cliffs, NJ: Prentice Hall.

Zysman, J. (1994) 'How Institutions Create Historically Rooted Trajectories of Growth, *Industrial and Corporate Change*, 3, pp. 243–83.

Zysman, J. (1995) 'Institutions and Economic Development in the Advanced Countries', in Dosi, G. and Franco, M. (eds) *Organization and Strategy in the Evolution of the Enterprise*, Basingstoke: Macmillan, pp. 410–55.

2
Global Change Management Approaches in MNCs and Distinct National Trajectories: Britain and Germany Compared

Mike Geppert, Dirk Matten and Karen Williams

Introduction

The discourse on globalization has been a field of research in international business for quite some time. Within the large body of literature there seems to be a rather strong, if not dominating, school of thought, which argues that globalization will ultimately result in the worldwide convergence of organizational patterns. There is talk of the 'stateless' enterprise (Parker, 1998) and the 'transnational' organization (Bartlett and Ghoshal, 1989), to name just two examples. The general argument is that the proliferation of worldwide, homogeneous economic and technological rationales is leading to a more or less worldwide standardization of organizational structures and processes. This view coincides with, and has been strongly encouraged by, a considerable bias on evolutionary concepts, which have clearly dominated theory building in the field of the multinational business organization over the last two decades. The most prominent example of this is the 'transnational solution' proposed by Bartlett and Ghoshal (1989: 66–71).

This view has, however, come increasingly under scrutiny since it neglects – if not totally ignores – the fact that business organizations are still remarkably different from country to country and region to region (see Mayer and Whittington's introduction in this book). Without going to the extreme of completely denying the influence and phenomenon of globalization (see Rugman, 2000, as a prominent example of this), our chapter starts from the assumption that global organizational strategies and processes are significantly shaped by concrete national environments and that the unified, globally harmonized and standardized organization is clearly a myth and an oversimplification of a generally more complex reality (Doremus et al., 1998; Ruigrok and van Tulder, 1995: 152–69). While the chapter acknowledges the forces and constraints of the globalization process and its manifestation within MNCs, we contend that the implementation of globalization policies is significantly shaped and influenced by the respective national environment.

The empirical background of this Chapter is based on the lifts and escalator sector, which as an industry is presently undergoing strong pressure towards globalization (see Iwer, 2000). The world market for these products has seen a significant concentration process, with only four major competitors now in the sector. There is a strong tendency towards globally standardized products and production technologies and the international competition between the four players has increased sharply. All these companies have undertaken, and are still undertaking, significant rationalization measures, which affect their worldwide organization. We had access to three of these MNCs and investigated their global strategies, as well as the implementation of these strategies in the host subsidiaries. In order to identify the effect of national environments on globalization strategies, we compared their subsidiaries in the UK to their subsidiaries in Germany.

On a concrete level, we focused on the global strategies of these MNCs with regards to the effect on their work systems. These strategies are globally homogeneous and could be seen as a manifestation of globalization forces at group level. We then analysed how these strategies were implemented at subsidiary level and how the work systems had effectively changed as a consequence of the global strategies. In order to investigate the influence of national environments, we specifically focused on the institutional framework of the national business system. By calibrating our research to these objectives, we were then able to ask the following four research questions, which we will address in the following chapter. These research questions are interlinked and gradually build on each other.

1. First, we pose the general question of whether global rationalization strategies and policies, which in most cases are developed in the HQ of the MNC, lead to homogeneous change management approaches and global effects in the host country subsidiaries. The subsidiaries are themselves embedded in different national contexts, such as Germany and the UK in our empirical case studies.

2. Next, we compare different rationalization logics of the host country subsidiaries and analyse the differences in the approaches of local managers to globalization policies.
3. Building on these findings, we then address the question of how differences in the embeddedness of the host country subsidiaries within their national institutional framework lead to different results in terms of the impact of change management approaches on work systems.
4. This finally leads to the question of whether the global change strategies of MNCs involve the erosion of national-specific patterns in the work systems and the emergence of global or transnational structures and networks, as the evolutionary model in international business would suggest.

Globalization, national institutions and work systems

In order to investigate the research questions above, we need to clarify and define some of the constructs used in our case studies. First of all, there is the issue of globalization as it influences and shapes work systems. There is considerable debate about the definition of globalization and the concept generally seems to be rather elusive (Ruigrok and van Tulder, 1995: 119–51; Scholte, 2000: 41–6; Rugman, 2000). In this chapter, we refer to globalization as an ongoing corporate discourse resulting in policies within MNCs to introduce world- and group-wide rationalization, restructuring and ultimately convergence of work systems. This discourse, at different levels and in different intensities, integrates some of the features which are commonly attributed to globalization in the academic debate. It includes the *internationalization* of production and marketing of goods and services (Rugman, 2000: 5; Prakash and Hart, 2000: 5) and the *universalization* and *standardization*, as well as *westernization*, especially *Americanization*, of management practices (see Mayer and Whittington in this volume). It also includes the element of *denationalization* (or deterritorialization; see Scholte, 2000: 46–61), which becomes particularly evident in some areas of our research, where the global strategies of MNCs clashed quite significantly with certain aspects of the work systems, which were subject to strong national influences. Globalization, in this general sense of an ongoing discourse, is what basically underlies the strategies formulated in the HQ of MNCs, which are then to be implemented in the respective national subsidiaries (for an empirical view on globally diffused language constructs, see Ganter and Walgenbach in this volume).

Our approach is similar to that of Mueller (1994) and Lane (2000), who assume that globalization not only affects the national business environment, but also shapes the processes within the multinational group. Thus, for example, Mueller stresses that the organizational development of global manufacturing strategies and the diffusion of technologies, knowledge or best practices, such as benchmarking, will undermine national institutions and societal effects (Mueller, 1994: 419–21). Lane, in her study on Germany and the UK, criticizes the fact that researchers of national societal effects ignore the impact of global multinational strategies 'on domestic institutional structures and the danger that it might blow apart the whole societal syndrome and thus undermine the social coherence of current German models of production organization and industrial relations'. (Lane, 2000: 207). However, our research, which focuses on the concrete level of work systems and the impact of globalization on this level, suggests that globalization forms part of corporate policies, which help to shape work systems on the surface but are far shorter lived and less powerful than the national institutional framework and its influence of the design of work systems (Whitley, 1997).

Our second point is that we draw on the conceptualization of work systems outlined by Sorge (1993) and Whitley (1999) in our comparative analysis of work systems design in British and German subsidiaries of MNCs. Work systems are the central object of our study, since this is where the impact of globalization becomes visible. Work systems can be conceptualized in more general terms as distinctive patterns of interconnected characteristics of (a) task organization and control, (b) workplace relations between social groups, and (c) employment practices and policies (Whitley, 1999: 90). More specifically, work systems have their concrete manifestation in (1) the organizational structure (which can be differentiated by function, market, geographical region or products), (2) the organizational processes which comprise communication flow, coordination control mechanisms, political and power relations, (3) the technologies used, and (4) the employment practices and policies of the MNC (Sorge, 1993: 4–5).

In the empirical discussion of our company case studies, we relate our analysis of change management approaches to these four components of work systems in the German and British subsidiaries. Despite our analytical focus on an Anglo-German comparison, we are aware that change management approaches, as reflected in the subsidiaries' work systems design, cannot be described without reference to the economic and social relations within the MNC as a whole. Thus, the function, design and performance of a particular national subsidiary influence its power potential and scope for strategic choices within the multinational group as a whole (Geppert et al., 2001). Far from neglecting the MNC level of analysis, we see a strength of our perspective in the fact that we investigate how global forces and national influences come together and shape the design of change management approaches at the national plant level. At the same time as investigating change in work systems, we also include an emphasis on elements of continuity in work systems, most notably in those cases where the intended change management approaches failed to achieve their objectives.

Thirdly, in analysing these work systems, we draw extensively on a stream of research known as the 'national business systems approach', which is linked to the names of Whitley (1992, 1999: 34–44), Lane (1992) and Sorge (1995). This approach helps us to focus specifically on the national institutional environment, such as the legal framework, ownership structures, educational system, industrial relations and so on of the subsidiary's host country and investigate their effects on the work systems. Furthermore, this perspective may be helpful in explaining the significant differences in how the multinational groups in our research share work and competencies internally. Recent research into the institutional foundations of the comparative advantages of national varieties of capitalism (Hall and Soskice, 2001) clearly points to a significant link between the national business system and the specific competitive advantages of corporations operating within these business systems. By looking at these different institutional backgrounds, we show that national business systems play a crucial role in the strategies of MNCs by 'orchestrating' (Casper and Whitley, 2002) different competencies within the multinational group. These competencies depend on the institutional characteristics of the respective national business systems of their subsidiaries.

Research design and methodology

Global change management processes are determined by the group-wide strategies of the MNC, mainly at HQ level. Subsequently, these changes are implemented in the subsidiaries, in our case, the subsidiaries in Germany and Britain. These change processes decided at corporate level should then become manifest in concrete changes to the work systems of the subsidiaries. In our research, we identify the various change management approaches taking place in the MNCs under investigation and their specific effects on the work systems. However, we assume that these change management approaches are influenced and shaped not only by the global strategies but also by the national business systems, which have a significant influence on the way in which these change management approaches result in actual change or continuity at the level of the work systems. A comparison of these results in the German and British subsidiaries will enable us to draw some conclusions about the role of national business systems in the globalization process.

The idea and design of the research project to analyse change management approaches in MNCs was jointly developed by our research group in Swansea and a research group in Humboldt University in Berlin. The chapter by Becker-Ritterspach et al. and ours are the direct outcomes of an intensive collaboration between the groups in Berlin and Swansea throughout the research process. However, differences in interpretations of the same empirical material reflect both the different conceptual perspectives and research interests of the two groups, as well as the interpretative methodology of our comparative study. A comparison of the two papers shows a lot of agreement on the essential research questions, but also different interpretations of some empirical findings. In such cases, the research teams have 'agreed to disagree'. As the Berlin group has outlined the methodology in detail in their chapter in this volume (see Becker-Ritterspach et al.), we can be fairly brief on our research methodology. We selected three of the four major global players of a relatively small business sector, lifts and escalators. All have headquarters in different host countries: *Amy* in the USA, *Jukka* in Finland and *Karl-Heinz* in Germany. All three companies have national subsidiaries in Germany and the UK. We applied mainly qualitative research methods. As an Anglo–German research team, we developed interview guidelines and semi-structured questionnaires in German and English for managers involved in or responsible for change management measures in their companies. Our analysis is based on in-depth expert interviews with CEOs and managers responsible for change management both at MNC level (in the headquarters and its functional subunits) and at subsidiary level in both countries. Moreover, works councillors and union representatives of the lifts and escalators industry were interviewed in both countries. In cooperation with our German partners, we have conducted ca. 25 interviews so far and studied official documents of these companies, as well as newspaper and internet sources. In the interviews the following topics were covered:

- *General information about the company*: Questions were related to issues such as education and career background of the interviewee, company performance and profile, number of employees and qualification structure, assessment of the company's competitive situation

- *Past, present and planned reorganization and change*: Questions were related to issues such as reasons for adopting these measure, actual aims of these measures, who was involved, obstacles and barriers to the change approach, emergence of different views about these measures and the scope of these measures (whether it affects the MNC as a whole and other subsidiaries or just the local plant)
- *Starting points of change*: Questions were related to issues such as who initiated these measures, the role of the headquarters, the role and influence of local management, key actors in this process and who communicated with whom
- *Assessment of what are the positive and negative aspects of the plant's location in a particular national context*: Here, questions were asked about the influence of the MNC's country of origin.

The case studies

In the following, we will analyse the three MNCs in our sample in the light of our theoretical framework. This will, first of all, involve an analysis of the globalization policy of the entire multinational group as it manifests itself in change management approaches later implemented at subsidiary level. Secondly, we analyse how these global strategies and their global effects, as defined above, are implemented in the different national subsidiaries in Germany and Britain.

Amy : the American MNC

Globalization as a continuous process towards organizational convergence

Globalization in *Amy*'s policies manifests itself as an ongoing process to achieve worldwide convergence of markets and globally standardized products. The extent of insensitivity to national differences is quite significant, being visible in the enforcement of one common business language and also in the fact that the UK is organized in the same group as the Southern European countries, a fact which was commented on by managers as being absurd. Among our sample, *Amy* is the company with the longest legacy of a globalization strategy and the German, as well as the UK interviewees, both stressed that, rather than having discrete changes in work systems (as in the Finnish MNC in our sample), in *Amy*, change is an ongoing, constant pressure in the drive to greater efficiency. Given recent pressures from the multidivisional group, *Amy* is part of a MNC-wide rationalization effort and has decided to cut a significant number of jobs, reducing its global manufacturing plants by more than half (to 16) and reducing its research and development (R&D) sites by more than two thirds to 6 worldwide (Iwer, 2000).

The form that globalization takes within *Amy* shows some typical signs of Americanization and all interviewees perceived the corporate culture as being dominantly American. This applies not only to the general culture in the company but also to the style of management and decision-making and use of American English, the latter point being particularly stressed by the German interviewees.

The global, group-wide strategies are also strongly influenced by a dominant focus on the (American) stock market. As a division of the 57th largest American corporation, *Amy* is part of a typical (Chandlerian) multidivisional corporation, with other divisions operating in technology-oriented branches, most notably the aircraft industry. Managers perceived the accounting and budgeting systems of the company to be the dominant coordination and control mechanism throughout the multinational group. Shares in *Amy*'s group are broadly scattered and their performance on the stock market has a direct influence on the short-term plans of managers in the subsidiaries. Recently, this pressure has intensified as other divisions in the conglomerate have suffered from downturns in the economy and *Amy* is now under even more pressure to make good the losses of those divisions in order to maintain the conglomerate's standing on Wall Street.

In *Amy*, globalization manifests itself strongly as the centralization of strategies, leaving little scope for bottom-up initiatives. A recent example is the closure of the European headquarters of *Amy* in Paris and the centralization of its former functions in the HQ in the US. In this way, *Amy* further centralized the strategic elements of the work system and prevented stronger regional (in this case European) influences. Numerous managers in the subsidiaries endorsed the view that *Amy* is anxious to prevent the creation of another centre of power outside the US. This strong centralization of strategy, however, is linked to a decentralized approach to operative decisions in the subsidiaries (see Becker-Ritterspach et al. in this volume).

Amy's British subsidiary: getting rid of a 'poor' manufacturing image by developing a strong service orientation

In the UK subsidiary, globalization has resulted in one major change management approach in recent years (apart from the continued enforcement of a one-brand strategy achieved in conjunction with the other change management approaches): *Amy* UK closed down all manufacturing sites and restructured the entire organization as a sales and service only organization with a centralized customer-care centre. The background to this is that the UK subsidiary had been underperforming for some time and, given the ongoing rationalization pressure within the whole MNC, it was clear that significant changes had to be made.

These changes affected all areas of the work system. In the area of organizational structure, an entire functional section of the organization was removed and two former brands merged into one organization. Organizational processes were also affected, especially the coordination and control mechanisms and communication flows, since the new organization operates with only one centralized customer-care call centre. The most radical changes, however, took place in the area of employment, as most of the manufacturing staff in the old organization were made redundant and new staff recruited for the newly enlarged service centre. Although the pressure from the headquarters to enhance profitability was quite high, the member of the board interviewed in the British subsidiary stressed that they had had considerable liberty in how to achieve a better performance; the decision to close down the manufacturing sites in Britain was not taken in the US but by the British management.

The reasons given for the British decision were, on the one hand, the perception that 'we in Britain' are not good at manufacturing and, most interestingly, the fact that in the UK the institutional framework makes redundancies an easy option:

> In the UK, it is probably the easiest country in Europe to do different kinds of things. We really didn't have many obstacles, the way we approached it is obvious you have to go through the formal process. Even in the UK, information consultations, discussions, union agreement and then dealing with the individual employee and what we try to do is to make sure that the employees are treated as best as we can.
>
> (Human Resource Director, *Amy* UK)

The way *Amy*'s British subsidiary implemented the change management approaches required by the HQ's global strategic requirements reveals that the national business system had a significant influence on the process. UK managers clearly took into account the constraints and weaknesses (poor manufacturing performance, low level of skill development, low social esteem for manufacturing and engineering in the UK) and the strengths (weak institutional barriers to redundancies, Anglo-Saxon service culture) of the national institutional framework in their decision-making at subsidiary level.

With regard to our research questions, globalization does result in significant pressure for global convergence, standardization and rationalization. However, when we focus on the way different areas of the work system have been changed, we see that local actors have a choice and that these choices reflect their perception of the national background. In *Amy* UK, major changes took place in the area of the technologies used and employment and human resources. In explaining the change from manufacturing to exclusively service technologies, all our interviewees emphasized characteristics of the British business system, such as the low level of skills, low productivity of manufacturing and the trend towards service industries in general (Lane, 1992). Furthermore, the weak regulatory environment allowed global strategies to have a direct and significant impact on the subsidiary. In a business environment characterized by weak national institutions, therefore, globalization policies have a strong impact. However, local managers do still have choices about how they implement change management approaches and the choices that they make reflect the actors' perceptions of the major strengths and weaknesses of the national business environment in which they operate.

Amy's German subsidiary: cultivating German 'virtues' in an American MNC

On the surface, our research in *Amy*'s German subsidiary shows a quite different picture. The most striking difference is that, apart from the removal of the second more minor brand besides *Amy*, there has been no identifiable discrete change management approach in the two manufacturing plants or in the administrative centre of *Amy* Germany. Despite considerable pressure from the HQ level, German managers responded to questions about change by referring to 'general', 'continuous' or 'permanent' pressure to change rather than actual concrete change measures taken within recent years.

The German subsidiary of *Amy* shows the strongest levels of continuity in the face of the global strategies, which in other parts of the group have resulted in significant change processes. Despite a clear global strategy espoused by the American HQ, *Amy*'s German management has considerable liberty with regard to the methods and technologies used to realize HQ goals. This leads to the most significant differences between the work systems of *Amy* in the UK and Germany. The most significant differences lie in the technological and human resources areas. Germany has two production sites, one producing mostly key electronic components for the entire multinational group and another specializing in heavy-duty escalators, for which it is the only remaining production unit within the whole multinational group. Furthermore, they also have extensive R&D capacities at both plants and the German managers regard their country as the leading unit worldwide in terms of their technological level. When asked about the reasons for this, all interviewees refer to the textbook features of the German business system: high level of skills, excellent vocational system and high productivity. Indeed, many of the managers, particularly those on the second hierarchical level below the national board, still regard themselves as a German company with its roots in the company *Amy* acquired no less than 50 years ago. Human resource practices also reflect the same strong national orientation.

The influences of the HQ global strategy are, however, more significant in the area of coordination and control mechanisms. The German chairman claimed to have 'no organization chart', as the company is a 'dynamic' entity not restricted by formal hierarchies, a view which other managers identified as a clear influence from their headquarters. The same applies to other structural elements of the coordination and control system, which were clearly seen by managers as 'American' in their emphasis on control by financial benchmarks, budgets and performance targets. The same applies to the short-term orientation of business decisions which German managers found particularly constraining and inappropriate:

> We have 80,000 elevators in maintenance. I cannot renovate them all at once. That is an investment programme for 10 years. And, given the shortsightedness of our American friends, they simply do not take any notice of this situation. You know, we are now forced to think much more short-term in introducing new procedures.
>
> (Director, Service Centre Division, *Amy* Germany)

Comparing the UK and German subsidiaries in the light of our research questions, we would argue that the case of *Amy* demonstrates that globalization does not lead to homogeneous change management approaches in different host country subsidiaries. National contexts still have a very strong effect on the realization of the global strategy, and, within the multinational group, the national peculiarities are 'used' in ways which best contribute to the overarching corporate goals. Due to their embeddedness in quite diverse national business systems in Britain and Germany, the resulting organization of the subsidiaries and their work systems are equally diverse. On the one hand, we have an example of the new British service economy and, on the other, a typical German manufacturing and technology-driven organization.

Jukka: the Finnish MNC

Globalization as group-wide standardization of management processes

Jukka has had its most significant growth phase during the last ten years as a result of acquisitions. The dominant strategic orientation is the global integration of the MNC with a clear view of globalization as the dominant imperative behind all impending change processes in the corporation. This is illustrated in the following quotes from three senior executives in the HQ, in Germany and Britain:

> 'Global' means trying to standardise not only products but processes throughout the world operations of the corporation.

> Globalization does lead to convergence eventually, it's not divergence, ... convergence definitely.

> The CEO calls it 'globalization' but I see it as a 'harmonization', harmonization of business processes.

The recent strategy to bring about the global standardization of management processes made it necessary to relocate the HQ to Brussels, although the company still has a HQ in Finland where the owning family lives (controlling two-thirds of the voting shares). Many respondents characterized the organization as strongly 'controller'-driven and *Jukka* appears to be aiming for a level of global integration, which a company like *Amy* achieved quite some time ago.

The strong globalization pressures manifest themselves in the ongoing change management processes in the company. Both subsidiaries have had to implement what we identified as three major change management approaches, which have led and still are leading to major changes in the work systems of the respective subsidiaries. Firstly, there has been the implementation of what is known as the '*Jukka* model' of doing business. Basically, this concept differentiates the organization into those functions which are oriented towards the market (the 'front line') and those oriented towards manufacturing (the 'supply line'). The aim of this model is to standardize all business processes worldwide and as such it affects almost all aspects of the entire work system in the subsidiaries. It also aims to abolish national entities and subsidiaries and orientate the corporation towards either the (globally integrating) market or the economic rationalities of the internal production processes. Consequently, this model manifests the MNC's orientation towards the low-context environments of global economic and business rationalities. The second major change management approach operates along similar lines (for a slightly different interpretation see Becker-Ritterspach et al. in this volume) and consists of the global introduction of a standardized financial reporting and controlling system based on tools provided by the software company SAP. Apart from encouraging further convergence of global business processes, this change management approach shows *Jukka*'s strong orientation towards the use of financial performance indicators as the central tool for management control within the MNC as a whole. The third significant change management approach is the implementation of a worldwide standardized escalator product line, which again reflects the corporate drive towards convergence and harmonization through-out all its subsidiaries.

Jukka in Germany: national specific patterns of resistance to change

The introduction of the new *Jukka* model and SAP, which were implemented more or less simultaneously, had a massive influence on the work systems in *Jukka*'s German operations, particularly their organizational processes and the technologies used. The general impression from our research is that, from the very beginning, the German subsidiary has been extremely successful in resisting and obstructing these changes. It is now the last entity in the entire multinational group where the changes are still being implemented, and senior management were still struggling with major problems at the time of our interviews. The reasons given by the HQ for the problems in Germany were twofold: on the one hand, they see the *Jukka* model as codifying the Anglo-Saxon orientation towards management processes, which clashes strongly with the German functional approach to management. The globalization policies of the MNC meant significant changes to major, nationally embedded areas of the subsidiary's work system, such as the organization of production and planning processes and accounting structures. The second group of reasons was more politically motivated as strong resistance came from among the senior management of the German company, formerly an independent, profitable company with international expertise in escalators before being taken over by *Jukka* in 1996. The enforcement of the *Jukka* model and the new software system was eventually only achievable by the almost complete replacement of the first and second tiers of management in Germany by '*Jukka*-ites' (as one interviewee put it), senior executives from other parts of the multinational group, the majority being Finnish nationals.

These findings shed specific light on our research questions. Globalization policies as imposed on the work system of the German subsidiaries faced strong and successful resistance. The power base of the German management clearly lay in the fact that the R&D know-how, engineering capacity and highly skilled and efficient production workforce in the subsidiary were key to *Jukka*'s global strategy. Germany provides the entire multinational group with engineering know-how and is the leading R&D location worldwide. These features of the company reflect the strengths of the German business system and can be clearly identified as national effects (NEs) (Warner and Campbell, 1993). German managers were quite skilful in playing on their specific, nationally influenced power resources: in the third change management approach based on the introduction of a global standardized escalator, they were able to ensure that their location in Germany was one of the three plants worldwide to produce the new product. Here, we see similarities between *Jukka* and *Amy*'s German subsidiaries: national strengths are explicitly not 'standardized', or 'harmonized' out of existence, but there is a struggle to integrate them into the global strategy of convergence of management systems. This struggle is well documented in our data: *Jukka* wants to preserve German know-how and expertise on the one hand, but wants to make them fit into standardized, globally harmonized work systems on the other. The case of *Jukka* reveals the recourse to the use of power in order to achieve this transition in a strong institutional and cultural context, such as the German one. Strong national resistance was also visible in the human resources area, where the German codified system of industrial relations, most notably the works council (*Betriebsrat*), was regarded by the Finnish managers as a major obstacle to the implementation of the new work system.

Jukka in the UK: Why are they still manufacturing there?

One of the most striking research questions during our field work focused on why *Jukka* UK has the only large-scale manufacturing operation in the UK of the whole lift and escalator sector. When comparing *Jukka*'s subsidiary in Britain with the one in Germany, it is striking how little difference there is between the two, given the different national contexts in which they operate. The reason lies in the fact that the British subsidiary has been part of what is now the German subsidiary of *Jukka*, formerly an independent German escalator producer, since 1973. The managing director of *Jukka*'s plant in the UK still referred to his company as a 'German' company, particularly in terms of the work system used in the UK. Over a period of more than ten years after the UK acquisition the former German owners built up a very efficient production and engineering plant in the UK, investing heavily in the vocational training of workers, production facilities and engineering skills. In fact, the British technicians in the plant still use German measures, standards and much of the 'technical language' is German as well. This strong influence of the former German owners established a subsidiary whose entire work systems, especially in the area of the technologies used and its employment policies and practices, in no way reflects the peculiarities of the British national context outlined earlier.

Consequently, the resistance to the change management approaches of *Jukka* was as high in the UK subsidiary as it was in Germany. It was only the retirement of the UK managing director in 1999, which enabled the massive reorganization process associated with the *Jukka* model and the new software systems to go ahead. In particular, the engineering and manufacturing staff perceived the new policies as 'edicts' imposed on them so that *Jukka*'s globalization strategy had to be implemented quite forcefully. However, our impression, especially when interviewing the new UK managing director, was that in the end senior management in the UK had identified considerable strategic advantages for the UK operations in complying with the global strategies. The engineering and manufacturing know-how in the UK subsidiary is proving to be a powerful asset for its role within the entire multinational group, now it is no longer a part of a German SME, but a direct subsidiary of a global group. In fact, the group made the decision to produce all heavy-duty and specialized escalators for the entire *Jukka* group in the UK. This massive change in the structure of the work system, most notably in the area of products and markets, puts the British plant in a position of relative power. There is also another aspect of globalization, which works to the advantage of the British subsidiary:

On the strategic level, that's quite interesting, we probably have a position and influence much greater than you might expect. The reason is because the working language of the company is English, and of course we are English, so the consequence of that is that the Finns are very logical and they say: 'Well, if you want to do something internationally and you need to get the message over properly then use an English guy because he speaks the language, hopefully, the best.'...Even in the US, they use English people, not US people. So they kind of capitalise on the language skills of the people here.

(Managing Director, *Jukka* UK)

So, in the concrete case of a British plant within a MNC, there seems to be considerable gain in the fact that globalization leads to convergence towards a 'global' culture with their own (English) national language as its base.

The case of *Jukka* UK shows that neither globalization nor national business systems influence work systems in subsidiaries in a deterministic way. On the one hand, we observe the same patterns towards global convergence of work systems as in the German subsidiary. Although the resistance in Britain seemed not to be as strong as in Germany due, we believe, to the fact that the globalization strategies brought considerable advantages to the management of the British subsidiary. On the other hand, we do not see the same results of the globalization process in the other British subsidiaries in our sample, which became purely service centres. Obviously, the pattern of globalization and the effects of national institutions also depend on the role of individual actors in this process and the specific backgrounds of the companies concerned: since *Jukka* UK historically had a strong manufacturing culture, the management was able to build on this profile and respond to globalization pressures in a way that does not indicate a deterministic effect of UK national institutions on change processes.

Karl-Heinz: the German MNC

Diversified quality production and the limits of globalization

In a certain sense, the German MNC in our sample provided the least evidence of globalization forces at work. Looking to the strategies of the MNC as a whole, our data showed less evidence of any moves towards global convergence than in the other two MNCs. The headquarters has tried to link certain coordination processes by recently introducing a standardized system for all subsidiaries' reports to the headquarters in Germany. Furthermore, there is some awareness of the need for a global market presence, which led to the acquisition of one of America's biggest lift and escalator companies and the first non-German board member – a first step, perhaps, in 'denationalizing' the leadership structure.

Apart from this, however, *Karl-Heinz* has a highly decentralized governance system with a rather loosely knit network of national companies, which, in their respective countries, work in accordance with the (perceived) national business context. There is little central R&D, no global standardization of products and, even though the general focus is on the more expensive, upmarket product range, this is not a generally enforced strategy throughout the group, which allows for different market strategies in different countries such as, for instance, France. However, the group-wide strategy of decentralization, although it lacks many of the common features of globalization, is nevertheless the espoused 'global' strategy of the group. Senior management in the headquarters, as well as in the German and British subsidiaries, deliberately adopt this approach by stressing extensive national differences in market requirements, production systems and, last but by no means least, language barriers, which are seen to make a more standardized approach to leadership within the multinational group impossible. As long as the budgeted financial targets are met nationally by the subsidiaries, they are granted a maximal amount of liberty. The reason for this decentralized strategy lies in the fact that, unlike the two other MNCs in our sample, *Karl-Heinz* focuses on the more valuable, customized upper market segment in the lift and escalator industry. This does not allow the same approach as *Amy* and *Jukka* take when they target the standard products segment of the market. In this, *Karl-Heinz* reflects the pattern of diversified quality production (DQP), identified as typical of German manufacturing companies in earlier research in the field (Sorge, 1991). In comparison to the other two cases, the globalization policies of *Karl-Heinz* differ significantly and, therefore, its change management approaches do not emphasize convergence or rationalization, but rather differentiation strategies to capture an upper market segment. This approach requires a more decentralized and less standardized strategy and is also reflected in the reorganization of the entire service operation in both Germany and Britain into regionalized, highly flexible and customer-focused networks of small service centres – although none of the managers involved saw this as the result of a top-down initiative by the HQ.

Karl-Heinz in Germany: a German SME

The German subsidiary of *Karl-Heinz* in many respects shows the typical characteristics of a medium-sized German company (*mittelständisches Unternehmen*). The one main manufacturing plant operates rather autonomously as a German company, with only limited awareness among management that they are part of an MNC. There have been very few changes in the work systems, the main one being a reorganization of the manufacturing plant into smaller units, which are managed as independent cost centres, but still follow 'craft' production strategies, as one interviewee put it. There is also an intense focus on continuous improvement processes, a remarkable level of R&D input in components, a high degree of horizontal integration and generally a rather participative management style with considerable emphasis on a constructive approach of management towards the works council and joint involvement in improving the manufacturing processes. Furthermore, as would be expected with a differentiated manufacturing strategy, there was an extremely high awareness of customer needs and a strong customer focus shown throughout the interviews. Management approaches to change in work systems patterns can be seen as the attempt to combine more effectively highly customized production with high output. Thus, change management approaches in this case are very much related to DQP, which is seen as typical for key segments of the German manufacturing sector (Sorge, 1991).

Karl-Heinz in the UK: the most 'British' subsidiary of our company case studies

Unlike the German subsidiary, significant changes had taken place in the British subsidiary of *Karl-Heinz* during the last three years. Shortly after the acquisition of a medium-sized company in the UK, *Karl-Heinz* closed down its entire manufacturing operations in the UK and reorganized the work system into a sales and service only organization. Our interviews with different actors involved in this change process revealed that the main initiative for the change and the key actor in this process was the managing director of *Karl-Heinz* UK. A German-owned company was transformed into a company which almost typically reflects key textbook features of the British business context with rather individualistic change management approaches, top managers who are highly experienced in job-hopping and rather short-term and financial-driven business planning perspectives (Tayeb, 1993). Apart from the need to bring the subsidiary back into profit, the British subsidiary had complete freedom as to how they realized this aim. There was absolutely no interference from headquarters, with headquarters guidelines for the subsidiary's operation said to fill no more than *'maybe three to four sheets of paper'*. However, the UK operations retained a very small workshop-based manufacturing unit needed to customize lift cabins for special design requirements of their customers. This, again, reflects the group-wide orientation of *Karl-Heinz* towards high-value customized products.

Thus, in the UK, the work system was changed in a very short period of time. In sales, there was a complete shift towards high-value products with a small workforce involved in customized work to meet client's specific wishes. For the rest, the formerly centralized service organization was completely transformed into a network of regional service centres, which can flexibly react to clients' wishes. The main reasons given by the managing director for these changes were that: *'we are not good in manufacturing'* and that servicing lifts and escalators in Britain is a very profitable business, not least because British law, unlike in Germany, requires users of lifts and escalators to have their equipment serviced on a regular basis. With regard to new products, the UK subsidiary buys them on the internal *Karl-Heinz* market from Germany, Spain, Italy or France. In this sense, the multinational group and its resources, although not forcing the British company down a particular route, played an enabling role for their strategy.

The entire process of communication and control in the reorganized company appeared to be very informal, personalized and built around the managing director, a fact confirmed by our interviews with other actors in the organization. The changes also affected employment issues, since about 12 per cent of the workforce had to be laid off. This was, however, unproblematic according to the managing director since: *'To fire persons went much faster than the German headquarters expected'*. The entire change management approach adopted in the UK was well adapted to the low level of institutionalization of the British business system in general.

Concluding discussion

The literature on the development of globalization and its impact on change management approaches has been preoccupied by evolutionary models based on the distinction between the traditional 'multinational' and newly emerging 'global enterprises' (see, for example, Bartlett and Ghoshal, 1989; Parker, 1998). It is assumed that HQ global strategies and policies will weaken the impact of local rationalities on host country subsidiaries and lead to similar patterns of work system design across national borders. In our case studies, there is some evidence of an 'ongoing process of rationalization' and 'continuous globalizing' (Mueller and Loveridge, 1997: 152) in the lifts and escalators sector. However, this has not led to the establishment of change management strategies to create a single standard work system pattern across national institutional borders. Instead, distinct business contexts in Britain and Germany have prevented convergence of work systems patterns, even in MNCs, where HQ change management policies specifically focus on the development of more globalized structures and processes, as in the cases *Amy* and *Jukka*.

Our research indicates, first of all, that global rationalization of patterns of work system design is influenced by sector specialization and national institutions. The comparison of German and British subsidiaries shows that the global policies of HQ, such as the development of global products, global manufacturing strategies and the implementation of 'best practices' or international accounting systems have not led to convergent change management patterns at the subsidiary level. National business systems help to explain different patterns of work system design found in British and German subsidiaries. Weak labour market institutions, strong academic stratification and the lower degree of integration of R&D and manufacturing functions within the work system in the UK (see Whitley, 1997) meant that the change management approaches in the British subsidiaries were much more straightforward and radical compared to the German cases. This was illustrated in the cases of *Amy* UK and *Karl-Heinz* UK in the strategic decision to close their manufacturing sites and in the way this was implemented.

Our data does not confirm recent work by Mueller and Loveridge (1997), which identified an erosion of national institutions due to globalization in the German automobile industry sector. Rather, in line with Schmidt's chapter (in this volume) on the 'German model', our empirical findings show that the impact of globalization rationalities on national work system patterns varies depending on the industrial sector. Certain patterns of sector specialization, which have been established historically, are likely to continue to last, whatever the arguments of globalization proponents (Quack and Morgan, 1999: 47). This finding is supported by our research in the lift and escalator sector. There is a danger of overgeneralizing from research in a particular industrial sector, whether in the automobile or pharmaceutical industries, seen as a sort of avant-garde of globalizing industrial sectors (for example Mueller and Loveridge, 1997; Lane, 2000), or in traditional engineering sectors, which, in Germany, strongly reflect German business system characteristics (see Schmidt later in this volume). Globalization has a different effect in different sectors and it cannot be argued that it generally results in the undermining of key institutions in highly integrated business systems, such as the German one.

Secondly, we have seen that work system patterns were strongly influenced in detail by national institutional features. As discussed elsewhere (Geppert et al., 2001), work system patterns in host country subsidiaries are neither determined by the global policies of MNC HQ, nor are they entirely shaped by the societal context. Local managers, therefore, have some degree of strategic choice to develop distinct change management approaches, even within the same national business system. Thus, the fact that *Jukka* is the only company in the lifts and escalators sector that has still significant manufacturing facilities in the UK, cannot be fully explained either by the global strategy of the company or by the typical national institutional patterns in the UK. National effects do not cause an isomorphism of identical organizational forms, but allow different managerial change strategies in companies in the same sector and society. Sorge distinguished between identical and non-identical reproduction of work systems in his comparison of machine-tool companies in France, Germany and the UK (Sorge, 1995). The non-identical focus of *Jukka* UK on manufacturing, compared to the other two British subsidiaries, can be better understood by the company's history during its ownership by the former German mother (now *Jukka* Germany). In this case, the company's specific engineering culture was, and still is, heavily influenced by its German counterpart. However, at the same time, the work systems of the two *Jukka* subsidiaries in Germany and the UK still represent distinct national patterns in terms of their structure, employment relations and qualifications of managers and employees.

Thirdly, we have seen that the more work systems are interlocked with their national business systems, the less likely they are to change radically (see, for example, Grabher, 1993; Schienstock, 1997; Whitley, 1999). Our comparison has shown that radical change management strategies are more likely to be found in the Anglo-Saxon business context, such as the UK, where the weaker interdependence of national institutions and work systems facilitate drastic measures, such as the closure of manufacturing sites or fundamental changes to customer service functions involving large scale redundancies. Change management in a more densely institutionalized societal context, such as Germany, however, seems to be more incremental and mirrors specific national work system patterns. *Karl-Heinz* Germany, for example, is located in the industrial district of Baden-Württemberg. Compared to the other German subsidiaries, this had the most integrated work systems design and followed the most distinct business strategy based on DQP by combining cost leadership and differentiation (Porter, 1980). An Anglo-German comparison of work systems design at the subsidiary level shows the significance of this lock-in effect. Due to *Karl-Heinz's* global strategy which contrary to the other two MNCs, targets the higher customized market segment, the company has a highly integrated, multifunctional, flexible specialized work system in Germany with a low level of separation of worker and management functions and a high level of worker participation in local decision-making processes. In contrast, in its British subsidiary, we found a weakly integrated work system focused on regional customer service centres with a strict separation between management and workers and a rather authoritarian management hierarchy.

This leads to our final conclusion. As shown earlier, our research does not support the implicit assumption of leading scholars that MNCs are evolving from the 'outdated' multinational model towards the global enterprise (for a critical perspective on the evolutionary framework see also Westney and Zaheer, 2001: 369ff.). Indeed, in *Jukka*, the attempt to develop towards the model of the global enterprise and *Amy's* attempts to continuously improve on the model resulted in a rather paradoxical effect: the global change management policies developed by HQ management elites only increased the local managers' awareness of their national culture and institutions. We did not find much evidence that national business systems had lost their significance in the change of work systems patterns. If we look at the two extreme types in the evolutionary framework of Bartlett and Ghoshal (1989: 65): on the one extreme, there is the case of the 'global company' such as *Amy*. Here, we would expect a significant amount of convergent and homogeneous business practices; however, our empirical findings on the work systems and the change processes in its German subsidiary show an almost textbook case 'German' company. The stunning contradictory – if not 'dialectical' (Sorge, 2000) – finding in our research seems to be that the more globalized the strategies and structures of a MNC become, the more the MNC allows, and indeed relies on, national specifics to play a key role in its global portfolio of national subsidiaries. From this perspective we could even argue that globalization policies will ultimately reinforce the importance of different national contexts. For example, the importance of national business system patterns became visible when local managers in *Amy* UK explained why they were relieved to close their low performing manufacturing units as part of their ongoing change management approach and instead focus their business strategy wholly on service and sales functions, seen as particular British strengths. In contrast, the structure of the work system in *Amy* Germany and their relatively powerful position in the MNC's decision-making process are indicators of German business system influences. The geographical HQ role of *Amy* in Germany, its increased geographical responsibilities (such as in Eastern Europe) and its strong position in the strategic tasks of the MNC as a whole, such as in R&D, are not just power resources, as recently argued (Geppert et al., 2001). *Amy* Germany's work systems design can be clearly related to the German institutional context.

At the other end of Bartlett and Ghoshal's spectrum (1989: 65), there is a company such as *Karl-Heinz*, which can be seen as a multinational company with a decentralized organizational structure dominated by its specific national background and local opportunities. The analysis of *Karl-Heinz's* operations in the UK, however, reveals a highly flexible, innovative organization capable of efficiently adapting to the local specifics of the market and focusing on high-quality upmarket products and services. One would not naturally expect a high potential for innovative change processes on the work systems level in a multinational-style company now regarded as a rather inefficient, outdated organizational structure. Our data suggests that the organizational design of *Karl-Heinz* and, especially, its German subsidiary significantly reflects German business system patterns. Its strong strategic orientation in the lifts and escalators division towards the customized quality market segment, reflected not only in the German but also in the British subsidiary, significantly shows its institutional origins in Germany. In this sense, it is no surprise that the German multinational group, not the American multinational, is the leader in this upper market segment. Moreover, the highly decentralized governance structure of the MNC not only permits the British plant to be very British in its work system design in terms of its service orientation, but also allows the German plant to operate as a textbook case German company with craft production, product-led rather than market-led work systems and highly skilled, professional managers (Warner and Campbell, 1993).

We would position *Jukka* in the middle of Bartlett and Ghoshal's spectrum. Here we might expect to see the strongest trend towards a true global convergence of organization-wide work systems, which might support Mueller's argument that there is a third, distinct 'organization effect' on MNCs (Mueller, 1994). Nevertheless, our case study shows that even the strongest organizational implementation of global standards by no means exercises an independent, deterministic effect. Instead, in our case study, *Jukka* faced strong resistance from constraints based on the history of the company (UK) and on the national business system (Germany). It is open to debate in which direction the strongly standardizing strategy in *Jukka* will finally move the MNC.

All in all, it can be concluded that national institutions still matter and are important in understanding change management approaches of MNCs in sectors such as the lift and escalator industry. Despite the popularity of globalization policies among management elites in this sector, national patterns of work system design in the German and British subsidiaries of these MNCs appear to be long lasting and deeply entrenched, particularly in core segments of the German manufacturing sector. This is an important facet of globalization, which is often undervalued by researchers attracted by the idea of new transnational and globally convergent organizational forms.

Acknowledgements

The authors are grateful for the challenging and stimulating comments of participants of the Research Conference, 'Management of Change in Multinational Companies: Global Challenges and National Effects' held in November 2001 at the Humboldt University in Berlin. We would especially like to thank Christel Lane (University of Cambridge) and Gert Schmidt (University of Erlangen) for their comments on an earlier draft of this chapter.

References

Bartlett, C. and Ghoshal, S. (1989) *Managing across borders: The transnational solution* (2nd edn), Boston: Harvard Business School Press.

Casper, S. and Whitley, R. (2002) 'Competency Orchestration within Entrepreneurial Technology Firms: A Comparative Institutional Analysis', Paper presented at the ESRI Thematic Research Workshop on Changing Contextual Constructions of Economic Rationality, September 15–18, 2001, Portoroz, Slovenia.

Doremus, P. N., Keller, W. W., Pauly, L. W. and Reich, S. (1998) *The myth of the global corporation*, Princeton, NJ: Princeton University Press.

Geppert, M., Williams, K. and Matten, D. (2001) *The social construction of change management in MNCs: an Anglo-German comparison*, Swansea: EBMS Working Paper 2001/9.

Grabher, G. (1993) 'The weakness of strong ties: The lock-in of regional development in the Ruhr area', in Grabher, G. (ed.), *The embedded firm*, London: Routledge, pp. 255–77.

Hall, P. A. and Soskice, D. (eds) (2001) *Varieties of capitalisms*, Oxford: Oxford University Press.

Iwer, F. (2000) *Innovationstrends in der Aufzugsindustrie und Folgen für die Beschäftigungssituation. Projektabschlußbericht*, Stuttgart: IG-Metall.

Lane, C. (1992) 'European business systems: Britain and Germany compared', in Whitley, R. (ed.), *European business systems*, London: Sage, pp. 64–97.

Lane, C. (2000) 'Understanding the globalization strategies of German and British multinational companies', in Maurice, M. and Sorge, A. (eds), *Embedding organizations: societal analysis of actors, organizations, and socioeconomic content*, Amsterdam/Philadelphia: John Benjamins, pp. 188–208.

Mueller, F. (1994) 'Societal effect, organisational effect, and globalization', *Organization Studies*, 15(3): pp. 407–28.

Mueller, F. and Loveridge, R. (1997) 'Institutional, Sectoral, and Corporate Dynamics in the Creation of Global Supply Chains', in Whitley, R. and Kristensen, P. H. (eds), *Governance at Work*, Oxford: Oxford University Press, pp. 139–57.

Parker, B. (1998) *Globalization and business practice: managing across boundaries*, London: Sage.

Porter, M. (1980) *Competitive strategy: Techniques for analysing industries and competitors*, New York: Free Press.

Prakash, A. and Hart, J. A. (eds) (2000) *Coping with globalization*, London: Routledge.

Quack, S. and Morgan, G. (1999) 'National capitalisms, global competition and economic performance: an introduction', in Quack, S., Morgan, G. and Whitley, R. (eds), *National capitalisms, global competition and economic performance*, Amsterdam/Philadelphia: John Benjamins, pp. 3–52.

Rugman, A. M. (2000) *The end of globalization*, London: Random House.

Ruigrok, W. and van Tulder, R. (1995) *The logic of international restructuring*, London: Routledge.

Schienstock, G. (1997) 'The transformation of regional governance: Institutional lock-ins and the development of lean production in Baden Württemberg', in Quack, S., Morgan, G. and Whitley, R. (eds), *National capitalisms, global competition and economic performance*, Amsterdam/Philadelphia: John Benjamins, pp. 190–208.

Scholte, J. A. (2000) *Globalization. A critical introduction*, Basingstoke: Palgrave.

Sorge, A. (1991) 'Strategic fit and societal effect – interpreting cross-national comparisons of technology, organization and human resources', *Organization Studies*, 12(2): pp. 161–90.

Sorge, A. (1993) *Arbeit, Organisation und Arbeitsbeziehungen in Ostdeutschland (Antrittsvorlesung 24. Mai 1993)*, Berlin: Humboldt-Universität.

Sorge, A. (1995) 'Cross-national differences in personnel and organization', in Harzing, A.-W. and van Ruysseveldt, J. (eds), *International human resource management. An integrated approach*, London: Sage, pp. 99–123.

Sorge, A. (2000) 'The diabolical dialectics of societal effects', in Maurice, M. and Sorge, A. (eds), *Embedding organizations: societal analysis of actors, organizations, and socio-economic content*, Amsterdam/Philadelphia: John Benjamins, pp. 37–56.

Tayeb, M. (1993) 'English Culture and Business Organizations', in Hickson, D. J. (ed.), *Management in Western Europe. Society, culture and organization in twelve nations*, Berlin/New York: De Gruyter, pp. 47–64.

Warner, M. and Campbell, A. (1993) 'German management', in Hickson, D. J. (ed.), *Management in Western Europe. Society, culture and organization in twelve nations*, Berlin/New York: De Gruyter, pp. 89–108.

Westney, D. E. and Zaheer, S. (2001) 'The multinational enterprise as an organization', in Rugman, A. M. and Brewer, T. (eds), *The Oxford handbook of international business*, Oxford: Oxford University Press, pp. 349–79.

Whitley, R. (ed.) (1992) *European business systems*, London: Sage.

Whitley, R. (1997) 'The social regulation of work systems: Institutions, interest groups, and varieties of work organization in capitalist societies', in Quack, S., Morgan, G. and Whitley, R. (eds), *National capitalisms, Global competition and Economic performance*, Amsterdam/Philadelphia: John Benjamins, pp. 227–60.

Whitley, R. (1999) *Divergent capitalisms. The social structuring and change of business systems*, Oxford: Oxford University Press.

3

Control Mechanisms and Patterns of Reorganization in MNCs

Florian Becker-Ritterspach, Knut Lange and Karin Lohr

Introduction

Current management and organizational research seems to agree in one respect: that management faces new challenges resulting mainly from globalization, whether it is real or perceived. Clearly, national corporations as much as MNCs feel the need to respond to new market conditions by reorganizing their businesses on a permanent basis. These changes concern structural configurations as much as flows of all kinds of resources including products, people and capital. However, in our empirical research we looked more closely at such reorganizations and found that even MNCs operating in the same industry were by no means responding to the challenges of globalization in a uniform or convergent way. Despite some similar trends, the types of reorganization, as well as the way the reorganization process developed, diverged from one company to the other. Searching for answers, we found that different dominant control mechanisms were key factors in explaining the divergent patterns of reorganization. Although our research topic is only indirectly linked to the general convergence–divergence debate in the context of globalization (see Ohmae, 1990; Maurice and Sorge, 2000; Morgan et al., 2001), we may nevertheless contribute to it. As will be outlined in our chapter, our findings on the connection between control mechanisms and patterns of reorganization indicate that there is as much convergence as divergence. In line with this, we suggest that the question should be less one of whether there is convergence or divergence among MNCs, but rather in which respects and why. Instead of looking for either-or, we opt for a more differentiated picture and agree with Lane (2000, 2001), who also favours a more actor-centered approach, both individual as well as collective, which includes an analysis of their structural embeddedness which may extend beyond the nation state.

From the outset, one of the main goals of our project was to explore the surmised relationship between changes in work systems, constituted by structural configuration, process organization, technical equipment and human qualifications (Sorge, 1993) and control mechanisms. Interestingly, this is a relationship that has found no attention so far in organizational research; while there is an extensive body of literature on organizational change and control mechanisms, little or no deliberate effort has been made to explore their connection. It is this connection that we wish to explore in this contribution. Empirically, our research is based on an in-depth analysis of three multinational corporations in the heavy engineering industry: a Finnish corporation (*Jukka*), a German corporation (*Karl-Heinz*) and an American corporation (*Amy*).

The contribution is structured as follows: following the introduction, the second section briefly recapitulates the debates about organizational change and control. In the third section, we elaborate our methodology and research design; whilst in the fourth, we develop a categorical framework to reflect the different patterns of reorganization. This is followed by an empirical description of the dominant patterns of reorganization observed in the MNCs. In the fifth section, analytical categories for describing control mechanisms are briefly introduced and this is again followed by an empirical outline of the dominant forms of control mechanisms in the respective MNCs. We then analyse the connection between control modes and certain aspects of the reorganization patterns and finally, summarize the major findings and draw some tentative theoretical conclusions to guide further research in the field.

The connection between reorganization and control mechanisms: an unexplored field

To our knowledge, neither the debates about change management and organizational change nor the growing body of contributions in the field of control mechanisms have explored the connection between reorganization and control mechanisms. Although the discourse on organizational change, on the one hand, and control, on the other, overlap in some respects, an explicit connection has neither been theorized nor empirically investigated.

Research on organizational change, which is often related to changing market conditions in the wake of globalization, can focus on two levels: changes in work organization and production systems is one level and changes in the whole structural configuration of corporations the other. In the early 1980s, the move away from the traditional Fordist–Taylorist production paradigm started to be discussed (Kern and Schumann, 1984; Altmann et al., 1986; Boyer, 1992; Hammer and Champy, 1993; Nippa and Picot, 1995). Among other terms, 'functional reintegration', 'job rotation', 'job enlargement', 'quality circles' and 'teamwork' were key-words describing these changes inside the firms. Although discussion of lean production and lean management in the 1980s already focused on the organization as a whole, it was mainly from the 1990s onwards that the core of the organizational change debate shifted away from a production and work organization focus towards the overall organiza-tional configuration of firms (Macharzina, 1996; Hirsch-Kreinsen, 1997; Cooper, 1998). Major findings in this research context reverberated around the terms 'decentralization' and 'dehierarchization', as well as increasing internal marketization through segmentation, profit centres and so on. In this context, control modes were also increasingly a focus, as changes in production paradigms and whole organizational structures were accompanied by new control concepts at the level of behavioural control, that is, an increase in self-control to replace formal bureaucratic control.

With the up and coming globalization debate throughout the 1990s, research on organizational change turned increasingly towards configurational changes in MNCs. This concerned itself with the discussion about a changed international division of labour in MNCs and changes in the flow of all kinds of resources (for example, capital, human resources, parts and products). Growing competition between globally dispersed production sites, outsourcing, business process reengineering, supply chain management, transnational networks and an increased focus on core competencies were all buzzwords, which attempted to encapsulate the empirically observed changes taking place in MNCs (Ruigrok and van Tulder, 1995; Hirsch-Kreinsen, 1997; Morgan, 2001). Along with the globalization debate and changed configurations in MNCs, changes in corporate governance systems also became an issue. An increase in Anglo-American governance sys-tems was claimed and seen to be manifested in growing shareholder value orientations, mainly in the form of output control by financial indicators, which were replacing or supplementing traditional forms of control (Rappaport, 1998; Hirsch-Kreinsen, 1998). Contributions to the debate often characterized the spectrum of possible control modes in terms of hierarchy, network and market, without, however, reaching agreement on which of the modes was acquiring new dominance (Ouchi, 1980; Thompson and Frances, 1993; Hennart, 1993; Hedlund, 1993).

In summary, whenever the issue control was raised in the context of organizational change, it was seen as part of, or a concomitant of, a new structural configuration resulting from liberalization and globalization of markets.

A review of the literature on control mechanisms, however, also reveals (Dunning 1994; Becerra, 1998; Harzing, 1999) that little or no attention has been given to the connection between coordination mechanisms and processes of change in MNCs. In a comprehensive analysis, Becerra (1998) reviews the extensive body of literature on the control of national subsidiaries and identifies the following dominant issues:

- Organizational structure as a control mechanism
- Contingencies, such as type of activity or function to be controlled and country of origin, influencing the extent of control
- Studies on and categorizations of control systems, including types of control and specific control mechanisms
- The connection between different strategies and control and coordination at the MNC level
- The connection between different strategic roles of subsidiaries and their control.

Both the individual studies as well as the summaries of various aspects of control mechanisms in MNCs show that research in the field has mainly centred around the influence of various contingencies (for example, size, environmental conditions, subsidiary and headquarters–subsidiary interdependence, function or activity to be controlled, headquarters as well as subsidiary characteristics) on the use of different control mechanisms. In contrast to this, no effort has been made so far to systematically link different aspects or types of control with different paths or patterns of reorganization in MNCs.

Our reflection on the connection between control mechanisms and patterns of reorganization is based on the following guiding assumptions:

- Reorganizations develop through social interaction and negotiation between different inter- and intra-corporate actors positioned at different hierarchical and functional levels (headquarters, subsidiaries, consulting firms).
- Processes of reorganization constituted by the interaction of different actors are power-asymmetric, since this interaction is strongly related to the exchange and exchangeability of resources (see Geppert et al. forthcoming).
- In reorganizations, actors pursue more or less diverging or conflicting goals, which are related to their different rationalities. Different rationalities, in turn, have to be seen as an outflow of different types of micro- (for example, hierarchical position, functional position, dominant form of control in a firm), meso- (for example, typical task environments and competitive dynamics of an industry) and macro-structural embeddedness (for example, national legislation, supranational accounting principles).
- Linking reorganization patterns and control mechanisms is the core assumption that control mechanisms strongly influence the distribution of resources, particularly of decision-making powers. This may, in turn, explain the different actors' level of involvement and autonomy in shaping different aspects of reorganization.

To distinguish control mechanisms from patterns of reorganization is, to some extent, an analytical process, as the reorganizations themselves may be a mode of controlling, for example, certain corporate units. Equally, to state that control mechanisms impact patterns of reorganization is not to deny the reverse influence, as a change in control mechanisms may be the very goal of the reorganization itself. However, despite being aware of these intricacies and cross-relations, we chose the overall dominant control mechanisms in the respective MNCs as a starting point and sought to identify if and how they impacted certain aspects of the reorganization projects.

Methodology

The study adopts a multiple *case study approach*. More precisely, the study involves not only multiple cases but also, within these cases, multiple units of analysis (Yin, 1994). The justification for this embedded case study approach is found primarily in two aspects of the research question: firstly, the required depth of analysis and secondly, the process perspective involved. Given our prime research interest of investigating patterns and interactive processes that are seen to underlie the formation and development of work systems, qualitative case studies appeared to be an appropriate means to gain an in-depth and holistic understanding of such intricate processes.

The selection of *research cases* was aimed at choosing a small population of MNCs in one industry. The cases mentioned in this chapter are three multinationals operating in a specific branch of the heavy engineering industry. *Data collection* rested primarily on qualitative data supplied by guided interviews (Flick, 1996). However, other sources of data collection were also employed such as group discussions in the corporations, a wide variety of documentary information and diagrammatic material provided by interviewees (Eisenhardt, 1989; Patton, 1990). All in all, 28 guided interviews were conducted lasting one to three hours. In *Jukka*, eight interviews were conducted and in *Karl-Heinz* and *Amy*, nine interviews. The interviews were always conducted by a team of two to allow the case to be 'viewed from the different perspectives of multiple observers' (Eisenhardt, 1989: 541). The *data analysis* was strongly informed by guidelines on qualitative data content analysis outlined by Miles and Huberman (1994): these are data reduction, data display and conclusion drawing and verification. In accordance with Miles and Huberman, we do not see these steps as sequential but rather as interactive and intertwined throughout the research process. In terms of *verification*, we followed the validity criteria suggested by Yin (1994), namely construct validity, internal validity, external validity and reliability. In line with these criteria, we can claim construct validity, internal validity as well as reliability of our data. External validity, however, which refers to whether the findings can be generalized via replication, cannot be stated (Yin, 1994): as no replication has been conducted in other industries, we cannot claim to be able to generalize the findings beyond the branch of industry researched.

Patterns of reorganization

Analytical framework

According to Ortmann, processes of organizational change can be analytically distinguished by whether they represent an 'evolution' or a 'reorganization' (Ortmann et al., 1997: 333). Whereas processes of evolution are understood as unintended and unplanned changes mainly via selection, reorganization is seen as an intended and reflected restructuring of the organization. In this chapter, we are concerned only with reorganizations and define them in line with Ortmann et al. (1997) as those organizational changes that are based on a minimum of intended, planned and reflective restructuring of an organization. To analytically grasp different *patterns of reorganization,* we differentiate between reorganizations depending on their *type* and their *process of development.* While the first aspect concerns *what* changes, the second considers *how* the organization changes.

Types of reorganization

In terms of what type of reorganization takes place, the *reach* and *depth* are distinguished. The *reach* of a reorganization refers to the question of whether a reorganization affects the MNC as a whole (far-reaching or global) or whether only some units or parts are involved (limited or local). If a reorganization is far reaching, that is, involves all units of a corporation and, particularly, the whole configuration of the MNC, we talk about strategic reorganization. In contrast, those reorganizations that are limited to one or only a few units are termed operational or local.

The *depth* of a reorganization concerns the question of how deeply it induces change or how radically it cuts into existing structures and processes of a local unit and/or the corporation as a whole. Table 3.1 illustrates different types of reorganization based on their depth and reach.

Development of reorganization

In terms of how the reorganization developed, we looked at reorganization processes. Reorganization processes are seen to be typically constituted by three *phases*: inducement, conceptualization and implementation and can be differentiated on the basis of the actors involved, their resources and their rationalities.

In the different phases of reorganization, there can be substantial variance in terms of how long, how planned and how reflected the respective phases are. While in some cases the inducement to introduce a reorganization may be easily traced back to a person or an event, it may be less obvious and more emergent in other cases.

Table 3.1   Types of reorganization based on depth and reach

Reach/ Depth	Far-reaching/global	Limited/local
Low	Modest-strategic	Modest-operative
Deep	Radical-strategic	Radical-operative

Likewise, in some cases, the phase of conceptualization may be long, well planned and reflected upon, whilst in another there is barely any planning and it resembles more an ad hoc implementation by trial and error. It is also important to note that the three different phases have to be seen as an analytical distinction, as in practice they may be tightly inter-woven.

In distinguishing the analysis of reorganization processes in terms of actors, resources and rationalities, we were influenced by structuration theory. In line with Giddens (1984) and Ortmann et al. (1997), we understand processes of reorganization as structuration processes. Structures are seen to be the framework in which social interaction is embedded but structures do not determine action, action always remains contingent. Whilst, on the one hand, structures simultaneously enable and delimit action, on the other, they are the very result and creation of human action (duality of structure). Thus the actors' behaviour relates to structures in a recursive way.

Ortmann et al. (1997), who have, among others, applied Giddens' structuration theory to organization research, distinguish in this context two aspects of structure: the rules of signification and legitimation on the one hand and allocative as well as authoritative resources on the other. Again, the two aspects are seen to be recursively interconnected. In the following analysis of reorganization patterns, we refer to core ideas and categories of structuration theory, albeit with some modifications.

As we were mainly concerned with analysing reorganizations at the level of interaction, the first step was to identify the relevant *actors* involved in the interactive processes of reorganization and, more concretely, the extent to which internal and external actors or central and local actors are involved in the inducement, conceptualization and implementation of a reorganization. This involves both the question of their organizational (central vs. local) and their societal embeddedness (which countries) and what function or role they play in the reorganizations.

Also in line with Giddens (1984) and Ortmann et al. (1997), we understand that the actors' behaviour and interaction always mirrors structural opportunities and limitations, although they may not be consciously reflected upon but rather take on the form of 'generalizable procedures applied in the enactment/reproduction of social practices' (Giddens, 1984: 21). What is more, structural opportunities and limitations on action were seen to be crucially mediated by the resources available to the actors, as well as by the rules of signification and legitimation that find expression in the behavioural rationalities of actors.

We have chosen the term 'behavioural rationalities' instead of rules at the level of interaction, as it seems to be more appropriate for expressing crystallized patterns of behaviour. It also avoids the formal structural connotation of the term 'rules and norms'.

Thus, also in the context of reorganizations we expect *resources* to play a key role. Processes of reorganization, as any other process of social interaction, are power-asymmetric due to the uneven distribution of resources (see Geppert et al. forthcoming). This implies that, depending on their access to and availability of resources, actors can, to a greater or lesser extent, enforce their goals. Borrowing loosely from Giddens, we can distinguish authoritative and allocative resources (Giddens, 1984). *Authoritative resources* basically concern an actor's decision-making rights and derive mainly from the actor's hierarchical position, but also from the legitimacy of traditional habits or personal charisma (Weber, 1922/1972). In contrast, *allocative resources* refer to the availability of capital, technical equipment, staff, skills and knowledge and so on; they derive from an actor's function or task, but also the hierarchical position in a corporation. Another sort of resource needs, however, to be mentioned: the availability of time. Different kinds of resources, which are seen to be crucial for reorganization, can be allocated at different spaces, that is, locally or centrally, inside or outside the organization.

Besides resources, the *rationalities* of actors were also seen to play a strong role in the processes of reorganization. Rationalities imply that which the actors consider legitimate, right and appropriate. Behavioural rationalities of actors strongly express norms and rules or the governing logic in specific areas of corporate activity. Such areas can be, for example, specific task environments of local units. The rationalities of actors also have an impact on their priorities in terms of goals and interests. In processes of reorganization, the rationalities of actors can compete and conflict to a greater or lesser extent (Deutschmann et al., 1995), for example, technical vs. financial rationality or local vs. global rationality (Table 3.2).

Empirical findings: patterns of reorganization

The three MNCs investigated were all facing a similar strategic challenge to strike a balance between local responsiveness to specific needs of local customers and global efficiencies to drive down costs and live up to capital market profitability expectations (Becker-Ritterspach et al., 2001a,b). In response to these strategic challenges, we saw a trend towards convergence and common strategic answers in the

Table 3.2 Development of reorganization

Phases/ Inputs	Inducement	Conceptualization	Implementation
Actors	Location and type of actors in the respective phases		
Resources	Allocation, type and amount of resources involved in the respective phases		
Rationalities	Diverging and/or conflicting rationalities in the respective phases		

industry under review (Iwer, 2000). Although varying in degree, all the major players sought:

- to realize a stronger customer orientation by separating production, R&D and customer services and by decentralizing the latter.
- to realize scale economies by downsizing and concentrating R&D and production units.
- to combine flexibility and scale economies by introducing modularized products based on standardized components.

All the MNCs were about to reorganize their internal division of labour, which essentially meant more internationalized supply chains. However, the strategic challenges in the industry only defined a corridor of potential strategic action and reorganization, they did not determine it. Comparing our three corporations more closely, we saw that they differed markedly in terms of the dominant patterns of reorganization. These three different patterns can be summarized as follows.

Jukka: *dominance of top–down, radical–strategic reorganization*

During the 1990s, *Jukka* witnessed a series of mainly radical–strategic reorganizations. Under the corporate heading of 'integration' and 'harmonization', the major strategic goal was the realization of scale economies. At the heart of the most recent reorganization lay the introduction of an IT-based organizational model that aimed at integrating and standardizing major business processes, as well as all kinds of administrative procedures throughout the corporation. All in all, the strategic reorganizations changed the configuration of the corporation as a whole and cut deeply into the organization of the local units. For the local units, these changes meant, more than anything else, a decrease in functional differentiation and autonomy. As a result, local units were allocated a much more operational role. What is more, as the local units were kept busy with implementing centrally devised reorganizations and had to adapt their structures and processes to the whole corporation, little or no operative reorganization took place.

With regard to the development of the reorganizations, HQ inducement and central conceptualization, as well as long-term orientation, were characteristic. Equally, the forceful top–down manner in which past and present reorganizations were induced, devised and implemented was typical for *Jukka*. Moreover, a very high level of planning was identified as all phases of the implementation were meticulously standardized and prescribed. The key players in the reorganization were HQ based and mainly supported by IT experts as well as external consultants. The reorganization also involved a substantial mobilization of resources (allocative, authoritative and time), most of which, however, were centrally allocated. As opposed to the HQ based players, local actors (also called 'process owners') were only involved in the implementation phase, where their intricate knowledge of locally specific processes was needed. The heteronomous nature of the reorganization measures, in terms of inducement, development and implementation, triggered hefty resistance in local units. The loss of autonomy, the cultural imposition, cost pressures, the degradation of formerly strategic roles all led to a strong clash of local and central rationalities. While the headquarters' actors were dominated by an overall corporate and economic-technological rationality, mirrored in their goals of integration, optimization and cost reduction, the local units' rationalities were shaped by their former autonomy, their local task environment (customer-specific products) and traditions, which were strongly related to their past national (that is, the German made-to-order engineering culture) and organizational embeddedness.

Karl-Heinz: *dominance of top–down, bottom–up, moderate–strategic reorganization*

Compared to *Jukka, Karl-Heinz* saw only limited comprehensive reorganization activity before the mid-1990s. Thereafter, the mostly moderate–strategic reorganizations in corporation *Karl-Heinz* centred around the introduction of a unified reporting system, the changeover to the US-GAAP accounting system and the segmentation of practically all corporate units, including small production units within the factories. Taken together, these measures were aimed at establishing the conditions for the implementation of a 'value-oriented control system'.

In other words, the major goal was to introduce an Anglo-American governance system together with the structural preconditions for it. Unlike *Jukka*, *Karl-Heinz* was much less interested in defining, standardizing and prescribing structures and processes. Although standardization may have been the result to some extent, the reorganization measures – particularly the segmentation – were implemented differently in the respective local units. This was mainly due to the rather open conceptual framework of the reorganization, which left concretization and implementation measures to the local units' discretion. From the local units' perspective, the strategic reorganization, and in particular the segmentation, called for local reorganization and some degree of functional disintegration (separation of service and production). However, compared to *Jukka's* corporate-wide reorganization, *Karl-Heinz's* local units not only enjoyed relative freedom and autonomy to realize moderate-strategic reorganizations, but also had the necessary organizational slack to undertake, in addition, their own moderate-operative reorganizations.

In terms of the reorganization development, *Karl-Heinz's* strategic reorganizations were centrally induced with the support of internal and external consultants. Although external consultants introduced the reorganization concepts, their actual shaping and concretization took place in the local units. Also, in terms of the implementation process, the corporate headquarters neither initiated nor prescribed a strictly phased action plan. On the contrary, it was clearly seen as a local task to shape and implement the reorganization. The extent to which local concept development and implementation took place was, to a certain degree, a matter of garbage-can logic (March and Olsen, 1972); that is, dependent on the availability of powerful local promoters supporting the reorganization concepts at a given point in time. Typical for *Karl-Heinz's* conceptualization and implementation processes was a broad participation of different actors from different organizational levels in the local units (including top and middle management and the works council). All in all, the shaping and implementation of the concepts took on the form of a bottom-up dynamic, following top-down inducement from the headquarters. The local units also appeared to have sufficient allocative, authoritative and time resources to realize the reorganization autonomously. Although different rationalities, mainly based on different national industry dynamics were observed, conflict between central and local actors did not appear to be particularly strong. On the one hand, the relatively low level of conflict in the coexistence of the different rationalities was due to the remaining autonomy of local units, on the other hand, it was also due to the headquarters' explicitly expressed attitude that local rationalities and embeddedness play a vital part in organizing the business in different national spaces.

Amy: *dominance of ad hoc operative reorganization*

Compared to the other two corporations, we found hardly any strategic reorganization in *Amy*. The only strategic reorganizations were centrally induced best practice initiatives such as QCPC (quality control process charts), TPM (total productivity maintenance), 5S (strengthen, sort, straighten, standardize, sustain) and EH&S guidelines (environment, health and safety), which aimed at improving all kinds of processes with regard to quality, safety at work and environmental protection. By and large, these process improvements were moderate, as they did not cut deeply into the way corporate and local processes were organized. In terms of implementation and further development, local units also had a substantial degree of freedom. Apart from these very limited global initiatives, a dominance of local or operational reorganization was observed in *Amy*. However, with regard to the content or depth, there was a variation between moderate and radical reorganizations. Whilst in the first unit, the local service business was restructured, production was outsourced in another and closed altogether in a third case.

The inducement of these operational reorganizations followed a similar path or mechanism in most cases; the reorganizations were indirectly induced through the existence or imposition of highly ambitious profitability indicators. If these financial targets were not met, local management had to initiate more or less radical changes. Which measures were taken, however, was up to the local management. Thus, within the local units it was, unlike the case of *Karl-Heinz*, mainly the local top management who devised the reorganization measures or, in some cases, invited external consultants to support them. Those affected by the reorganization measures, for example middle management, other employees and the works councils, were hardly involved at all. It was also a characteristic of these local reorganizations that the allocative and time resources were extremely scarce, which also contributed to an overall low level of participation in the local units. As a consequence, reorganizations in *Amy* were short-term oriented and showed a low level of planning in their mainly ad hoc and trial and error characteristics. The dominant rationalities of actors involved in the local reorganizations were strongly based on internal competition and target figure oriented. Local and HQ rationalities complemented each other to the extent that profitability indicators and other quantitative performance indicators were a strong point of common reference. In line with this HQ based rationality, local units were granted autonomy and authoritative resources for the conceptualization and implementation of reorganizations as long as profitability and internal competitiveness were secured. The permanent pressure for profitability and the lingering fear about their continued existence motivated key local actors to induce and implement reorganizations. Lack of time and low participation levels, however, triggered a fair amount of conflict within the local units (due to job loss, non-involvement and so on). In contrast to the high level of local conflict, little overt headquarter–subsidiary conflict was observed.

Concluding the empirical outline of the reorganizations, different patterns of reorganization were found along the analytical dimensions developed beforehand. There were not only differences in terms of the dominant types of reorganization (radical and moderate) – ranging from strategic to operative – but also in terms of their development (Table 3.3). The question is how to explain these diverging patterns of reorganization. One of our core theses is that a closer look at the control mechanisms in the respective MNC will yield some explanatory power.

Control mechanisms

Analytical categories

Before we try to outline the connection between patterns of reorganization and control mechanisms, the latter have to be looked at more closely. This requires a more refined conceptualization of control mechanisms, which goes beyond the rather broad distinction of hierarchy, market and network. Our conceptualization is based mainly on Harzing's (1999) analytical categories, which are derived from an intensive review of the vast number of contributions in the field of control.

Generally, two control mechanisms, direct and indirect control mechanisms, can be broadly distinguished (Baliga and Jaeger, 1984; Harzing, 1999). Whereas direct control mechanisms aim at directly controlling behaviour, indirect mechanisms aim at controlling only the outcome of behaviour. Besides the distinction between direct and indirect mechanisms, Harzing further distinguishes, on another dimension, whether control mechanisms are personal/cultural, that is

Table 3.3 Summary of empirically observed reorganization patterns

Corporation/ Pattern	Jukka	Karl-Heinz	Amy
Type of reorganization	Radical-strategic	Moderate-strategic (Some moderate-operative)	Radical as well as moderate-operative (Some moderate-strategic)
Reach	The whole corporation	Corporation-wide but locally differentiated	Locally differentiated
Depth	Strongly impacts all structures and processes	Mainly impacts corporate governance	Differs strongly from case to case
Development of the reorganization			
Dominant Actors	HQ induced through top management	HQ induced through top management	HQ induced through ambitious financial indicators
	Mainly conceptualized and implemented by central experts and external consultants	Some involvement of external consultants in broad concept development	Mainly conceptualized and implemented by local top management
	Selected local actors take part in implementation, otherwise very low level of participation within local units	Mainly conceptualized and implemented by local actors	Low degree of participation within local units
		High degree of participation within local units	Involvement of consultants varies by location

Resources	Based on substantial resources of all kinds HQ allocated	Based on authoritative resources in HQ	Based on authoritative resources in HQ
	Limited allocative resources and a very low level of authoritative resources in local units	A fair amount of authoritative, time and allocative resources in local units	A fair amount of authoritative resources in local units
			Very limited amount of time and allocative resources in local units
Conflicting rationalities	Overall corporate and economic-technical rationality in HQ conflicting with local rationalities of tradition, task and national industry environment	Different rationalities (mainly based on different national industry dynamics perceived) between HQ and local units coexist	Local and central rationalities similar or complementary, based on internal market orientation and performance indicators
	High conflict between HQ and local units	Moderate conflict between HQ and local units	Little overt local vs. central conflict was observed
Dominant pattern	Radical-strategic	Moderate-strategic	Operative
	Top-down	Top-down, bottom-up	Ad hoc

Table 3.4   Classification of control mechanisms on two dimensions

Personal/Cultural (founded on social interaction)		Impersonal/Bureaucratic/ Technocratic (founded on instrumental artifacts)
Direct	Personal centralized control	Formal bureaucratic control
Indirect	Socio-integrative control	Output control

Source: Modified from Harzing (1999: 21).

founded on social interaction, or impersonal/bureaucratic/techno-cratic, that is founded on instrumental artifacts. Combining these two dimensions, Harzing develops the following taxonomy, which has been modified slightly and serves as a reference point for our own research questions.

Direct control mechanisms

Table 3.4 indicates that direct control mechanisms can take the form of either *personal centralized control* or *bureaucratic formalized control*. Personal centralized control is based on the social interaction between actors (superior and subordinate) and comes in the form of personal directives, personal supervision (Blau and Scott, 1963; Mintzberg, 1979, 1983), top level decision-making (Harzing, 1999), management transfer and rotation. *Formal bureaucratic control* implies control through programmes, plans (March and Simon, 1958), standardization (Thompson, 1967), formalization (Child, 1973) and rules and regulations (Harzing, 1999).

Indirect coordination and control mechanisms

As opposed to direct control mechanisms, indirect mechanisms encompass either *socio-integrative* control, as Harzing (1999) puts it 'socialization and networks', or *output control*. Both mechanisms imply strong elements of self-coordination (Kieser, 1998) and self-organization.

Socio-integrative control mechanisms are based on socialization processes that find expression in shared *meanings, rationalities and goals*. They can also be understood as, what Bartlett and Ghoshal call, 'cooption' or the 'matrix of the mind' (Bartlett and Ghoshal, 1998: 226). That is, they achieve inter-unit integration and cooperation through 'a common understanding of, identification with, and commitment to the corporation's objectives, priorities, and values' (Bartlett and Ghoshal, 1987: 78).

As opposed to socio-integrative mechanisms, output control is mainly based on 'objective' figures and indicators. This control form is based on the idea of management by objectives, that is, goal setting without defining ways of attainment. They find expression in the agreement on, or imposition of, strategic goals, budgets, indicators (financial as well as non-financial) and specific ratios indicating profitability (for example, return on capital employed). As opposed to direct mechanisms, indirect control mechanisms are theoretically based on self-control within decentralized corporate units.

Empirical findings: control mechanisms

According to our findings, and supported by other research (Jürgens et al., 2000), the adoption of indirect, result-oriented control mechanisms is on the rise within MNCs (Sauer and Döhl, 1997; Hirsch-Kreinsen, 1999; Morgan, 2001; Tainio et al., 2001). This tendency was most obvious in case of *Karl-Heinz*. Although *Karl-Heinz* had coordinated and controlled for some time using output control, it was not until the late 1990s that an elaborate and integrated output control was implemented, which more closely reflected Anglo-American governance. Moreover, the move towards Anglo-American corporate governance was also manifested in the introduction of stock option programmes in early 2000 in *Jukka* as well as in *Karl-Heinz*, whereas *Amy* already had a long tradition of elaborate output control.

The changes in corporate governance have to be seen in the wider context of changing societal governance or changing 'business systems' (Cerny, 1997; Dore, 2000). Following Hirsch-Kreinsen, we would agree that the 'shareholder value concept' is the driving force behind the increased introduction of indirect control mechanisms (Hirsch-Kreinsen, 1998). The erosion of nationally specific capital market structures, caused primarily by deregulation and the globalization of capital investments, is the key factor behind the push for shareholder value orientations within MNCs. As important, however, is probably the MNCs' ever increasing need for capital to finance globalization and innovation activities and, concomitantly, their ability to attract the sought-after capital on a global scale. Capital can, in turn, only be attracted if control mechanisms are in place, which supposedly give capital investors the transparency and ability to compare different types of capital investment. Thus, indirect control mechanisms can be seen as a precondition for attracting capital investment, as they make it easier for capital market investors to seek out the most profitable form of capital investment.

However, despite some convergence towards result-oriented control mechanisms, we did not find an all-out convergence in the investigated MNCs (see also Harzing et al.'s contribution in this volume). This is mainly because result-oriented control mechanisms were, to a greater or lesser extent, combined with other control mechanisms, which sometimes even contradicted each other. The empirical evidence for this is presented below.

Jukka: *dominance of formal bureaucratic control and personal centralized control*

Subsidiaries of *Jukka* were coordinated and controlled by the most comprehensive control scenario of all three MNCs. Elaborate output control, financial as well as non-financial, was combined with far-reaching formal bureaucratic control, personal centralized control as well as socio-integrative control. However, although *Jukka* had a long tradition of output control and had deliberately stepped up its efforts to boost socio-integrative mechanisms in the early 1990s (for example, by creating a common corporate language, enforcing a common corporate logo and increasing the number of management meetings and workshops), formal bureaucratic control and personal centralized control, including the use of Finnish expatriates (termed the 'Finnish Mafia'), appeared to be the overriding control mechanisms (see Marschan et al., 1999: 429). Subsidiaries were even faced with contradictory control mechanisms, as certain output expectations were coupled with direct control and thus did not allow local management to achieve results in the way they deemed most appropriate. In sum, *Jukka*'s subsidiaries had the least amount of autonomy with respect to organizing operations and activities.

Karl-Heinz: *dominance of output control, supplemented by some informal personal centralized control*

Subsidiaries of *Karl-Heinz* were exposed to the least amount of formal bureaucratic control. At the time of research, a common IT reporting system had just been introduced into all subsidiaries. Apart from a fixed set of reporting policies guiding output control, *Karl-Heinz* did not impose any standardized procedures, processes or policies on its subsidiaries. Informal personal centralized control, in the form of regular visits by senior HQ managers, supplemented what was otherwise a dominance of output control.

Socio-integrative control mechanisms, such as management rotation or common value creation, were not observed. *Karl-Heinz*'s mix of control mechanisms was based on output control, supplemented by some informal personal centralized control. Informal personal centralized control became more pronounced when subsidiaries underperformed, that is, when they had problems achieving the centrally determined profitability indicators. Thus, the subsidiaries had a relatively far-reaching autonomy in the organization of their operations, as long as output was in line with the financial targets.

Amy: *dominance of output control, with a strong emphasis on internal market competition*

In *Amy*, we saw the strongest focus on output control, combined with deliberate efforts to foster internal market competition. The local units were not only coordinated and controlled by short-term profitability targets, but also faced a situation of permanent competition with other corporate units. Apart from a strong emphasis on output control, a moderate amount of formal bureaucratic control, in the form of some globally defined policies and procedures, and some limited personal centralized control were evident. Personal centralized control in the form of expatriates played practically no role in the local units investigated; not a single expatriate was found. However, a few areas, such as R&D, were under personal centralized control. In terms of socio-integrative mechanisms, the picture was somewhat mixed. On the one hand, little deliberate common value creation was observed. On the other hand, globally standardized policies and, above all, the strong culture of internal competition, manifested, for example, in the distribution of gold, silver and bronze performance awards, were sure to have had a socializing effect in terms of creating common understandings. All in all, the direct control mechanisms in *Amy's* case hardly interfered with the subsidiaries' organization of operations (Table 3.5). In other words, apart from a very focused set of corporate-wide standards and policies on quality, health and the environment, *Amy's* units had a relatively high level of autonomy to organize their operations.

The connection between control mechanisms and patterns of reorganization

After outlining control mechanisms as well as patterns of reorganization, we now seek to identify some connections between the two. To begin with, one of the initial findings was that, in some cases, the control mechanisms themselves had become the object of change and this

Table 3.5   Summary of empirically observed control mechanisms

Corporations/ Control Mechanisms	Jukka	Karl-Heinz	Amy
Direct			
Personal centralized	Very Strong	Considerable	Existent
Formal bureaucratic	Considerable	Not observed	Existent
Indirect			
Socio-integrative	Existent	Not observed	Existent
Output	Considerable	Strong	Very strong
Dominance	Personal centrallized plus formal bureaucratic control	Output plus informal centralized control	Output plus strong internal market competition

made it somewhat difficult to relate these reorganizations to specific control mechanisms. Apart from this finding, it appeared that the patterns of reorganization differed most strongly depending on whether the respective companies relied more on direct or indirect mechanisms of control.

Direct control mechanisms and patterns of reorganization

Where direct control mechanisms dominated, their effect on patterns of reorganization was such that local units had only limited autonomy in the inducement, conceptualization as well as the implementation of reorganizations. *Jukka* was a case in point, where the dominance of direct control mechanisms (personal centralized and bureaucratic) delimited the authoritative resources available to local units in the process of reorganization. Whilst personal centralized control curtailed local participation and decision-making rights due to direct HQ intervention, the strong formal bureaucratic controls (for example, management handbooks, roll-out procedures) also limited local actors' authoritative resources through their detailed descriptions and plans for the change processes. What is more, direct mechanisms, in general, and personal centralized control modes, in particular, seemed to make a clash of different rationalities more likely, as local actors were left with little or no freedom to bring in their own ideas and concepts. However, our findings suggest (see also *Karl-Heinz* and *Amy*) that specifically the inducement for strategic reorganizations is generally directly controlled, that is, by personal centralized control, no matter what the dominant control mechanisms otherwise are in the corporation. Some explanations for this include their reach, their perceived importance, the anticipated conflict and, above all, the simple fact that authoritative resources for strategic reorganization tend to be centrally allocated. This, however, is not to say that all phases of strategic reorganization will necessarily be directly controlled, although this was the case with *Jukka*. Particularly the case of *Karl-Heinz* showed that, although the inducement for strategic reorganization was directly controlled, the phases of conceptualization and implementation were left to the local units and thus reflected the dominance of output control in this corporation. The focus on the dominant control mechanisms in the two contrasting cases offers some explanation for the divergence. Whereas *Jukka's* dominant control mode was direct mechanisms, *Karl-Heinz* relied more on indirect mechanisms, namely output control. As a result, the two corporations differed markedly with regard to the allocation of authoritative resources and this had a strong impact on their patterns of reorganization. In addition, there was also a much lower level of headquarter–subsidiary conflict in the case of *Karl-Heinz* as its mode of control interfered much less with local rationalities. We can thus tentatively infer that, although the inducement for strategic reorganization tends to be directly controlled, the way the conceptualization and implementation processes develop through the involvement of central or local actors may vary depending on the otherwise dominant control mechanism in the MNC.

Indirect control mechanisms and patterns of reorganization

As opposed to direct mechanisms, indirect control mechanisms generally leave more authoritative resources to local actors in both operative and strategic reorganizations. As output control is based on the idea that specific goals have to be met, without, however, defining the way of achievement, there is naturally less interference in how local units structure or restructure themselves. The cases of *Karl-Heinz* and *Amy* showed that subsidiaries were generally free to reorganize autonomously; direct control was only observed when output did not meet the targets set at central level. Even when operative reorganizations were centrally induced, as in the case of *Amy*, conceptualization and implementation were left in the hands of the local unit actors. What is more, the clash of central and local rationalities resulting from reorganizations appeared to be much less serious in corporations like *Karl-Heinz* and *Amy*, which are dominantly controlled by output. This is mainly due to the fact that indirect mechanisms, by their very nature, do not impose specific concepts and ideas upon other actors.

However, the effects of output control on patterns of reorganization need to be further distinguished. It is important to note in this context that output control can vary to a certain degree. In corporation *Amy*, where output control went hand in hand with strong internal marketization and competition, local units seemed to have little or no time and allocative slack resources to invest in long-term and planned reorganization measures. As any utilization of scarce resources was seen as endangering short-term profitability and weakening the unit's internal competitive position, no large-scale mobilization of resources for reorganization was observed. Empirically, the difference in output control was most evident in the cases of *Karl-Heinz* and *Amy*, two MNCs with pronounced output control. As opposed to *Amy*, *Karl-Heinz* had neither a longstanding tradition of complex and elaborate output control nor a particularly strong level of internal competition. As a consequence, the availability of allocative and time resources for reorganizations was much higher in the local units of *Karl-Heinz*.

Finally, the effect of socio-integrative control mechanisms on reorganizations also has to be considered. With socio-integrative control mechanisms, we have to distinguish between whether they are deliberately employed or fostered or whether they just happen to be at work.

Corporation *Jukka* was a good example of the deliberate employment and fostering of socio-integrative mechanisms, albeit with contradictory effects in terms of reorganization. The fostering of a common corporate language and culture had limited impact on the integration and creation of common rationalities between local and central actors in the reorganization processes. On the contrary, local units rejected the measures, experiencing them as cultural imposition from the Finnish HQ. This resistance, however, was countered with yet another mechanism that was both socio-integrative and direct control: Finnish managers, who had been socialized into corporate culture at HQ level, were sent into local units to control them directly and overcome the disintegrative effects of diverging local rationalities in order to implement the same reorganization throughout the corporation. The case of *Amy* also suggests that socio-integrative control mechanisms were implicitly at work. The strong culture of internal competition most probably created a certain acceptance on the part of local management of performance-related reorganization inducement. In summary, socio-integrative control mechanisms work to create more or less converging rationalities of actors. This, in turn, has a very significant effect on the level of contestation in the process of reorganization.

Theoretical conclusions and final reflections

Our contribution has tried to explore the connection between control mechanisms and patterns of reorganization. Within this explanatory context – albeit for a small population of MNCs – we have shown that different dominant mechanisms of control strongly influence patterns of reorganization, through the allocation and availability of resources, as well as their impact on the level of conflict between different rationalities. Due to the small sample of companies investigated, the connections observed allow no generalizations. They may, however, allow us to derive some tentative theoretical conclusions to guide further research in the field.

1. High levels of personal centralized control – be it in the form of expatriates or directives – tend to curtail local authoritative resources. As a result, local participation and initiative in the development and implementation of reorganization, certainly at a strategic level and probably also at operative levels, appear to be limited, no matter the extent of allocative and time resources available locally. The likelihood of conflicting rationalities is also high, as the latitude for local units to achieve specific targets is narrow.
2. Strong formal bureaucratic control mechanisms tend to strongly prescribe and structure the development of reorganization in terms of the phases, participating actors and allocation of resources. In combination with centralized personal control, they diminish local actors' authoritative resources, particularly when procedures and plans are imposed, which prescribe all the steps in the development of the reorganization.
3. A dominance of output control generally allocates authoritative resources for the conceptualization and implementation of reorganization, mainly at an operative level but also at strategic levels, to local actors. As concepts and implementation tend not to be externally imposed, a clash between central and local rationalities in the reorganization process tends to be low. However, if output control is linked with strong competition among the subunits, local units may not be able to invest a substantial amount of allocative and time resources to the reorganization measures due to the lack of slack resources.

As a result, reorganization is more likely to be ad hoc, with little planning or broad participation levels, and carried out in a relatively short period of time. If output control, on the other hand, occurs without strong internal competition, more allocative and time resources appear to be available. Under these circumstances, local actors are also more willing to invest them and, as a consequence, reorganizations show a higher degree of development and planning, as well as broader participation levels. What is more, subunits are also more willing to share knowledge under conditions of low internal competition.

4. Socio-integrative control mechanisms, whether deliberately fostered or implicitly at work, can serve to create similar rationalities between different actors. In terms of reorganization, actors may have internalized a common understanding of what type of reorganization is needed and how it should be developed. Effective socio-integrative control mechanisms may, in this way, reduce the clash of rationalities and, thus, the level of conflict in the reorganization process. It is doubtful, however, whether socio-integrative mechanisms can be readily created by deliberate management initiatives.

Finally, having stated a connection between different control modes and patterns of reorganizations, we do not assume that dominant control modes develop in a vacuum. While it is not our intention to recapitulate the debate on control and all the possible contingencies that influence it, three areas, in which our MNCs differed sharply, emerged in our research as having a substantial impact on the dominating control mode in the respective MNC. These were: the internationalization strategy, ownership structure and the country of origin of the corporations (see also Harzing et al. and Geppert et al. in this volume).

References

Altmann, N., Deiß, M., Döhl, V. and Sauer, D. (1986) 'Ein "Neuer Rationalisierungstyp" – neue Anforderungen an die Industriesoziologie', *Soziale Welt*, 37, pp. 191–207.

Baliga, B. R. and Jaeger, A. M. (1984) 'Multinational Corporations: Control Systems and Delegation Issues', *Journal of International Business Studies*, 15 (Fall), pp. 25–40.

Bartlett, C. A. and Ghoshal, S. (1987) 'Managing across Borders: New Strategic Requirements', *Sloan Management Review*, 28, pp. 7–17.

Bartlett, C. A. and Ghoshal, S. (1998) *Managing Across Borders: The Transnational Solution*, Boston: Harvard Business School Press.

Becerra, M. (1998) *Control of National Subsidiaries: A Critical Assessment and Future Research Directions*, paper presented in 2001 at the Founding Conference of the European Academy of Management in Barcelona.

Becker-Ritterspach, F., Lange, K. and Lohr, K. (2001a) *Do European Corporate Coordination and Control Systems Converge?* Paper presented at the Founding Conference of the European Academy of Management in Barcelona.

Becker-Ritterspach, F., Lange, K. and Lohr, K. (2001b) *The Micro-Coevolution of an Organisational Model in a Multinational Corporation: Bringing Actors into the Coevolutionary Framework*, paper presented at the EGOS conference in Lyon.

Blau, P. M. and Scott, W. R. (1963) *Formal Organizations*, London: Routledge & Kegan Paul.

Boyd, G. and Dunning, J. H. (1999) *Structural Change and Cooperation in the Global Economy*, Cheltenham: Edward Elgar.

Boyer, R. (1992) 'Neue Richtungen von Managementpraktiken und Arbeits-organisation', in Demirovic, A. (ed.) *Hegemonie und Staat. Kapitalistische Regulation als Projekt und Prozeß*, Münster: Westfälisches Dampfboot, pp. 55–103.

Cerny, P. (1997) 'International Finance and the Erosion of Capitalist Diversity', in Crouch, C. and Streeck, W. (eds) *Political Economy of Modern Capitalism*, London: Sage, pp. 173–81.

Chandler, A. D. (1962) *Strategy and Structure: Chapters in the History of the Industrial Enterprise*, Cambridge, MA: MIT Press.

Child, J. (1973) 'Strategies of Control and Organization Behaviour', *ASQ*, 18, pp. 1–18.

Cooper, R. (1998) *Schlank zur Spitze. Mit Konfrontationsstrategien ins 21. Jahrhundert*, München: Vahlen.

Deutschmann, C., Faust, M., Jauch, P. and Notz, P. (1995) 'Veränderungen der Rolle des Managements im Prozeß reflexiver Rationalisierung', *Zeitschrift für Soziologie*, 24 (6), pp. 436–50.

Dore, R. (2000) *Stock Market Capitalism: Welfare Capitalism. Japan and Germany versus the Anglo-Saxons*, New York: Oxford University Press.

Dunning, J. H. (1994) *Multinational Enterprises and the Global Economy*, Reading: Addison-Wesley.

Eisenhardt, K. (1989) 'Building Theories from Case Study Research', *Academy of Management Review*, 14/4, pp. 532–50.

Flick, U. (1996) *Qualitative Forschung. Theorie, Methoden, Anwendung in Psychologie und Sozialwissenschaften*, Hamburg: Rowohlt.

Geppert, M., Williams, K. and Matten, D. (forthcoming) 'The Social Construction of Change Management in MNCs: An Anglo-German Comparison', *Journal of Management Studies*.

Giddens, A. (1984) *The Constitution of Society. Outline of the Theory of Structuration*, Cambridge: Polity Press.

Hammer, M. and Champy, J. (1993) *Reengineering the Corporation: A Manifesto for Business Revolution*, New York: Harper Business.

Harzing, A. K. (1999) *Managing the Multinationals. An International Study of Control Mechanisms*, Cheltenham: Edward Elgar.

Hedlund, G. (1993) 'Assumption of Hierarchy and Heterarchy, with Applications to the Management of the Multinational Corporation', in Ghoshal, S. and

Westney, D. E. (eds) *Organization Theory and the Multinational Corporation*, New York: St. Martin's Press, pp. 211–36.

Hennart, J.-F. (1993) 'Control in Multinational Firms: The Role of Price and Hierarchy' in Ghoshal, S. and Westney, D. E. (eds) *Organization Theory and the Multinational Corporation*, New York: St. Martin's Press, pp. 157–81.

Hirsch-Kreinsen, H. (1997) 'Weltmarkt und Wandel der Unternehmensstrategien. Grenzen der Globalisierung', in Hradil, S. (ed.) *Differenz und Integration. Die Zukunft moderner Gesellschaften. Verhandlungen des 28. Kongresses der Deutschen Gesellschaft für Soziologie in Dresden 1996*, Kongressbd. 1, Frankfurt a.M./New York, Campus, pp. 726–39.

Hirsch-Kreinsen, H. (1998) 'Shareholder Value: Unternehmensstrategien und neue Strukturen des Kapitalmarktes', in Hirsch-Kreinsen, H. and Wolf, H. (eds) *Arbeit, Gesellschaft, Kritik. Orientierungen wider den Zeitgeist*, Berlin: Edition Sigma, pp. 195–222.

Hirsch-Kreinsen, H. (1999) 'Shareholder Value. Zum Wandel von Unternehmenstrukturen und Kapitalmarktbedingungen', *WSI-Mitteilungen*, 5.

Iwer, F. (2000) 'Projektabschlußbericht. *Innovationstrends in der Aufzugsindustrie und Folgen für die Beschäftigungssituation*', Branchenstudie im Auftrag des Hauptvorstandes der IG Metall im Rahmen des Kooperationsprojekts RKE-DGB, Stuttgart.

Jürgens, U., Rupp, J., Vitols, K. and Jäschke-Werthmann, K. (2000) *Corporate Governance und Shareholder Value in Deutschland. Nach dem Fall von Mannesmann* – Paper revisited, WZB Discussion Chapter, FS II 00-202.

Kern, H. and Schumann, M. (1984) *Das Ende der Arbeitsteilung? Rationalisierung in der industriellen Produktion: Bestandsaufnahme, Trendbestimmung*, München: Beck.

Kieser, A. (1998) 'Über die allmähliche Verfertigung der Organisation beim Reden. Organisieren als Kommunizieren', *Industrielle Beziehungen*, 1, 1–40.

Lane, C. (2000) 'Understanding the Globalization Strategies of German and British Multinational Companies: Is a "Societal Effect" Approach Still Useful?', in Maurice, M. and Sorge, A. (eds) *Embedding Organizations: Societal Analysis of Actors, Organizations and Socio-Economic Context*, Amsterdam/Philadelphia: John Benjamins, pp. 189–208.

Lane, C. (2001) 'The Emergence of German Transnational Companies: A Theoretical Analysis and Empirical Study of The Globalization Process', in Morgan, G., Kristensen, P. H. and Whitley, R. (eds) *The Multinational Firm. Organizing Across Institutional and National Divides*, Oxford: Oxford University Press, pp. 69–96.

Macharzina, K. (1996) 'Globalisierung als Unternehmensaufgabe. Strategien und Organisation, Kriterien für Standortentscheidungen', in Steger, U. (ed.) *Globalisierung der Wirtschaft. Konsequenzen für Arbeit, Technik und Umwelt*, Berlin: Springer.

March, J. G. and Olsen, J. P. (1972) 'A garbage can model of organizational choice', *ASQ*, 17, 1–25.

March, J. G. and Simon, H. A. (1958) *Organizations*, New York: John Wiley.

Marschan, R., Welch, D. and Welch, L. (1999): 'In the Shadow: The Impact of Language on Structure, Power and Communication in the Multinational', *International Business Review*, 8, 421–40.

Maurice, M. and Sorge, A. (eds) (2000) *Embedding Organizations: Societal Analysis of Actors, Organizations and Socio-Economic Context*, Amsterdam/Philadelphia: John Benjamins.

Miles, M. and Huberman, A. M. (1994) *Qualitative Data Analysis*, Beverly Hills, CA: Sage.

Mintzberg, H. (1979) *The Structuring of Organizations: A Synthesis of the Research*, Englewood Cliffs, NJ: Prentice Hall.

Mintzberg, H. (1983) *Power In and Around Organizations*, Englewood Cliffs, NJ: Prentice Hall.

Morgan, G. (2001) 'The Multinational Firm: Organizing Across Institutional and National Divides', in Morgan, G., Kristensen, P. H. and Whitley, R. (eds) *The Multinational Firm. Organizing Across Institutional and National Divides*, Oxford: University Press, pp. 1–24.

Morgan, G., Kristensen, P. H. and Whitley, R. (eds) (2001) *The Multinational Firm. Organizing Across Institutional and National Divides*, Oxford: University Press.

Nippa, M. and Picot, A. (eds) (1995) *Prozessmanagement und Reengineering. Die Praxis im deutschsprachigen Raum*, Frankfurt/New York: Campus.

Ohmae, K. (1990) *The Borderless World*, New York: Harper Business.

Ortmann, G., Sydow, J. and Windeler, A. (1997) 'Organisation als reflexive Strukturation', in Ortmann, G., Sydow, J. and Türk, K. (eds) *Theorien der Organisation. Die Rückkehr der Gesellschaft*, Wiesbaden: Westdeutscher, pp. 315–54.

Ouchi, W. G. (1980) 'Markets, bureaucracies and clans', *ASQ*, 25 , pp. 120–42.

Patton, M. Q. (1990) *Qualitative Evaluation and Research Methods*, Newbury Park: Sage.

Rappaport, A. (1986) *Creating Shareholder Value – The New Standard for Business Performance*, New York: Free Press.

Ruigrok, W. and van Tulder, R. (1995) *The Logic of International Restructuring*, London: Routledge.

Sauer, D. and Döhl, V. (1997) 'Die Auflösung des Unternehmens? – Entwicklungstendenzen der Unternehmensreorganisation', in IfS, *Jahrbuch Sozialwissenschaftliche Technikberichterstattung. Schwerpunkt: Reorganisation*, München/Berlin, pp. 19–75.

Sorge, A. (1993) 'Arbeit, Organisation und Arbeitsbeziehungen in Ostdeutschland', *Berliner Journal für Soziologie*, Heft 4, pp. 549–67.

Tainio, R., Huolman, M. and Pulkkinen, M. (2001) 'The Internationalization of Capital Markets: How International Institutional Investors are restructuring Finnish Companies', in Morgan, G., Kristensen, P. H. and Whitley, R. (eds) *The Multinational Firm. Organizing Across Institutional and National Divides*, Oxford: University Press, pp. 153–71.

Thompson, J. D. (1967) *Organisations in Action*, New York: McGraw-Hill.

Thompson, G. and Frances, J. (eds) (1993) *Markets, Hierarchies and Networks: The Coordination by Social Life*, London: Sage.

Trist, E. (1981) *The Evolution of Socio-technical Systems. A Conceptual Framework and an Action Research Program*, Toronto: Ontario Quality of Working Life Center, Occasional paper no. 2.

Weber, M. (1922/1972) *Wirtschaft und Gesellschaft*, Tübingen: Mohr (Siebeck).

Yin, R. K. (1994) *Case Study Research: Design and Methods*, Beverly Hills: Sage.

4

Headquarters–subsidiary Relationships in Multinational Companies: A British–German Comparison

Anne-Wil Harzing, Arndt Sorge and Jan Paauwe

Introduction

One of the recurrent themes in international organization studies is what happens to organizational practices as enterprises are increasingly exposed to internationalizing influences. Such influences can be divided into two main areas:

1. On the one hand, enterprise activities are internationalized through exposure to customers, suppliers or alliances outside a society or domestic economy of origin, regulated by common and relatively homogeneous institutions. This kind of internationalization culminates in the formation of a multinational company if and when non-marginal company functions are localized in subsidiaries outside the country of origin.
2. On the other hand, even enterprises which are not internationalized or multinational are subject to competitive pressures, regulatory norms and imitation influences, which emerge from an international search for good or best organizational practices.

This debate continues, partly under new auspices, along a well-established track, which focuses on the extent of and explanations for *convergence* and *divergence*. The literature has used these concepts in different ways. An authoritative definition by reputed scholars states that: 'The subject of organizational convergence is concerned with how far organizations in different countries have traveled along a path to global convergence in operations and management and, conversely, how far the influence of specific cultural factors must be understood and planned for if the manager is to be effective in cross-cultural situations' (Pugh and Hickson 1996: 3899; see also the overview in Geppert et al. this volume, based on Child, 2000). This may imply a longitudinal argument or research design demonstrating convergence or divergence as happening over time, but it need not necessarily. Indeed, many publications debating the extent of convergence versus divergence have limited themselves to comparing and evaluating the extent of convergence or divergence in terms of the *results* that enterprise development has achieved at a given moment. Divergence is coterminous with the embeddedness of organizations and other actors in regionally or nationally different societies. Societies have characteristic and specific elements such as a normative institutional order, the cultural dispositions of different types of actor in different types of situation or across the board and also economic and industrial structures. Convergence, on the other hand, implies a relative degree of disembeddedness of practices or structures, which override more regionally or nationally specific institutions or behavioural predispositions.

More recently, the 'sharp end' of the convergence–divergence debate, where the issue of divergence versus convergence is most acute, has come to lie where internationalization is assumed to be most pervasive, in the functioning of the multinational enterprise. Here, internationalization attaches to all the 'hooks' of Porter's diamond: factor conditions; firm strategy; structure and rivalry; demand conditions; and related and supporting industries (Porter 1990: 72). Internationalization in the multinational enterprise, therefore, attaches to all the fields governing its structure and functioning: task and general environment, internal structure and process and generic strategies that establish meaningful relations between environment, context and internal structure and process.

This is the subject on which we focus in this chapter. More specifically, we concentrate on that part of the multinational enterprise that is its most international and potentially most de-contextualised one: the relationships between headquarters and their subsidiaries. By focusing on the international level in multinational enterprises, above the level of national subsidiaries and their internal organizational patterns, their own specific strategy and their immediate task and general environment within the country in which they are located, we examine that terrain in which the forces working towards convergence are potentially the strongest.

Given the focus of this volume, this chapter will investigate differences in headquarters–subsidiary relationships in MNCs from two European countries: Britain and Germany. We will also compare these countries to the US and Japan and assess to what extent convergence has taken place. For a more detailed discussion of the convergence versus divergence debate on a worldwide and European scale see Harzing and Sorge (forthcoming). The remainder of this chapter is structured as follows. In the next section, we discuss our concepts, review the literature on comparisons between British and German MNCs and derive a number of hypotheses. A methodology section then discusses the data collection, sample and measures used in the empirical study, while the results section presents the outcome of the testing of our hypotheses. In the final discussion and conclusion section, we argue that the generalization of the results from studies of individual European countries to suggest a wider European pattern is inappropriate, even for multinational companies. European MNCs cannot be seen as a homogeneous group and due attention should therefore be paid to the representation of European MNCs from different countries in any research design.

Conceptual background and hypotheses

Concepts

In this chapter we look at differences in the headquarters–subsidiary relationship between MNCs from different countries of origin. This relationship can be seen as a classic control problem, whose attributes are similar to principal–agent relationships (Nohria and Ghoshal, 1994). Headquarters, the principal, cannot make all decisions because it does not possess all the necessary knowledge or resources, but it cannot leave all decisions to the subsidiaries because the interests of subsidiaries might be different from those of the headquarters or the MNC as a whole. Therefore, the key aspect of the headquarters–subsidiary relationship is the way in which the headquarters ensures that subsidiaries are working towards common organizational goals. The different types of *control mechanisms* are the tools used by the headquarters to achieve this alignment. Hence, the level of control exercised by the headquarters by means of the different types of control mechanisms is the first element of the headquarter–subsidiary relationship that we will investigate. As we will see below, there is a range of control mechanisms available that goes beyond the level of autonomy granted to subsidiaries. The second element that we will look at is the level of *expatriate presence* in subsidiaries. Expatriates can perform many roles in the headquarters–subsidiary relationship, among them control and knowledge transfer. The *level of interdependence* between headquarters and subsidiaries in comparison to the level of interdependence *between* subsidiaries is a third important element of the headquarters–subsidiary relationship. The final element that we will study is the *level of local responsiveness* – in terms of local production, local R&D and adaptation of products and marketing to local conditions – that the headquarters allows the subsidiary.

Britain and Germany: differences in culture and business systems

Two European countries that are often singled out as being very different from each other are Germany and Britain (see also Mayer and Whittington, this volume). Germany and Britain differ considerably in terms of their national culture and business system. Culturally, Germany and Britain are always found in different country clusters. Ronen and Shenkar (1985) discussed nine different studies that investigated cultural differences and identified clusters of countries. In seven of these studies the UK was included and in all of the studies it was classified in the Anglo-Saxon cluster, together with the US, Canada, Australia and New Zealand in studies where these countries were also included. Germany was included in seven of these studies and was classified in the Germanic cluster in five studies, in the Nordic cluster in one and in the independent cluster in another.

Looking at their business systems, Germany and Britain also differ dramatically (see also Tempel, this volume, for a description of the differences between the two countries with regard to industrial relations). Britain shares with the US an adherence to consumer capitalism, which is in strong contradiction to the producer capitalism more typical of both Germany and Japan (see also Mirza, 1998). With the first comes a focus on marketing excellence, while the second is characterized by manufacturing excellence and German companies have indeed been shown to be significantly ahead of British companies in adopting world-class manufacturing practices (Voss and Blackmon, 1996). There are also major differences between Germany and Britain with regard to capital structure and the importance of stock markets. British and American companies raise their funds mainly by selling stock (equity-based), while German and Japanese companies are mainly credit-based (Prowse, 1994). In 1985, stock market capitalization as a percentage of GNP amounted to 81 per cent in Britain compared with a mere 14 per cent in Germany, while the USA and Japan fell between these two with

48 and 37 per cent respectively (Prowse, 1994: 30, Table 6). These different capital structures are also reflected in different philosophies about the management of companies. While Anglo-Saxon companies are mainly managed in the interests of shareholders and focus on the maximization of short-term profits, German and Japanese companies are more concerned about long-term viability and stability. In German and Japanese companies, the interest of stakeholders other than shareholders (for example employees, unions, community, government) is given serious consideration and companies are seen more as social institutions than as profit-generating machines. This phenomenon is reinforced by the fact that in the Anglo-Saxon countries, around 80 per cent or more of the shares are held for trading purposes, while in Germany and Japan the overwhelming majority of shares are held for control purposes (Prowse, 1994: 24, Table 3). Obviously, investors holding shares for trading purposes are more likely to focus on short-term returns than on long-term stability. As Lane (1995: 50) indicates, in British companies 'every major financial decision has to be taken with an eye on the movement of the stock market'.

An earlier comparison of British and German multinationals showed that the British companies are stronger in their marketing and financial functions and these strengths show both at headquarters level and in the different subsidiaries. On the other hand, the German multinationals are stronger in production and engineering functions (see also Geppert et al. this volume, whose comparative case studies on change provide a good illustration of these different strengths). Policies in the respective subsidiaries outside the country of origin devote particular attention to remedying perceived deficiencies in those functions, which are comparatively underemphasized in the country of the subsidiary's location. This picture reinforces the view that British companies, among them multinationals, strategically emphasize the more commercial and financial functions, whereas German companies emphasize the more technical functions, including the links between development and production (Ebster-Grosz and Pugh, 1996).

The consequence of these differences might be the following: since the product and its production and development are more important for the corporate identity of a multinational from Germany, it will be more likely to promote an international strategy in the process of going international. This means it will attempt to perform on the basis of an existing product template and its advantages. It will try to replicate this product template abroad and emphasize interdependencies or the common basis of the country of origin template and the subsidiary template and it will not go for multi-domestic or other locally responsive strategies abroad. The British multinational, on the other hand, will see the enterprise as hanging together around financial flows and measures and encourage marketing postures, which are more multi-domestic or locally responsive in an integrated form. In this way, internationalization strategies of MNCs are likely to be the consequence of deeply rooted, societally embedded strategies in the country of origin. All this follows from differences already established in their early history of industrialization: German companies grew by internal growth, on the basis of a specific technical template, whereas British companies, to a greater extent, featured growth by mergers and acquisitions, which more often led to conglomerates with different technical and product templates (Landes, 1960).

Finally, both German and Japanese companies are much more embedded in industrial networks and have close ties with buyer and supplier firms, while British and American companies operate much more independently. So, as indicated by Lane (1998: 463):

> Given the striking difference in business systems between Britain and Germany...we can expect different responses in the ways companies have managed the tensions between pressures for globalization and established nationally shaped business strategies and patterns of behaviour.

We would, therefore, expect MNCs from Germany and Britain to differ in the way they internationalize and hence in their headquarters–subsidiary relationships.

Hypothesis 1: The HQ–subsidiary relationship in German MNCs will be more similar to the HQ–subsidiary relationship in Japanese MNCs than to the HQ–subsidiary relationship in British MNCs. The HQ–subsidiary relationship in British MNCs will be more similar to the HQ–subsidiary relationship in US MNCs than to the HQ–subsidiary relationship in German MNCs

Previous research on British and German MNCs

As far as we know, there are no previous studies that compare the headquarters–subsidiary relationships between British and German MNCs on the range of variables we discussed above. There are, however, some studies that provide us with pointers to possible differences between British and German MNCs with regard to individual elements of the headquarters–subsidiary relationship: control mechanisms, expatriation, interdependence and local responsiveness. Although not all these studies include a direct comparison between German and British MNCs, they often compare one of these countries with the US and/or Japan, so that some indirect conclusions can be drawn. We will review these studies below.

With regard to control mechanisms, Coates et al. (1992) indicate that British and US MNCs usually control their subsidiaries by means of budget-setting and monitoring systems, oriented to short-term financial performance, while German MNCs seem to rely more on personal feedback and communications than on formal financial measures. The latter is also typical for Japanese MNCs who rely much less than Anglo-Saxon MNCs on arms-length formal systems and more on face-to-face assessment. Egelhoff (1984) found that American MNCs used more output control of their subsidiaries than European MNCs. British MNCs tended to fall between these extremes, but in the finance area, output control was equal to American MNCs. Neghandhi (1987) finds the frequency of reporting to be higher in American than in German and Japanese MNCs. We would, therefore, expect a greater reliance on direct personal control in German MNCs and less reliance on impersonal control than in British MNCs.

> *Hypothesis 2*:   German MNCs will apply a higher level of direct personal control and a lower level of impersonal control to their subsidiaries than British MNCs

The reliance on face-to-face assessment is one of the reasons why Japanese MNCs are expatriate-intensive. Given that German control systems appear to be more like the Japanese model, Ferner (1997) expects a similar reliance on control through expatriation in German MNCs. In Dobry's (1983) study of American and German MNCs, the German MNCs were more likely to employ parent country nationals (PCNs) in their American subsidiaries than American MNCs in their German subsidiaries. Negandhi and Welge (1984) found that both Japanese and German MNCs had host country nationals (HCNs) in only 2 per cent of the top positions in their foreign subsidiaries, while American firms had HCNs in 28 per cent. Egelhoff (1988) indicates that, in general, European MNCs make greater use of expatriates than both American and British MNCs. In Wolf's (1994) study, German MNCs had the largest number of PCNs in the managing director position, while there was no major difference between American and the remaining European MNCs in this respect. Although these studies do not directly compare German and British MNCs, the indirect comparisons would lead us to expect that:

Hypothesis 3: German MNCs will show a higher level of expatriate presence in their subsidiaries than British MNCs

Several studies have indicated that German MNCs display a lesser geographical reach than British MNCs and, until recently, relied more heavily on export than on FDI; they are also deeply embedded in their domestic business system, producing far more value from their domestic base than their foreign affiliates (Ruigrok and van Tulder, 1995; Dörre 1996; Hirst and Thompson, 1996; Lane, 1998; Whitley, 1998). According to Lane (1998), the foreign affiliates of German MNCs are replicas of the parent company rather than adapting to host country features, while British MNCs tend to follow more of a conglomerate strategy with many subsidiaries resulting from acquisitions. These differences would point in the direction of a lower local responsiveness and higher dependence on headquarters for German subsidiaries, while the reverse would be true for British subsidiaries. Whitley (1999) emphasizes this point even more directly when he describes German MNCs as 'co-operative hierarchies', in which most foreign subsidiaries of any significance will be quite closely supervised and integrated into parent activities and where the integration of foreign subsidiaries into host economies is limited. Whitley sees the isolated firm type as more typical of American and British companies. In this type of firm, subsidiaries are managed at a distance and, provided the formal procedures and targets are followed, units are allowed some local adaptation and will not be as fully integrated into their parents' operations, as is the case with cooperative firms. The result may be higher integration into host economies with local sourcing and adaptation of products to local markets. Subsidiaries from cooperative hierarchies will, in contrast, rely more on products and technologies from the parent. More direct support for a potential difference in interdependence is found by Pauly and Reich (1997), who showed that both Japanese and German investors in the USA were characterized by a higher level of intra-company purchases than French and British investors. We will therefore put forward the following hypotheses:

Hypothesis 4: German MNCs will show a higher level of interdependence with HQ than British MNCs

> *Hypothesis 5*: German MNCs will show a lower level of local
> responsiveness than British MNCs

Sample and methodology

Data collection and sample description

Our data on Britain and Germany, and on the USA and Japan, resulted
from a much larger study. Our chapter here thus presents results
extracted from the larger study. The data was collected by means of
a large-scale international mail survey. Questionnaires were mailed
to the managing directors of some 1650 wholly owned subsidiaries of
122 multinationals in 22 different countries. The selection of the 122
multinationals was based on the 1994 *Fortune* Global 500 list. Eight
manufacturing industries with a good representation of multinationals
from different countries were selected and the largest multinationals in
these industries were included in our sample.

A pilot mailing was sent to 96 subsidiaries in 12 different countries at
the beginning of June 1995. Questionnaires for the final mailing were
mailed in two batches: one in October 1995 and one in January 1996.
Incentives to increase response rates included an announcement post-
card, a reminder, an offer of the results, an international committee of
recommendation and several methods of making the relationship
between researcher and respondents less anonymous and more interactive than in the usual mail questionnaire approach. The overall
response rate at subsidiary level was 20 per cent, ranging from 7.1 per
cent in Hong Kong to 42.1 per cent in Denmark. Since this variance in
response rates across countries might introduce a response bias, the
country of subsidiary location will be included as a control variable in
our analysis.

Table 4.1 summarizes the response rates and number of respondents
by industry, country of location of headquarters and subsidiary country. The total number of 287 subsidiary responses represents 104 different headquarters and the number of responses per headquarters varied
from 1 to 11. This study only uses the data collected for British,
German, US and Japanese MNCs.

Variables and measures

Corporate control mechanisms can be defined as the instruments used
to make sure that all units of the organization strive towards common
organizational goals. Numerous control mechanisms have been
identified. But, following a synthesis of authors such as March and

Table 4.1 Number of respondents by industry, subsidiary country and head-quarters country

	Number of respondents	Response rate (%)
Industry		
Electronics	41	17.1
Computers, office equipment	26	16.2
Motor vehicles and parts	30	20.4
Petroleum (products)	20	21.4
Food and beverages	34	18.4
Pharmaceutical	46	23.8
Paper (products)	25	20.6
Chemical (products)	55	21.3
Various	10	17.1
Country of location of headquarters		
Finland	23	24.0
France	26	18.6
Germany	32	21.8
Japan	38	16.7
Netherlands	16	31.5
Sweden	41	24.6
Switzerland	31	30.4
UK	25	19.7
USA	55	14.3
Subsidiary country		
Argentina	4	12.9
Austria	8	19.0
Belgium	14	20.3
Brazil	15	22.1
Denmark	16	42.1
Finland	8	32.0
France	14	13.6
Germany	16	15.5
Hong Kong	5	7.1
Ireland	11	30.6
Italy	21	24.4
Japan	16	28.6
Mexico	10	15.2
Netherlands	25	26.6
Norway	13	40.6
Singapore	10	13.6
Spain	14	15.9
Sweden	11	20.4
Switzerland	14	29.8
UK	25	18.8
USA	13	11.4
Venezuela	4	13.8

Simon (1958), Lawrence and Lorsch (1967), Child (1973, 1984), Galbraith (1973), Ouchi (1977, 1979, 1980), Mintzberg (1979, 1983), Merchant (1985), Kenter (1985), Bartlett and Ghoshal (1989), Martinez and Jarillo (1991) and Hennart (1991), they are mainly structured along two dimensions: directness and explicitness of control on the one axis and impersonality of control on the other (see also Becker-Ritterspach et al. this volume, who use the same taxonomy). This allows us to identify four major types of control mechanisms as summarized in Table 4.2. Based on the literature review, several constituent elements were defined for each of the four control mechanisms. Expatriate control was added to the direct personal control category, since for multinationals this will be an important way of realizing direct supervision or centralization of decision-making by creating mini-headquarters at subsidiary level.

To measure the various constituent elements of the different control mechanisms, we adapted and supplemented the questions used by Martinez and Jarillo (1991) and subjected them to a factor analysis. An oblique rotation, direct oblimin, was used instead of one of the more common orthogonal rotations (equamax, quartimax, varimax), since correlation between the different control mechanisms could be expected. Bartlett's test of sphericity was highly significant (609.778, $p = 0.00000$). KMO's measure of sampling adequacy was 0.69, which is considered acceptable for the application of factor analysis. Three factors were extracted that had an eigenvalue of larger than 1. These three factors explained 58.7 per cent of the variance.

The factor analysis (See Table 4.3) clearly distinguished the indirect and direct personal categories, with high loadings on its constituent

Table 4.2   Classification of control mechanisms on two dimensions

	Personal/Cultural (founded on social interaction)	Impersonal/ Bureaucratic/ Technocratic (founded on instrumental artifacts)
Direct/Explicit	Centralization, direct supervision, expatriate control	Standardization, formalization
Indirect/Implicit	Socialization, informal communication, management training	Output control, planning

Table 4.3 Factor analysis of ten questions measuring control mechanisms

Variable	Impersonal	Indirect personal	Direct personal
Output control	.766	–.043	.081
Planning	.727	.134	.124
Procedures	.702	.065	.199
Standardization	.647	.029	.270
Informal communication	–.226	.792	.078
Shared values	.196	.777	.000
International training	.246	.688	.114
Centralization	.234	.075	.744
Personal surveillance	.185	.141	.717
Expatriate control	.249	.164	.657

elements and loadings below 0.30 on the other items. Questions for the two impersonal control mechanisms, however, all loaded on the same factor, so the first factor was identified as impersonal control.

Actual expatriate presence is a more direct way to measure expatriate control, as identified above. Three questions were used to assess the presence of expatriates in a given subsidiary. These questions asked respectively for the nationality of the managing director, the number of top five jobs held by expatriates and the total number of expatriates working in the subsidiary. The latter was subsequently divided by the total number of employees to arrive at the share of expatriates in the subsidiary's workforce. The nationality of the managing director was recoded into 0 if the managing director was a local and 1 if the managing director was a parent country national. The small number of third country nationals was disregarded.

Interdependence was operationalized using the percentage of intracompany sales and purchases. Respondents were asked to differentiate between their purchases from or sales to headquarters and subsidiaries, so that we could verify the relative importance of their interdependence with both the headquarters and other subsidiaries. As respondents would not be likely to know the exact percentages, six answer categories were included: 0, 1–25, 26–50, 51–75, 76–99 and 100 per cent. Local responsiveness was measured with four items asking for the percentage of local R&D and local production incorporated into products sold by the subsidiary and the percentage of products and marketing that were substantially modified for the local markets. As for interdependence, six answer categories were created.

The study used a key-informant approach and our results are there-fore based on the information of a single respondent in each organiza-tion. This is a limitation that this study shares with virtually all large-scale studies of multinationals. The prevalent response rates in international mail surveys make another approach practically infeas-ible. Another factor we need to mention is that, although every care was taken to formulate questions as unambiguously as possible, our study used perceptual measures to operationalize some of the constructs. This was done because of the nature of concepts, such as control mechanisms, which are not immediately quantifiable. The result is that the answers to our questions might contain an element of perception, which may reduce the validity of our findings. However, the questions elicited information on actual practices and policies, rather than opinions of such practices, which might be personally influenced and, therefore, depend on the person of the respondent instead of on the organization. Finally, although our sample was relat-ively large compared to other studies, sample sizes for individual countries were still relatively small, which means that the peculiarities of individual multinationals might influence the results.

Results

In the literature review, we indicated that, given the very different cultural and institutional background of Britain and Germany, we would expect these two European countries to systematically differ from each other on the aspects of headquarters–subsidiary relationships included in our study. At the same time, given the similarities in cultural and institutional background between Britain and the USA and Germany and Japan respectively, we would expect these country pairs to show fewer differences. In order to test this, we compared the three country pairs on each of the 14 variables included in our study. Table 4.4 shows the results of these tests.

German and British multinationals differ significantly from each other on nine of our 14 variables, while differences are insignificant for the remaining five variables. However, in only two of these cases, impersonal control and the percentage of expatriates in workforce, do any of the other country pairs differ significantly from each other. In addition, one of these five variables, marketing modification, does not show a significant country of origin impact for any country. German and Japanese multinationals differ significantly from each other on only four of our 14 variables. These differences, however, are equally spread over all four clusters of variables, so that in each cluster there is no difference for the majority of variables. German and Japanese multi-nationals, therefore, do not seem to have any systematic differences. American and British multinationals differ significantly from each other on only one variable, the extent of local manufacturing, which is higher for the British companies. The number of significant differences between German and British multinationals is nearly twice as high as the *combined* number of differences between German and Japanese multinationals and American and British ones.

The only area where there do not seem to be significant differences between German and British enterprises is control mechanisms. This, however, is not to say that coordination and control in British and German multinationals are likely to be the same throughout the enter-prise. Our analysis is focused on the international level of control, between headquarters and subsidiaries. Furthermore, it may well be that other comparative indicators of control would yield larger differences. Indeed, other comparative research on Britain and Germany strongly suggests this possibility (Maurice et al., 1980; Sorge and Warner, 1986; Ebster-Grosz and Pugh, 1996). But, with the indicators we used, it appears that internationalization strategies and transactions between headquarters and subsidiaries differ between Britain and Germany much more than control mechanisms. We can, therefore, accept hypo-thesis 1 and safely conclude that German and British multinationals bear a closer resemblance to Japanese and American ones respect-ively than to their European counterpart. In fact, British and German MNCs often take up an even more extreme position than US and Japanese MNCs. This is reflected in the fact that there are only six significant differences between Japanese and US MNCs, while there are nine significant differences between British and German MNCs. The fact that both the German–US and the British–Japanese comparisons show significant differences for seven of the 14 variables corroborates this picture.

Turning to our hypothesis about specific differences, *hypothesis 2* is not confirmed by our data. Although the differences are in the expected direction, they are not significant and German MNCs *do* differ significantly from Japanese MNCs in that they rely more heav-ily on impersonal control. A recent qualitative study of German MNCs (Ferner and Varul, 1999) confirms this specific combination of impersonal and personal control for German MNCs. As expected, however, British MNCs did not differ from their US counterparts. Even though the specific hypothesis could not be confirmed, we do

Table 4.4 Comparisons between British and German, German and Japanese, and British and US multinationals

Variable	Mean scores for different aspects of the HQ–subsidiary relationship in British, German, Japanese and US MNCs				Significance of difference between British and German MNCs		Significance of difference between German and Japanese MNCs		Significance of difference between British and US MNCs	
	British MNCs	German MNCs	Japanese MNCs	US MNCs	p-values	Sign. at 0.05	p-values	Sign. at 0.05	p-values	Sign. at 0.05
Control mechanisms										
Impersonal control	0.51	0.20	−0.60	0.38	0.211	No	0.001	Yes	0.546	No
Direct personal control	0.10	0.41	0.23	−0.09	0.273	No	0.450	No	0.469	No
Indirect personal control	−0.10	−0.18	−0.11	0.14	0.734	No	0.765	No	0.296	No
Expatriate presence										
Percentage of expatriates in workforce	1.2%	1.8%	5.4%	1.4%	0.376	No	0.035	Yes	0.767	No
Managing director PCN	27%	56%	58%	19%	0.049	Yes	0.827	No	0.453	No
Number of expatriates in top 5	1.00	1.66	2.16	0.98	0.034	Yes	0.156	No	0.944	No

Table 4.4 (continued)

Interdependence										
Purchases from HQ	1.36	3.81	3.54	1.78	0.000	Yes	0.416	No	0.108	No
Sales to HQ	1.12	1.56	1.27	1.44	0.005	Yes	0.062	No	0.139	No
Purchases from subsidiaries	2.72	1.94	2.38	3.11	0.021	Yes	0.076	No	0.299	No
Sales to subsidiaries	2.58	1.59	2.57	2.02	0.044	Yes	0.004	Yes	0.364	No
Local responsiveness										
Local manufacturing	4.08	2.55	2.92	3.13	0.000	Yes	0.336	No	0.026	Yes
Marketing modification	3.68	3.58	3.32	3.39	0.824	No	0.519	No	0.456	No
Product modification	3.12	2.00	2.51	2.71	0.001	Yes	0.043	Yes	0.222	No
Local R&D	2.48	1.90	1.92	2.19	0.035	Yes	0.942	No	0.329	No
Differences significant at 0.05						9/14		4/14		1/14

find a confirmation of previous research in that direct personal control is the most important control mechanism for both Japanese and German MNCs and that impersonal control is the most important control mechanism for both British and US MNCs. *Hypothesis 3* is confirmed to a large extent: German MNCs do differ significantly from British MNCs on two of the three measures of expatriate presence and the difference for the third measure is in the expected direction. *Hypothesis 4* is fully confirmed, with subsidiaries of German MNCs showing a significantly higher dependence on the HQ for both sales and purchases. It is interesting to see that subsidiaries of British MNCs are more likely to be dependent on other subsidiaries for their sales and purchases. Whilst subsidiaries of German MNCs tend to function mostly as pipelines for their HQs, subsidiaries of British MNCs can be important nodes in the corporate network. *Hypothesis 5* finds a high level of support as well: subsidiaries of German MNCs tend to be far less locally responsive than subsidiaries of British MNCs. The only measure of local responsiveness that does not show a difference is marketing adaptation, but, as we mentioned before, this measure did not show any differences between countries. Overall therefore, we find a high level of support for our hypotheses on specific differences between German and British MNCs.

Discussion and conclusion

The results of this study provide further support for the existence of unique country patterns, even for the most internationalized companies in the world. This extends the applicability of the societal effect approach to MNCs and provides a strong counter-argument against Ohmae's (1990) picture of the 'nation less' corporation. In line with Hu (1992), we think it is more appropriate to describe MNCs as national firms with international operations.

A clear conclusion of our study is that there are large differences in nearly all aspects of the headquarters–subsidiary relationship between German and British MNCs. In terms of control mechanisms, we did not find any significant differences, but, as expected, the dominant control mechanism was direct personal control for German MNCs and impersonal control for British MNCs. Subsidiaries of German MNCs also showed a higher level of expatriate presence than subsidiaries of British MNCs. On average, subsidiaries of British multinationals have a *lower* interdependence with headquarters, a *higher* interdependence with other subsidiaries and a *higher* local responsiveness than subsidiaries of German MNCs.

We can detect a broad pattern in which German companies most closely resemble Japanese companies, while British companies are very similar to their American counterparts. It would, therefore, seem inappropriate to either generalize findings from one or two European countries to suggest a European pattern or to consider European countries as a homogeneous group. Although Europe is becoming more economically and politically integrated, this has not yet resulted in a similarity of management practices, not even for the most internationalized companies. Indeed, we may ask, why should it? If political and economic integration does take place, it may very well lead to different specializations in sectoral, product and product/market combinations of multinationals from different nations. Within Europe, we have only investigated differences between German and British MNCs. However, even if we exclude these two very different countries, this still leaves a significant difference between the remaining five European countries for seven of the 14 variables at a 0.05 level of significance. We would, therefore, express strong reservations against a continued use of the label 'European' as a catch-all for a highly varied group of countries.

It would seem inappropriate to generalize results from a small number of European countries to suggest a European pattern, as is the case, for instance, in Bartlett and Ghoshal (1989), who investigated three European MNCs, of which one was Dutch, one Dutch/English and one Swedish. Their conclusions about European companies might have been substantially different if they had investigated German, French and Spanish MNCs instead. Equally inappropriate are attempts to generalize findings into a European pattern from a very unbalanced European sample, where one or two countries constitute a large part, or even the majority, of the sample, as is the case in Kopp (1994) and Peterson et al. (1996). However, even a balanced sample could present problems, since the overall mean could hide large underlying differences. Picard (1977), Haar (1989) and Swamidas and Kotabe (1993), for instance, draw conclusions from samples which include a comparable number of German and British MNCs: given the differences described above, their results might have been very different had one of these countries not been included. Unfortunately, in many studies the samples for individual countries are too small to permit a country-by-country analysis of European MNCs. However, even where this is the case, researchers should at least try to exclude countries, such as Germany and Britain, from their European sample to see whether this has a significant effect on the overall mean.

We can, of course, ask to what extent the differences uncovered in this article are enduring and whether convergence might indeed become more important in the twenty-first century. Lane (2000) suggests that German multinationals might have deviated from established societal patterns in the second part of the 1990s. She mentions that subsidiaries of German multinationals have been allocated more resources and granted more autonomy as the organizations move towards a decentralized network structure and subsidiaries become more embedded in the local environment. Her conclusions, however, are weakened by the nature of the underlying material. Firstly, this comprises mainly documents supplied by headquarters of MNCs, which tend to express intentions rather than actual practice sustained over time, and unpublished studies, where we cannot verify the reliability of their conclusions. Secondly, the material stems from six flagship companies in highly internationalized industries. It remains to be seen what an *empirical* investigation after the implementation of the policies would show: whether actual practice at subsidiary level follows the declarations of intent made earlier and what practice in a larger, and conceivably expanding population of multinationals would look like. Where developments are empirically observed, such as in the level of local responsiveness of VW, the question remains whether this is much of a change compared to the past. VW Mexico and VW Brazil have traditionally been given more of a free hand in developing models or modifications to suit regional markets, more so than the subsidiaries of Mercedes-Benz and BMW with their luxury brands, where customers would be annoyed if the German home standard were to be compromised by more extensive local responsiveness. Also, we must bear in mind the extent to which the rhetoric and both the momentary theory-in-use and nascent theory-in-practice of multinationals are subject to radical fluctuation over time. In the mid-1980s, the proclaimed strategy and structure of Daimler-Benz was to become a differentiated technology conglomerate, making cars, lorries, airplanes and armaments, as well as electronic consumer and investment goods. All that has now disappeared; the firm is back to being a car and lorry making concern and is much more multinational through its merger with Chrysler and the acquisition of Mitsubishi Motor. Thus, momentary individual vignettes resulting from randomized or matched-pair comparisons of multinationals of different origin cannot be extrapolated into comparative tendencies.

This leads us to plead the case for the longlasting stability of comparative differences over time. They are not only striking but also clearly rooted in different postures and strategies of national and multinational enterprises, which have remained remarkably stable throughout an extensive period of industrialization and post-industrialization. This is due to the fact that they are the result of different conceptions of what the identity and comparative advantage of the firm should be built on: such as the product and engineering template in Germany and the differentiated marketing plus integrated financial management approach in Britain. Such postures and strategies make different paths of internationalization possible and they are not necessarily specific to each historically successive phase of internationalisation. The British multinational will, therefore, almost always seek to make its highest profit in a conglomerate, which is locally responsive, whereas the German MNC will concentrate on a specialist technical template that can basically be implemented across different locations.

Consequently, we extend a strong plea for more empirical research into the country of origin effect in MNCs in general and the study of previously neglected MNCs of European origin in particular. As argued in earlier publications (Harzing, 1995, 1997), a lack of empirical research in international business and management in general and a lack of non-US research in particular have created several myths. We do not want the myth of the European monolith to continue to be one of them. Neither do we want the idea that internationalization implies one best way of doing things, so that we mainly distinguish between forerunners and followers, to acquire mythical quality.

References

Bartlett, C. A. and Ghoshal, S. (1989) *Managing across borders. The transnational solution*, Boston, MA: Harvard Business School Press.

Child, J. (1973) 'Strategies of control and organization behavior', *Administrative Science Quarterly*, 18, pp. 1–17.

Child, J. (1984) *Organization: A guide to problems and practice*, London: Harper & Row.

Child, J. (2000) Theorizing about organizations cross-nationally, in Cheng, J. L. C. and Peterson, R. B. (eds) *Advances in international comparative management*, Stamford, CN: JAI Press, pp. 27–75.

Coates, J., Davis, E., Emmanual, C., Longden, S. and Stacey, R. (1992) 'Multinational companies' performance measurement systems: international perspectives', *Management Accounting Research*, 3, pp. 133–50.

Dobry, A. (1983) *Die Steuerung ausländischer Tochtergesellschaften – Eine theoretische und empirische Untersuchung ihrer Grundlagen und Instrumente*, Giessen.

Dörre, K. (1996) 'Globalstrategien von Unternehmen – ein Desintegrationsphänomen? Zu den Auswirkungen grenzüberschreitender Unternehmensaktivitäten auf die industriellen Beziehungen', *SOFI Mitteilungen*, 25, pp. 43–70.

Ebster-Grosz, D. and Pugh D. (1996) *Anglo-German business collaboration*, London: Macmillan.

Egelhoff, W. G. (1984) 'Patterns of control in US, UK, and European multi-national corporations', *Journal of International Business Studies*, 15, pp. 73–83.

Egelhoff, W. G. (1988) *Organizing the multinational enterprise*, Cambridge: Ballinger.

Ferner, A. (1997) 'Country of origin effects and human resource management in multinational companies', *Human Resource Management Journal*, 7, pp. 19–37.

Ferner, A. and Varul, M. Z. (1999) *The German Way: German Multinationals and Human Resource Management*, An Anglo-German Foundation Report, Anglo-German Foundation for the Study of Industrial Society.

Galbraith, J. R. (1973) *Designing complex organizations*, Reading, MA: Addison-Wesley.

Haar, J. (1989) 'A comparative analysis of the profitability performance of the largest US, European and Japanese multinational enterprises', *Management International Review*, 29, pp. 5–19.

Harzing, A. W. K. (1995) 'The persistent myth of high expatriate failure rates', *International Journal of Human Resource Management*, 6, pp. 457–75.

Harzing, A. W. K. (1997) 'Response rates in international mail surveys: Results of a 22 country study', *International Business Review*, 6, pp. 641–65.

Harzing, A. W. K. and Sorge, A. (forth coming) 'The relative impact of country-of-origin and universal contingencies on internationalization strategies and corporate control in multinational enterprises: worldwide and European perspectives', *Organization Studies*.

Hennart, J.-F. (1991) 'Control in multinational firms: The role of price and hierarchy', *Management International Review*, 31, pp. 71–96.

Hirst, P. and Thompson, G. (1996) *Globalisation in question*, Cambridge: Polity Press.

Hu, Y.-S. (1992) 'Global or stateless corporations are national firms with international operations', *California Management Review*, Winter, pp. 107–26.

Kenter, M. E. (1985) *Die Steuerung ausländischer Tochtergesellschaften. Instrumente und Effizienz*. Frankfurt am Main/Berlin/New York: P. Lang.

Kopp, R. (1994) 'International human resource policies and practices in Japanese, European and United States multinationals', *Human Resource Management*, 33, pp. 581–99.

Landes, D. L. (1960) *The structure of enterprise in the nineteenth century: The cases of Britain and Germany*. Berkeley, CA: Institute of Industrial Relations, reprint no. 152.

Lane, C. (1995) *Industry and society in Europe: Stability and change in Britain, Germany and France*, Aldershot: Edward Elgar.

Lane, C. (1998) 'European companies between globalization and localization: a comparison of internationalization strategies of British and German MNCs', *Economy and Society*, 27, pp. 462–85.

Lane, C. (2000) 'Globalisation and the German model of capitalism – erosion or survival?', *British Journal of Sociology*, 51, pp. 207–34.

Lawrence, P. R. and Lorsch, J. W. (1967) *Organization and Environment: Managing Differentiation and Integration*, Boston: Harvard University Press.

March, J. G. and Simon, H. A. (1958) *Organizations*. New York: John Wiley and Sons.

Martinez, J. I. and Jarillo, J. C. (1991) 'Coordination demands of international strategies', *Journal of International Business Studies*, 33, pp. 429–44.

Maurice, M. and Sorge, A. (eds) (2000) *Embedded organizations. Societal analysis of actors, organizations and socio-economic context*, Amsterdam/Philadelphia: Benjamins.

Maurice, M., Sorge, A. and Warner, M. (1980) 'Societal differences in organizing manufacturing units. A comparison of France, West Germany and Great Britain', *Organization Studies*, 1, pp. 59–86.

Merchant, K. A. (1985) *Control in business organizations*, Cambridge, MA: Balinger.

Mintzberg, H. (1979) *The structuring of organizations*, Englewood Cliffs, NJ: Prentice Hall.

Mintzberg, H. (1983) *Structure in fives. Designing effective organizations*, Englewood Cliffs, NJ: Prentice Hall.

Mirza, H. R. (1998) 'The emerging cultures of capitalism: From the "clash of civilizations" to "unity in diversity"', *Issues & Studies*, 34, pp. 25–47.

Negandhi, A. R. (1987) *International Management*, Newton, MA: Allyn & Bacon.

Negandhi, A. R. and Welge, M. (1984) 'Beyond theory Z: Global rationalization strategies of American, German and Japanese multinational companies', *Advances in International Comparative Management*, Greenwich, CA: JAI Press.

Nohria, N. and Ghoshal, S. (1994) 'Differentiated fit and shared values: alternatives for managing headquarters–subsidiary relationship', *Strategic Management Journal*, 15, pp. 491–502.

Ohmae, K. (1990) *The borderless world: Power and strategy in the interlinked economy*, London: Collins.

Ouchi, W. G. (1977) 'The relationship between organizational structure and organizational control', *Administrative Science Quarterly*, 22, pp. 95–112.

Ouchi, W. G. (1979) 'A conceptual framework for the design of organizational control mechanisms', *Management Science*, 25, pp. 833–48.

Ouchi, W. G. (1980) 'Markets, bureaucracies and clans', *Administrative Science Quarterly*, 25, pp. 129–41.

Pauly, L. W. and Reich, S. (1997) 'National structures and multinational corporate behavior: enduring differences in the age of globalization', *International Organization*, 51, pp. 1–30.

Peterson, R. B., Sargent, J. Napier, N. K. and Shim, W. S. (1996) 'Corporate expatriate HRM policies, internationalization, and performance in the world's largest MNCs', *Management International Review*, 36, pp. 215–30.

Picard, J. (1977) 'How European companies control marketing decisions abroad', *Columbia Journal of World Business*, 12, pp. 113–21.

Porter, M. E. (1990) *The competitive advantage of nations*, Basingstoke: Macmillan.

Prowse, S. (1994) *Corporate governance in an international perspective: a survey of corporate control mechanisms in the United States, the United Kingdom, Japan and Germany*, Basle: Bank for International Settlements, BIS Economic Papers, no. 41 (July).

Pugh, D. S. and Hickson, D. (1996) 'Organizational convergence', in Warner, M. (ed.) *International encyclopedia of business and management*, London and New York: Routledge, 4, 3899–903.

Ronen, S. and Shenkar, O. (1985) 'Clustering countries on attitudinal dimensions: A review and synthesis', *Academy of Management Review*, 10, pp. 435–54.

Ruigrok, W. and van Tulder, R. (1995) *The logic of global restructuring*, London: Routledge.

Sorge, A. and Warner, M. (1986) *Comparative factory organisation. An Anglo-German comparison of management and manpower in manufacturing*, Aldershot: Gower.

Swamidas, P. M. and Kotabe, M. (1993) 'Component sourcing strategies of multinationals: An empirical study of European and Japanese multinationals', *Journal of International Business Studies*, 24, pp. 81–99.

Voss, C. and Blackmon, K. (1996) 'The impact of national and parent company origin on world-class manufacturing', *International Journal of Operations and Production Management*, 16, pp. 98–115.

Whitley, R. (1998) 'Internationalization and varieties of capitalism: the limited effects of cross-national coordination of international activities on the nature of business systems', *Review of International Political Economy*, 5, pp. 445–81.

Whitley, R. (1999) 'How and why are international firms different? The consequences of cross-border managerial coordination for firm characteristics and behaviour', *Paper presented at the 15th EGOS Colloquium*, 4–6 July, Warwick.

Wolf, J. (1994) *Internationales Personalmanagement. Kontext – Koordination – Erfolg*, Wiesbaden: Gabler, MIR Edition.

5
Extending the Perspective: Small and Medium-sized Enterprises as Competitors and Network Partners of MNCs

Martin Brussig and Lutz Gerlach

Introduction

Multinational corporations (MNCs) are in a division of labour with small and medium-sized enterprises (SMEs): on the one hand, globalizing SMEs are increasingly becoming competitors of the MNCs, and on the other hand, they are also network partners for MNCs. For a better understanding of the strategies of MNCs, a closer look on their relationship with globalizing SMEs is required; this is the focus of our paper. Our investigation pertains to the German national business system with its consensual style of capitalism, but some of the results might well serve as hypotheses for other varieties of capitalism as well.

This contribution is structured as follows. In the next section, a brief overview is given of our theoretical bases and hypotheses. In the third section, the relationship between MNCs and SMEs as competitors is discussed, some results presented from research about globalizing SMEs in Germany and the implications for the relationship between MNCs and globalizing SMEs investigated. The fourth section is about the relationship between MNCs and SMEs as network partners and, again, some general trends about networks are introduced. However, it is much more difficult to find well-substantiated propositions about networks and relations between enterprises within networks. This is due to the great empirical variety of networks, the ongoing theoretical discussions about the nature of networks and the difficulties of empirically investigating networks, which encompass many enterprises. Some empirical evidence, however, is provided in the form of a case study about the transfer of an existing network relationship across national borders. The final section comprises the summary and final conclusion of our contribution.

Theoretical bases and hypotheses

Small and medium-sized enterprises not only receive attention because of their significant share of employment and, even more so, of firms in the German economy, they are also regarded as 'different' and fulfilling a 'special role', compared to the more famous large industrial enterprises. This special role of SMEs touches on many of the central topics in industrial societies, such as job-creation processes (Eckart et al., 1987; Kratzer, 1999), the diffusion of new technologies (Sorge, 1987; Acs and Audretsch, 1992) and industrial relations (Auer and Fehr-Duda, 1988; Höland and Eidmann, 1994). There is also the ongoing debate about whether SMEs are pioneers or latecomers, but all the discussions, since the 1980s, result in the finding that SMEs, as a group of enterprises, are extremely heterogeneous (for summaries see, for example, Bartel, 1990; Brussig, 2000).

Questions concerning the position and perspectives of SMEs gained momentum in the 1990s under the influence of globalization. For most SMEs, globalization presents more risks than opportunities. But for a small fraction of SMEs, especially innovative enterprises with a high specialization in niche markets, it offers new opportunities to compete successfully in international markets. In both public and political debates, these enterprises, seen as 'hidden champions' (Simon, 1996; Storey and Tether, 1996), often serve as a model to be followed by other SMEs.

However, research on globalization primarily focuses on large multi-national enterprises (Kreikebaum, 1998; Weber et al., 1998), which were the first companies for whom globalization was relevant. Consequently, investigation of the relations between the headquarters and subsidiaries started with the big MNCs and has looked at the influence of so-called global, national and country of origin effects on the organizational structure and strategies of MNCs (see Geppert et al. in this volume). However, organizational structures and strategies of MNCs are further shaped by their relationships with other enterprises. In this chapter, the discussion of the influence of these relationships is confined to a selected group of enterprises, namely globalizing small and medium-sized enterprises. By 'globalizing SME' we refer to enterprises with less than 500 employees, which export goods or capital and have the possibility of influencing each other, either directly or by learning from each other.

In the discussion about the influences in the relationship between MNCs and globalizing SMEs, a basic distinction should be made between whether the globalizing SME is a competitor or a network partner for the MNC. This does not mean that a given SME is either a competitor or a network partner; it might be both or neither. Enterprises are often competitors for one enterprise and network partners for another. Two enterprises may even compete in one field, such as R&D, and cooperate in another, such as the labour market (Streeck, 1992). Indeed, networking itself is not without competitive elements (Hessinger et al., 2000). The idea behind this basic distinction is that the relationship between an MNC and SME should be different depending on whether they are competitors or network partners to each other. The use of the term 'competing globalizing SME' refers to a goods or capital exporting SME, which competes with an MNC on export markets. SMEs which are only local competitors to MNCs are not included in our analysis.

The following discussion is based on two hypotheses, one for each type of relationship. For the competitor relationship, the hypothesis is borrowed from the popular discourse about globalizing SMEs, that is, that they have superior organizational principles, which enable them to link flexibility with efficiency and that MNCs should therefore learn from them and adapt to the models these SMEs embody. The influence of this relationship on MNCs is indirect and consists of learning from the SME and may be some reorganization within MNCs according to the typical (and supposedly superior) organizational principles of SMEs.

For the network partner relationship, the hypothesis is that the big network partner should have an interest in the successful globalization of the whole network, including the small and medium-sized network partners, and should provide some support for globalizing SMEs to increase their chances of a successful globalization strategy. The influence of this relationship on MNCs, but even more on the SMEs in the network, is direct and consists of the creation of communication and exchange structures, such as joint quality circles, steering groups and so on.

Admittedly, these are highly stylized hypotheses. For a thorough empirical testing much more data has to be collected and specifications made, but their function here is to identify the main arguments and initial references.

Small and medium-sized enterprises as competitors to multinational corporations

This section focuses on globalizing SMEs as competitors to MNCs, outlining some findings on globalizing SMEs and then discussing the hypothesis about the consequences for MNCs.

Recent trends in globalizing SMEs

Although the research on globalization and SMEs is often seen as lagging behind compared to studies about MNCs, many different studies were undertaken in the 1990s (see Weber and Kabst, 2000) and resulted in five main, and largely uncontroversial, points about globalization and SMEs:

- The organizational forms of internationalization activities of SMEs are influenced by the cultural and political conditions in the host country

There are not only global effects and national effects operating within a foreign subsidiary; even the organization of a subsidiary is influenced by the conditions in the host country and relations between the headquarters and the subsidiary (Table 5.1). Foreign European markets are usually served by the German home base. For the North American market, German firms often set up subsidiaries, where their perceived low language thresholds and an assumed cultural proximity allow to them to

Table 5.1 Different distribution channels when the export focus is on Europe, North America and East Asia

Distribution channels	Focus of export activities is on...		
	Europe N 5 197 (in %)	North America N 5 246 (in %)	East Asia N 5 78 (in %)
German home base	28	13	18
Subsidiaries abroad	57	72	49
In cooperation with German partners	7	11	18
In cooperation with local partners	29	38	47

Source: Lay et al. (2001: 21).

operate immediately in the market. In Asia, however, the dominant organizational form is cooperation with a native partner. Especially in China, this is due to local content regulations. To overcome cultural differences, cooperation with a native partner is generally highly recommended (Lay et al., 2001) not only for SMEs of course, but, due to their resource restrictions, one can assume that SMEs have to adapt to local conditions to a much stronger extent that MNCs.

- The main reasons for German firms to export capital are to find new customers and enlarge sales markets

The building up a new subsidiary abroad, the enlargement of an existing subsidiary or investment in a joint venture are all forms of capital export and may offer the opportunity for enterprises to find a more beneficial environment and escape problems at home. Export of capital may also offer the chance to get closer to the foreign customer and enlarge markets. Several studies show that the main reasons for German firms to export capital are to find new customers and enlarge sales markets (for example Schultz-Wild, 1997: 8ff.; see also Table 5.2). This is in sharp contrast to the public debate and the persistent claims of industrial lobbyists, not necessarily the entrepreneurs themselves, that firms export capital due to cost pressure as a result of the high wage conditions in Germany.

Although cost pressure is almost universally mentioned as a significant factor in capital export (Bamberger and Wrona, 1997: 721), few empirical studies argue that high wages, as the most important cost factor, are the main motive for capital export (see, for example, Lay et al., 2001: 26ff.). Lay et al. (2001) also reveal how limited solely cost-based considerations are. Firms which built or enlarged their subsidiary because of wage costs were not able to increase their sales, compared to those firms which did not export capital, whereas firms which built or enlarged their subsidiary because of the sales market increased their sales more often. Times for deliveries and the 'time to market' of innovations are also significantly longer in firms which transferred their production abroad for cost reasons, compared to those, which 'stayed home' (71 vs. 64 days; 16 vs. 14 months). As a consequence, some firms have started to relocate their production sites back to Germany (see Schulte, forthcoming). According to Lay et al. (2001: 26), the ratio between 'exporters' and 'relocaters' was 6:1 in 1995–97, but changed in 1997–99 to 4:1. The reasons for relocating production capacity reflect, at least in part, how limited pure cost considerations

Table 5.2 Reasons for capital export of German manufacturing firms with five or more employees

Reason for capital export	Number of answers
Customer and market	*3845*
Exploring new markets	1942
Securing existing markets	1308
Sourcing	595
Cost pressure	*1280*
Lower wage costs	893
More work hours	262
Longer machinery use time	125
Administration and regulation	*666*
Lower taxes	339
Lower administrative barriers	152
Less environmental protection regulation	175
Local conditions	*546*
To lower currency exchange fluctuations	236
Import restrictions	310
Other	*694*
Technology transfer	375
Other reasons	319

Source: IAB Panel (1998), projections, authors' own calculations.

are: the relocators mentioned the gain in flexibility (62 per cent in 1997 and 55 per cent in 1999) and quality problems (43 and 52 per cent) as the most important reasons. The third important reason for relocating, usage of existing capacity (47 and 45 per cent), shows that, in times of cyclical crisis in Germany, managers often try to avoid dismissals by relocating production to Germany. An isolated focus on wage costs leaves other aspects hidden, which nevertheless change when a subsidiary is built, aspects such as communication, coordination, flexibility and so on (Lay et al., 2001: 90ff.). Another important reason for relocating firms is to lower coordination costs (36 per cent in 1997 and 1999).

Cost pressure has a tremendous influence on firms, but it is often not the main reason German firms export capital. If capital export decisions are reduced to wage cost considerations, firms risk losing out in other fields, such as time for deliveries or time to market of innovations. Thus, even in a situation of high wage conditions, the enlargement of the sales market and the search for new customers are the main motives for capital export.

SMEs pursue fewer objectives with their globalization activities than large companies

There is no difference in the structure of reasons for capital export between small and big firms. Neither do small firms particularly try to escape high wage conditions in Germany, nor is the enlargement of the market an aim reserved for the big enterprises. But there is a remarkable difference in the complexity of the reasons for globalization: small and medium-sized enterprises focus on one or two reasons for going international; the number of reasons why enterprises export capital increases with firm size (Table 5.3). This size effect is already known from the investment behaviour of SMEs in comparison to larger enterprises (Fritsch, 1987). Nevertheless, it shows the stronger focus of the SMEs and the risks which are involved for SMEs. Several studies have shown that SMEs go global for different reasons and with different aims in mind (for example production, sourcing, selling) (Schultz-Wild, 1997; Bamberger and Wrona, 1997; Lay et al., 2001).

- Small and medium-sized enterprises are, to a large extent, internationally active

Generally, the export rate grows with firm size. In Germany, many small and medium-sized enterprises export. Statistically, if a firm has 100 or more employees, non-exporting firms are in the minority (22.9 per cent among the size group 100–249), while almost half of this size group export more than 15 per cent of their annual sales (see Table 5.4). There is, however, a sharp difference between East and West German enterprises: East German industry exports roughly only half of

Table 5.3 Number of reasons for capital export of German manufacturing firms with five or more employees

Size group (empl.)	Number of answers per firm
5–19	1.0
20–99	2.1
100–249	2.9
250–499	3.1
500–999	3.3
≥ 1000	4.3
Total	3.6

Source: IAB Panel (1998), projections, authors' own calculations.

Table 5.4   Export and firm size; German manufacturing firms with five or more employees

Size group (empl.)	No export 0%	Some export up to 15% of ann. sales	Strong export more than 15% of ann. sales	N
5–19	86.3	8.1	5.6	90572
20–99	61.6	25.3	13.1	51573
100–249	22.9	28.7	48.4	8386
250–499	18.3	19.9	61.8	2556
500–999	8.9	10.7	80.3	1220
≥ 1000	8.3	11.6	80.1	579
				154886

Source: IAB Panel (1998), projections, authors' own calculations.

the percentage of their total sales compared to West German industry (approx. 18 compared to 33 per cent). Low export activity is considered to be one of the main indicators for the ongoing need for industrial recovery in East Germany. But the much greater volume of exports from West German industry means that the low East German rate does not have much of an impact on the export rate for Germany as a whole. Widespread export activities, even among relatively small enterprises, reflect the fact that, in international comparisons, German SMEs are regarded as competitive and segmentation between firms is considered to be low (Lane, 1997).

● For SMEs, globalization activities are reactive rather than anticipatory

SMEs are more often latecomers than pioneers in the globalization process. This is in striking contrast to a near-consensus in the 1980s about the pioneering function of a great number of SMEs. However, quantitative and qualitative studies since then show that the globalization undertaken by SMEs often comes under pressure from competitors or customers (for example Miesenbock, 1988; Fieten et al., 1997; von Behr, 2001). Faced with an environment which requires globalization activities, they develop their strategies to cope with these challenges. Sometimes this leads to global activities of SMEs, but only in reaction to demand from suppliers or customers. Therefore, SMEs, on the whole, are less involved in export activities and are not the first to be exposed to global competition. There are, of course, small enterprises which are international from their inception, but these are few and far between.

Although these five points concerning the activities, motives and strategies of globalizing SMEs are widely agreed upon, many questions are left unanswered. Two important questions are, for example, how are globalization activities and globalization strategies of SMEs shaped and what are the extent and the dynamics of the international activities of SMEs? Despite the lack of knowledge about globalizing SMEs, some indicators have been presented as a basis for the discussion of the possible influence of SMEs on MNCs when both are competitors to each other.

Do globalizing SMEs have an impact on MNCs?

Is there something for MNCs to learn from the fact that SMEs compete on global markets with MNCs to a significant extent? Do globalizing SMEs represent a model and is it a model MNCs can profit from?

The implications for MNCs caused specifically by the global competition between MNCs and globalizing SMEs are hard to specify. This is partly due to the variety of SMEs and the variety of competitive relationships between MNCs and globalizing SMEs, but some general points can be made. Global SMEs do not cause intensified global competition. Typical 'drivers' for globalization, such as technological innovations and institutional reforms, affect every enterprise involved in global competition and every enterprise therefore has to search for a strategic response. SMEs and MNCs both build on different strengths and weaknesses (see Bartel, 1990; Acs and Audretsch, 1992).

The multiple globalization activities of SMEs are largely independent of what MNCs are doing. Globalizing SMEs look to what their competitors are doing, what the market offers and the customer demands. They do not look at a specific group of firms. This is also true of MNCs: MNCs look at the market and the competition, they look for the best in their field, but they do not look specifically at globalizing SMEs. May be they would, if all globalizing SMEs were fast, flexible and successful, but only some SMEs are pioneers, most are lagging far behind.

Therefore, there are few, if any, immediate consequences for MNCs, their globalization strategies and their internal organization, specifically resulting from the fact that SMEs are competing internationally.

Small and medium-sized enterprises as network partners of MNCs: a case study of a 'follow customer' relationship

Contrary to the limited influence of globalizing SMEs in a competitor role with MNCs, the hypothesis here is that globalizing SMEs as network partners do influence MNCs (and vice versa). Enterprises in a network should have an interest in the globalization of the other network partners and the big partners in the network should be interested in what the small partners are doing. We will start with the main arguments and selected empirical material about German SMEs in networks, then provide a case study about a globalizing network to discuss the above hypothesis.

What do networks offer?

Since the mid-1980s, the restructuring of supply chains has been increasingly under discussion (Altmann et al., 1986; Womack et al., 1990). Although the restructuring of supply chains is often presented as a coherent system (Toyotism, lean production, *systemische Rationalisierung*), the core elements of the restructuring processes are heterogeneous and partly contradictory. They include strategic sourcing, rationalization of the supplier base and segmentation among suppliers (Christensen, 1999).

The automotive industry is often cited as an example for the segmentation among suppliers, but strategic sourcing and the rationalization of the supplier base have been reported in other industries as well (Womack et al., 1990; Pries et al., 1990; Fieten et al., 1997). Japan is regarded as the paradigmatic example for lean production and, although some important national characteristics contribute to the Japanese system (Dore, 1987), such as a segmented labour market and strong regulative and public pressure for inter-firm relations, the core elements of lean production are seen as applicable to other national economies as well and have influenced the restructuring of supply chains since the 1980s.

The restructuring of supply chains was accompanied by an increased interest in networks (Semlinger, 1993). Relational contracting and intense communication between the partners, two typical characteristics of networks, seemed to make them a suitable organizational form for lean production. The consequences for small and medium-sized suppliers resulting from these changes in the division of labour are far from uniform. Some authors emphasize the risks (Semlinger, 1988; Harrison, 1994): first-tier suppliers have to invest massively, they have to organize the production of complex components, often under the conditions of just-in-time production, they have to organize manifold relations to their suppliers and, last but not least, they are forced to use economies of scale. This excludes SMEs almost by definition from a position as first-tier supplier. Within *segmented supply chains*, SMEs fall back into strategically unimportant positions and face immense cost pressures and high fluctuations in demand. Other authors, however, emphasize opportunities for SMEs in network relations beyond first-tier positions (Piore and Sabel, 1984). SMEs may benefit from *strategic sourcing*, when they develop core competencies and occupy strategic position in networks. In this scenario, SMEs do not have an advantage *per se*, but they are not *a priori* excluded from the benefits.

Empirical analysis in Germany shows that the regional embeddedness of enterprises pays off. Table 5.5 compares two performance indicators (productivity as added value per employee and time span from order to delivery – for both complex and simple products) for four groups of enterprises. The survey data is based on a representative group of German manufacturing enterprises from the capital goods sector. To sort each enterprise into each group, the regional distribution of sourcing (selling) was measured. An enterprise with a share of sourcing (selling) above the median of all the other enterprises is classified as an 'international' sourcer (seller), otherwise it is 'national/regional'. 'Home-based players', that is, regionally embedded enterprises with a strong export, show the highest productivity (value added per employee) when compared to all other groups. Moreover, 'home-based players' have faster delivery times than the 'global players', the other group with strong exports. Despite their strong exports, they are almost as fast in their deliveries as the 'national manufacturers' and the 'global sourcers', which concentrate on the national and regional market (see Table 5.5).

Network partners have to solve four problems in a coordinated way to realize the gains from the network relationship:

1. They have to coordinate the division of labour and organize the cooperation. In comparison to markets and hierarchies, networks are often characterized as beneficial in terms of the linkage between stability and flexibility.
2. They have to reach and to secure common standards. Usually, the big partner sets standards such as product quality and punctuality in deliveries and the small partner has to reach these standards to secure task fulfilment.
3. The interests of both partners have to be compatible with each other. This is especially the case for the small partner, which has to adapt to the big partner in many ways. Long-term gains should be possible for the small partner.
4. They have to protect themselves against each other. Two dangers are prominent: performance failure and misuse of trust by the misuse of privileged knowledge about the other partner.

Table 5.5   Performance of four types of regional embeddedness

	National manufacturer	Home-based player	Global sourcer	Global player
	N=281	N=266	N=363	N=342
Value added per employee (1000 DM)	102	140	144	137
Time to deliver (days), complex products, small batches	102	122	118	136
Time to deliver (days), simple products, large batches	21	20	29	26

Source: Dreher and Kinkel (2000: 37).

In the next section, we will present a case study about a globalizing medium-sized enterprise in a network relationship with a multinational corporation and see how it solves these problems.

The transfer of a service relationship in a 'follow customer' mode: a case study

The case study is about a transfer of a relationship in a 'follow customer' mode, where the medium-sized enterprise follows its customer, a multinational corporation, and builds, for the first time in its history, a subsidiary in a foreign country. The case study is not about a global network: it is about the 'going global' of an already existing network. According to the hypothesis, the MNC should have an interest in the successful transformation of the small network partner into an internationally acting enterprise.

The network consists mainly of three enterprises. The *first* is a medium-sized service supplier located in Chemnitz, Saxony in the southeast of Germany. This enterprise was founded in 1991, but, as many of the East German firms, builds on a predecessor enterprise, which does not exist today in its original form. The owner of the 'spin-off' is an industrial holding with headquarters in Munich. Today, about 300 employees are employed in several departments (machine building, industrial services, electrical engineering, steel construction). The strategic focus is on industrial services for other enterprises, especially in the automotive industry. The *second* enterprise in this network is Volkswagen, the largest German car producer. Volkswagen is a multinational corporation with subsidiaries virtually all over the world. One of them, an engine plant, is directly located in Chemnitz, the same city where the service supplier works. Another subsidiary, a big assembly plant, is in a small town nearby. The medium-sized service enterprise provides services in the VW production sites, such as tool management and fluid management. These tasks were formerly done by Volkswagen, but later outsourced to local firms. Over the years, a highly efficient relationship between the two was established. In 1998, the medium-sized service supplier in Chemnitz received the 'Value to the Customer' award, which indicated how well the cooperation between both partners was working. In 1998, Volkswagen planned to establish a new production site in Poland in Lower Silesia, an area characterized by a long industrial tradition and a great history as a mining region. This new production site in Poland produces engines. Of the above-mentioned subsidiaries of Volkswagen, the Polish subsidiary (VW Polska) is the focus of the case study. Here, the headquarters of Volkswagen in Wolfsburg planned an outsourcing of most service tasks, which are pooled in a 'technical services pool'. The service enterprise from Chemnitz became one the partners and had to found a new company in Poland. This subsidiary of the medium-sized service enterprise in Poland is the *third* enterprise in the network. Today, it has about 38 employees. Their task is the maintenance and repair of the manufacturing lines of VW Polska.

It is this relationship between the service enterprise from Chemnitz, its Polish subsidiary and the production plant of Volkswagen in Poland (VW Polska), which is the focus of the case study. Other firms are involved, especially the headquarters of Volkswagen in Wolfsburg and the Volkswagen subsidiary in Chemnitz, as well as the other firms in the 'technical services pool' in Poland, which are, like the service subsidiary from the parent company in Chemnitz, subsidiaries of independent suppliers.

It is important to stress that without the assignment from Volkswagen, the medium-sized service supplier in Chemnitz would not have built a subsidiary abroad. As mentioned above, globalization 'under pressure' is common for most small or medium-sized enterprises. The managers there know that they have to work in foreign countries and with foreign employees, customers and suppliers but only build new subsidiaries after they have secured orders in that country.

The decision for Poland was based on two simple considerations made by Volkswagen. On the one hand, there are the political and economic advantages for sales where there is a production base in the host country. On the other hand, Poland is, in principle, a good place to produce goods for export into the European Union: it is closely located to Germany and favourable in terms of its costs. The inclusion of Poland into the EU in the years to come will further improve the conditions of this production site.

The Polish service subsidiary works mainly with Polish employees. In the beginning, they used experienced pilot workers (*Anlaufunterstützer*) from the parent company in Chemnitz at the same time as they were introducing the Polish employees to their tasks. Gradually, the pilot workers went back to their home base in Chemnitz. In the last year, the Polish service subsidiary has enlarged its profile and offers services to customers other than VW in Poland. However, VW is still the most important customer, both in quantitative terms and strategically.

Organising the cooperation

As a first step, Volkswagen released 'invitations to bid' for the technical services and asked for offers. Especially with larger tasks, it is expected that the supplier designs a solution for the described purpose and the solution is part of the document, which the supplier offers to Volkswagen in its application for the bid. The next stage is negotiations between Volkswagen and one or more bidders, and then Volkswagen decides which bid to accept.

For task fulfilment, both service enterprises in Chemnitz and Poland work mostly independently of VW Polska. They communicate, however, on the operational level. Sometimes, negotiations between both partners are necessary, especially towards the end of the task and in unforeseen situations. With permanent ongoing tasks, such as maintenance, it is somewhat different. Here, there are regular meetings on the management level and the service supplier managers have operational decision-making rights over Volkswagen employees. Thus there is a 'blurring of organizational boundaries', but only on the operational level. The cooperation is also stimulated by the personal attitudes of the managers on both sides, who appreciate their autonomy from their respective parent companies.

The question, therefore, of how the cooperation is organized has to be answered differently for different stages and organizational levels. Volkswagen seeks to retain a competition during the first stage, bidding and negotiation, even if there are only a handful of enterprises which qualify for that competition. During the second stage, task fulfilment, cooperation prevails. Trust seems to play a role, especially on the operational level. On the organizational level, however, there seems to be little support of the big partner for the small partner.

Task fulfilment according to higher standards

To look how the SME reaches the required standards, it is necessary to look at what the specific strengths of the small and medium-sized service suppliers in Poland and Chemnitz are and which weaknesses they have to overcome.

The first strength is, of course, their competence in industrial services. This has to be seen in relation to possible competitors, not to Volkswagen. Experience in industrial services is the second strength, which goes hand in hand with competence. In recent years, the service supplier in Chemnitz acquired a good name for competent and efficient service. The third advantage is the cost structure. In services, costs mostly comprise wages. The medium-sized service supplier in Chemnitz pays according to existing payment schemes negotiated by unions and employer associations in the metalworking industry, where the pay level is well below the level of Volkswagen, which negotiates its own company agreement. The fourth strength is the flexibility provided by the supplier: it is much easier for Volkswagen to reduce, enlarge and change the demand for services by negotiation with another, comparatively weak, enterprise than to negotiate such changes within Volkswagen itself.

On the other hand, both suppliers face some problems which they have to overcome. Firstly, they act on a short-term basis, as the supplier can only operate 'within' the time span given by the customer. Secondly, they must not fail to meet the targets set them, for they do not have the resources to rectify mistakes nor does the customer (VW) have the necessary tolerance. They are under contract in nearly everything they do for Volkswagen. Thirdly, the Polish service supplier has only second choice of the resources. For example, in the local labour market in Poland, Volkswagen and the other networking firms were all looking for employees in the region where the investment took place at the same time. Volkswagen offered better conditions and they were well known to the Polish workers, so VW had first choice of labour.

These obstacles are overcome through the commitment of specific actors – managers, pilot workers and employees. Our interview partners in Chemnitz and Poland emphasized a good working atmosphere as critical for the success of the company. An external observer, however, notes that, to a large extent, the problems are overcome simply by 'extra work' being put in by the men. Volkswagen trusts that the managers from the Chemnitz service supplier will implement the same Volkswagen standards in their Polish subsidiary, as they had in Germany.

Gains and motives for the small partner

So far, the service suppliers seem to be play a more passive role, but certainly there are incentives for the parent company in Chemnitz to take part in the 'follow customer' strategy. By following the customer with their services, the service supplier in Chemnitz gains valuable experience in a future market. Another important aspect is the opportunity to learn from Volkswagen as experiences from the cooperation with VW Polska on the operational level 'trickle down' to the enterprise in Chemnitz. These experiences are rarely used in a strategic or conscious way; their usage depends on the proximity/distance from VW Polska. As a matter of course, the Polish service subsidiary uses some routines and organizational tools from Volkswagen, such as competence profiles for each employee and an assessment process to find out which additional competencies a given employee should learn. Such tools, simple as they are, find their way only slowly into the parent company in Chemnitz. But the departments of the parent company could gain from the opportunity to learn.

Mutual protection

The main problem for VW Polska is how to prevent performance failures of the Polish service enterprise. For the Polish service enterprise, the main problem is their dependence. Three different and independent groups of measures should be mentioned, which lower the risk for Volkswagen.

Firstly, Volkswagen distributes the manufacturing of identical products between a number of different locations. The engines, for instance, which are produced in Poland, are also produced in the Volkswagen plant in Chemnitz. In case of a production stop in one place, the production in the other plant can continue. Secondly, Volkswagen benchmarks its suppliers and subjects them to a constant monitoring on the basis of performance criteria. This may be the main reason for the introduction of the 'Value to the Customers award' mentioned earlier. Thirdly, all changes to the relations between Volkswagen and its suppliers are made gradually. Again, the motor engine plant in Poland is an example: the outsourcing of technical services is very extensive in Poland and VW will use their experiences there to draw conclusions about its use for other plants.

For the service enterprises in Chemnitz and Poland, the main problem is their dependence on Volkswagen. This dependence is mutual, although not symmetrical. To lower their dependence, they strive for a balanced structure of customers. The Polish service subsidiary, which started life as a 'follow customer' operation, now works for other firms in Poland besides VW Polska. VW Polska concluded a five-year contract with its service suppliers, which includes cost reductions targets for them. Moreover, Volkswagen and the Polish service supplier agreed that employees could not change jobs from the Polish service supplier to VW Polska. This prevents a constant and permanent loss of experienced employees for the small service supplier and safeguards their continued existence.

Discussion of the case

The relations between the MNC and the medium-sized service enterprise cannot be understood on the basis of a simple dichotomy of 'competition' and 'cooperation'. It is both, and the extent to which competition or cooperation dominates depends on the chronological stage of the relationship and the organizational level involved. But it is the MNC which decides which mode dominates because it sets the conditions under which the service enterprise has to operate.

Also, the popular question about mutual or one-sided dependence or independence cannot be answered as simply as the network discussion sometimes suggests. Greater independence of the small network partner by building a diversified structure of customers does not preclude (at least in our case study) a greater dependence in the sense of a tight adaptation to the needs of the main customer. The latter adaptation can be seen rather as a precondition for the former, the diversification of the customer base, since the Polish service subsidiary looks for new customers in Poland, but only insofar as the quality of their services for VW Polska is not endangered.

Nevertheless, every case study is confronted with the question how far the observations can be generalized. Usually this question is answered by linking the observations to the theoretical discussion.

The theoretical basis of the case study was an assumed interest of the big partner in a successful globalization of the small partner. There are some indicators for such an interest, such as experimentation of the MNC with make-or-buy decisions. But, in contrast to reports from Japan or other lean production examples, the support of the big partner for the small partner in our study was fairly weak. Communication between the big partner and the small partner in the selected case study was also not very developed.

Rather, the MNC seemed to trust that the small partner would reach the necessary standards within a short period of time. From the perspective of the societal effects approach, one could assume that this is linked to the low segmentation among German firms, whereby small and medium-sized enterprises are often serious partners for MNCs. The MNCs get to know the performance of the SMEs over a long period and this influences their strategies for actual and future cooperation with them. Stability of inter-firm cooperation and the non-exclusive nature of the high-quality segment for enterprises in Germany are two characteristics of German industry, which could help to explain the lack of active support of the MNC towards the SMEs within the networks.

In networks, property rights and transaction costs are differently distributed than they are in hierarchical organizations. Obviously, Volkswagen benefits from the network solution, especially in terms of costs and flexibility. From the point of view of the service supplier, the difference between being a network partner or an in-sourced service department within Volkswagen is less significant.

This reminds us that strategies can often be better understood if we understand their context. Strategies may be rooted in the visions of an Schumpeterian entrepreneur, but they may also be rooted in the perceived demands of suppliers and customers on an enterprise. Of course, the managers in the medium-sized service supplier in Chemnitz take an active approach to globalization problems, but, without the opportunities offered by Volkswagen, their 'follow customer' globalization strategy would be much harder to justify. Rather, it appears to be a gradual shaping of a strategy, which only later can be identified as a promising 'follow customer' strategy.

This leads us back to the starting point of the chapter. We will better understand the strategies of MNCs if we understand their context, and part of their context comprises globalizing SMEs, acting as either competitors or network partners.

Conclusion

This chapter focused on globalizing SMEs in Germany. Our starting point was that we can better understand multinational corporations when we include their relationships to other enterprises, and do not merely confine the analysis to global, national and country of origin effects on HQ–subsidiary relations. MNCs are in a division of labour with small and medium-sized enterprises and globalizing SMEs can, on the one hand, be competitors and, on the other, network partners. What are the consequences for MNCs and the relationship between MNCs and globalizing SMEs of both these 'roles'?

We argued that there are few, if any, consequences for MNCs resulting from the fact that globalizing SMEs are competitors. It is, however, somewhat different with SMEs as network partners and we introduced a case study about a transfer of a network relationship to another production site abroad (follow customer strategy). According to the case study, there are some actions and reactions, especially of the small partner, but also the big partner, which can be ascribed to their network relationship. But these actions and reactions (for example experimentation, especially with make-or-buy decisions, open and cooperative communication, especially on the operative level, but no common quality circles and no investment support) are weaker than one would expect from fully fledged lean production relations. This might be due to the peculiarities of the case study, which were not controlled for, but it might also be due, as we would suggest, to societal patterns of the German industry – long-term cooperation between firms and a large high-quality segment among small and medium-sized enterprises create long-term opportunities for mutual learning, trust and flexibility, which makes explicit support of large enterprises for their small network partners less necessary.

One of the characteristic features of the case presented was the extension of the network to Poland. We are unable to explore in this paper how the cooperation of both partners was influenced by the fact that the host country was specifically Poland (and not, for example, the Czech Republic). But with European integration, the extension of networks to Eastern Europe will increasingly occur. This will lead to the issue of the societal roots of well-established patterns of cooperation between enterprises becoming increasingly important.

References

Acs, Z. J. and Audretsch, D. B. (1992) *Innovation durch kleine Unternehmen*, Berlin: Edition Sigma.

Altmann, N., Deiß, M. and Döhl, V., Sauer, D. (1986) 'Ein "neuer Rational-isierungstyp" – neue Anforderungen an die Industriesoziologie', *Soziale Welt*, 37, pp. 191–207.

Auer, P. and Fehr-Duda, H. (1988) *Industrial Relations in Small and Medium-sized Enterprises. Final Report. Report to the Commission of the EC*, Berlin: WZB.

Bamberger, I. and Wrona, T. (1997) 'Globalisierungsbetroffenheit und Anpassungsstrategien von Klein- und Mittelunternehmen. Ergebnisse einer empirischen Untersuchung', *Zeitschrift für Betriebswirtschaft*, 67, pp. 713–35.

Bartel, R. (1990) 'Unternehmensgrößenvor- und Nachteile. Eine strukturierte Auswertung theoretischer und empirischer Literatur', *Jahrbuch für Sozialwissenschaft*, 41, pp. 135–59.

Behr von, M. (2001) 'Wissenstransfer bei internationaler Produktion', in von Behr and Semlinger, K. (eds) *Transfer und Steuerung von Wissen. Zur Internationalisierung kleinerer und mittlerer Unternehmen*, München: ISF, pp. 9–67.

Brussig, M. (2000) *Kleinbetriebliche Arbeitssysteme in den neuen Bundesländern. Theorie, Funktionsweise, Entwicklung*, Berlin: GSFP.

Christensen, P. R. (1999) *Challenges and Pathways for Small Subcontractors – in an Era of World-wide Restructuring of Supply Chains*, University of Southern Denmark: Centre for Small Business Studies.

Dore, R. (1987) *Taking Japan Seriously: A Confucian Perspective on Leading Economic Issues*, London: Athlone Press.

Dreher, C. and Kinkel, St. (2000) 'Die Bedeutung der regionalen Basis für Globalisierungsentscheidungen', in Hirsch-Kreinsen, H. and Schulte, A. (eds) *Standortbindungen: Unternehmen zwischen Globalisierung und Regionalisierung*, Berlin: Edition Sigma, pp. 29–60.

Eckart, W., von Einem, E. and Stahl, K. (1987) 'Dynamik der Arbeitsplatzentwicklung: Eine kritische Betrachtung der empirischen Forschung in den Vereinigten Staaten', in Fritsch, M. and Hull, C. (eds) *Arbeitsplatzdynamik und Regionalentwicklung. Beiträge zur beschäftigungspolitischen Bedeutung von Klein- und Großunternehmen*, Berlin: Edition Sigma, pp. 21–48.

Fieten, R., Friedrich, W. and Lagemann, W. (1997) *Globalisierung der Märkte-Herausforderung und Optionen für kleine und mittlere Unternehmen, insbesondere für Zulieferer*, Stuttgart: Schäffer-Poeschel.

Fritsch, M. (1987) 'Groß und Klein in der Wirtschaft? Was man darüber weiß und was man darüber wissen sollte', in Fritsch, M. and Hull, C. (eds) *Arbeitsplatzdynamik und Regionalentwicklung. Beiträge zur beschäftigungspolitischen Bedeutung von Klein- und Großunternehmen*, Berlin: Edition Sigma, pp. 175–95.

Harrison, B. (1994) *Lean and Mean. The Changing Landscape of Corporate Power in the Age of Flexibility*, New York: Basic Books.

Hessinger, P., Eichhorn, F., Feldhoff, J. and Schmidt, G. (2000) *Fokus und Balance. Aufbau und Wachstum industrieller Netzwerke*, Opladen: Westdeutscher Verlag.

Höland, A. and Eidmann, D. (1994) *Sozialwissenschaftliche Erkenntnisse zum Betriebsverfassungsrecht. Eine Literaturstudie*, Düsseldorf: HBS.

IAB Panel (1998) 'Arbeitgeberbefragung des Instituts für Arbeitsmarkt- und Berufsforschung'. (The IAB panel is a yearly investigation among representatively selected enterprises in Germany (since 1993) by the Institut für Arbeitsmarkt- und Berufsforschung (IAB) (Institute for Labour Market Research).

Kratzer, N. (1999) 'Beschäftigungseffekte von Existenzgründungen', in IAB et al. (eds) *Jahrbuch Sozialwissenschaftliche Technikberichterstattung 1998/99, Schwerpunkt: Arbeitsmarkt*, Berlin: Edition Sigma, pp. 113–56.

Kreikebaum, H. (1998) *Organisationsmanagement internationaler Unternehmen. Grundlagen und neue Strukturen*, Wiesbaden: Gabler.

Lane, C. (1997) 'Industrial reorganization in Europe: patterns of convergence and divergence in Germany, France and Britain', in Warner, M. (ed.) *Comparative Management. Critical Perspectives on Business and Management*, London/New York: Routledge, pp. 517–40.

Lay, G., Kinkel, S., Eggers, T., Schulte, A. and Le, P. (2001) *Globalisierung erfolgreich meistern*, Frankfurt/M.: VDMA.

Miesenbock, K. J. (1988) 'Small Business and exporting: A literature review', *International Small Business Journal*, 6, pp. 42–61.

Piore, M. J. and Sabel, C. F. (1984) *The Second Industrial Divide: Possibilities for Prosperity*, New York: Basic Books.

Pries, L., Schmidt, R. and Trinczek, R. (1990) *Entwicklungspfade von Industriearbeit. Chancen und Risiken betrieblicher Produktionsmodernisierung*, Opladen: Westdeutscher.

Schulte, A. (forthcoming) *Das Phänomen der Rückverlagerung – Eine Untersuchung zur Dynamik von Standortentscheidungen kleiner und mittlerer Unternehmen*, University of Dortmund: PhD thesis.

Schultz-Wild, R. (1997) *Herausforderung Internationalisierung der Produktion. Chancen für die mittelständische Industrie*, Karlsruhe: PFT.

Semlinger, K. (1988) 'Stellung und Probleme kleinbetrieblicher Zulieferer im Verhältnis zu großen Abnehmern', in Altmann, N. and Sauer, D. (eds) *Systemische Rationalisierung und Zulieferindustrie. Sozialwissenschaftliche Aspekte zwischenbetrieblicher Arbeitsteilung*, Frankfurt/M.: Campus, pp. 89–118.

Semlinger, K. (1993) 'Effizienz und Autonomie in Zulieferungsnetzwerken – Zum strategischen Gehalt von Kooperation', in Staehle, W. and Sydow, J. (eds) *Managementforschung*, Berlin: Walter de Gruyter, pp. 309–54.

Simon, H. (1996) *Die heimlichen Gewinner. Die Erfolgsstrategien unbekannter Weltmarktführer*, München: Heyne.

Sorge, A. (1987) 'Begünstigt der technische Wandel kleine und mittlere Produktionseinheiten?', in Fritsch, M. and Hull, C. (eds) *Arbeitsplatzdynamik und Regionalentwicklung. Beiträge zur beschäftigungspolitischen Bedeutung von Klein- und Großunternehmen*, Berlin: Edition Sigma, pp. 235–44.

Storey, D. and Tether, B. (1996) *New Technology Based Firms (NTBFs) in Europe*, Warwick Research Institute.

Streeck, W. (1992) 'Interest Heterogeneity and Organizing Capacity: Two Class Logics of Collective Action', in Streeck, W. (ed.) *Social Institutions and Economic Performance. Studies of Industrial Relations in Advanced Capitalist Economies*, London: Sage, pp. 77–104.

Weber, W. and Kabst, R. (2000) 'Internationalisierung mittelständischer Unternehmen', in Gutmann, R. and Kabst, R. (eds) *Internationalisierung im Mittelstand. Chancen – Risiken – Erfolgsfaktoren*, Wiesbaden: Gabler, pp. 3–89.

Weber, W., Festing, M., Dowling, P. J. and Schuler, R. (1998) *Internationales Personalmanagement*, Wiesbaden: Gabler.

Womack, J. P., Jones, D. T. and Roos, D. (1990) *The Machine that Changed the World*, Boston: MIT Press.

Part II

Human Resource Management and Industrial Relations in Europe: The Pressures of Globalization

6
Multinational Companies, Institutional Environments and the Diffusion of Industrial Relations Practices

Anne Tempel

Introduction

The process of globalization driven by the activities of multinational companies (MNCs) has led some commentators to argue that MNCs are footloose, sourcing, producing and marketing on a global scale, as dictated by their business strategy (Ohmae, 1990; 1993; Strange, 1997; *The Economist*, 1995) and that through these denationalized companies, a process of homogenization is at work.

However, contrary evidence indicates that the notion of the footloose enterprise remains a myth (Dörre, 1997; Hirst and Thompson, 1996), most MNCs being national companies with international operations rather than stateless corporations (Hu, 1992; Ruigrok and van Tulder, 1995). Moreover, there is a large body of authors who argue that there is continued diversity in the way in which societies solve similar problems (Lane, 1989; 1995; Whitley, 1992; 1994; Porter, 1990) and who therefore provide grounds for thinking that national models are likely to retain their specific institutional contexts.

At the same time, there are a number of authors who highlight processes which could lead to a decline in the significance of national economies and their institutions, whilst not necessarily leading towards a borderless world. Research has pointed to the power of MNCs to disseminate practices across national borders within their organizations despite national cultural and institutional differences (Mueller and Purcell, 1992; Coller, 1996; Mendez, 1995). Moreover, recent cases have shown that MNCs may increasingly be able to adopt globalization as a strategic option and thus appear footloose (Dörre, 1997; Mueller, 1996). The threats of MNCs to divest are sufficient in persuading local trade unions and worker representatives to concede to the introduction of new employment policies because nationally based trade unions and worker representatives are often not in a position to establish whether these threats are real or whether productivity comparisons have been carried out.

This chapter is centered at the heart of the debate around the denationalization versus national embeddedness of MNCs and their power to transfer practices across national borders. Focusing on the industrial relations practices of MNCs, it investigates the extent to which MNCs are informed by their country-of-origin national business systems in their industrial relations policies and draws on recent case study research into the industrial relations policies of German MNCs operating in Britain and British MNCs operating in Germany.

The country-of-origin effect and industrial relations in MNCs

Against the background of research highlighting the importance of national systems, Ferner (1997a) has proposed a framework of analysis to research the extent to which MNCs are informed by their national business systems in their industrial relations and HRM policies and whether they attempt to transmit industrial relations and HRM practices formed in their country of origin to their foreign operations or abandon what they regard as constraining features of their national business systems when operating abroad.

The extent to which MNCs are likely to transfer country-of-origin practices to their subsidiaries has been linked particularly to the nature of the host country environment (Ferner, 1997a; see also Marginson et al., 1993; Marginson and Sisson, 1994; Smith and Meiksins, 1995). It is argued that MNCs operating in 'permissive' host country systems which are based on custom and practice and less formal or 'sticky' institutions (Streeck, 1987) may be able to introduce country-of-origin practices with relative ease into 'permissive' host country systems, which pose few constraints and can sustain a range of alternative industrial relations practices and possibilities. MNCs operating in permissive host countries thus have the strategic choice to adapt to the environment of the host country and adopt local practices or to introduce country-of-origin practices into their subsidiaries.

In contrast, it is argued that MNCs operating in 'constraining' host country systems may be prevented from transferring country-of-origin practices by uniform and binding rules and formal and more 'sticky' institutions which impose a template on companies from wherever they originate. MNCs operating in constraining systems may attempt to circumvent the restrictions imposed by these institutions and introduce country-of-origin practices despite regulations.

Germany and Britain represent interesting national business systems to investigate the extent to which MNCs attempt to influence the industrial relations practices of their foreign subsidiaries for a number of reasons. Firstly, the industrial relations systems of the two countries are pole opposites (Edwards et al., 1998; Jacobi et al., 1998; Lane, 1995). The British system of industrial relations has traditionally been marked by the absence of legal regulations shaping industrial relations, patterns of labor relations being more contingent on negotiated regulation by the parties involved. In recent decades, legal, economic and political changes in Britain have led the industrial relations environment to become more permissive as traditional pluralist industrial relations have collapsed (Purcell, 1993) and the joint regulation of industrial relations through collective bargaining has increasingly given way to unilateral regulation by employers (Purcell, 1995; Dickens and Hall, 1995; Brown et al., 1997; 1998; Cully et al., 1999). In contrast, industrial relations in Germany are much more subject to uniform and binding regulations, based both on statute and formal agreements negotiated by encompassing actors. However, globalization and reunification have taken their toll on the stability and strength of key industrial relations institutions (Bispinck, 1997; Hassel 1999; Dörre, 1996). The transformation process in former East Germany in particular has led to a more decentralized, fragmented and internally differentiated German industrial relations system (Jacobi et al., 1998; Artus et al., 2000; Lohr et al., 1995; Schmidt, 1998).

Secondly, the permissive nature of the British system and the constraining nature of the German system provide ideal test beds to investigate the extent to which MNCs attempt to transfer country-of-origin practices, choose, or have no choice but to adapt to host country practices. More specifically, the investigation of the industrial relations practices of German MNCs in their British subsidiaries is useful in researching the extent to which MNCs, faced with the strategic choice offered by the permissive British environment, choose to transfer country-of-origin industrial relations practices to their British subsidiaries or to adapt to and take advantage of the British industrial relations system. The investigation of the industrial relations practices of British MNCs in their German subsidiaries is useful in testing the extent to which MNCs are prevented from transferring country-of-origin practices into a constraining environment and extent to which they seek and are able to find room for maneuver in a constraining industrial relations system.

Finally, in both countries, there are debates as to the influence of MNCs on industrial relations. In recent years, Britain has distinguished itself in the European Union as enjoying relatively low labor costs, freedom from social legislation, and a greatly weakened trade union movement. Although highly successful in attracting foreign investment, there are fears that Britain has become the location of labour-intensive, low skill 'branch plant' operations (Marginson, 1994; Lane, 1995). Moreover, recent decisions by MNCs to relocate investment planned in Britain to other European countries and a wave of plant closures and redundancies in foreign-owned subsidiaries in Britain (EIRO, 1997; EIRR, 2000; EIRO, 2001a) have highlighted the ease and speed with which workers can be dismissed in Britain (Ferner, 1997b; TUC Press Release, 2000). In contrast, high-labor costs and the detailed regulation of industrial relations have been at the center of the discussion about the international competitiveness of Germany and the location of industrial investment in that country over the last decade (Tüselmann, 1998; Jungnickel, 1996; Mueller, 1996; EIRR, 1994).

The study

Britain and Germany and British and German MNCs have been the focus of recent studies into the industrial relations and human resource practices of MNCs. Müller (1996, 1997, 1998) investigated the practices of American and British-owned MNCs in Germany whilst Beaumont et al. (1990), Dickmann (1999) Ferner and Varul (1999) (see also Ferner et al., 2001) and Tüselmann et al. (2001) conducted research into the practices of German MNCs in Britain. The research upon which this chapter is based aimed to combine the investigation of the industrial relations practices of German MNCs in Britain and British MNCs in Germany in one study. This chapter will discuss the pay determination and employee representation practices of two German-owned MNCs in their British subsidiaries and two British-owned MNCs in Germany (Tempel, 2001).[1]

Detailed case studies were carried out in these companies between September 1998 and January 1999. At total of 17 semi-structured interviews were conducted with HRM managers in the companies, both at headquarters and subsidiary levels. Interviews were conducted at the two levels in order to gain a more objective picture of parent company influence and subsidiary autonomy (Coller, 1996; Coller and Marginson, 1998) and to reveal whether micro-political processes promoted or inhibited the country-of-origin and host country effects (Edwards et al., 1993). The four companies are based in the chemical and pharmaceutical industry. The research was conducted in one industry in order to limit the influence of sectoral factors and the chemical and pharmaceutical industry was chosen because of its highly internationalized nature (Grant and Paterson, 1994; Lane, 1997), which facilitates the international integration of operations within MNCs and therefore the exercise of country-of-origin influence (Ferner, 1997a; Coller and Marginson, 1998).

The areas of pay determination and employee representation were chosen against the background of the contrasting institutional frameworks shaping these areas in Germany and Britain. In terms of pay determination, the British collective bargaining system has traditionally been voluntary, resting on the market strength of the bargaining parties. The economic, legal and political changes in Britain have since the 1960s led to the collapse of multi-employer bargaining, a reduction in the scope of collective bargaining and the increasing individualization of pay determination (Purcell, 1995). At the end of the 1990s, pay for the majority (65 per cent) of non-managerial employees in the private sector was determined unilaterally by management and for those covered by collective bargaining (28 per cent), single-employer bargaining was most common (Cully et al., 1999).

In contrast, the legal enforceability of collective agreements in Germany at the center of the German collective bargaining system has given employers associations and trade unions the status of law-creating institutions, able to socially generate legal norms. The provisions of industry-level collective agreements cover all organized workers and all employers affiliated to employers associations. In special circumstances, they may be extended to all employees and companies in an industry, regardless of trade union and employer association membership. However, since the 1970s, structural challenges and globalization and reunification have led to a decline in the capacity of the social partners to make binding collective agreements, particularly in former East Germany (Dörre, 1996). Moreover, there has been a growth in company-level collective bargaining and the emergence of a growing gap between highly regulated sectors with strong institutions and poorly regulated sectors with weak ones (Hassel, 1999). Despite this evidence that the German collective bargaining system is being undermined, the importance of collective bargaining shaping in pay determination in Germany is much higher than in Britain. In 1997, 65 per cent of employees in the West German private sector were covered by industry-level collective bargaining and in 1998, 8 per cent of all employees in West Germany were covered by company level collective agreements (Kohaut and Schnabel, 1998, 1999).

A key implication of the differences in the levels and methods of pay determination in Britain and Germany has been identified as being the extent to which payment can be related to performance in the two countries (Sparrow and Hiltrop, 1994; Lawrence, 1991). It is argued that the lack of control of German HRM managers over pay or reward decisions because of industry-level collective bargaining places performance management in a very different context to Britain, where appraisal and reward are under the direct control of the line manager (Sparrow and Hiltrop, 1994; see also Kurdelbusch, 2001).

Previous investigations of the collective bargaining practices of foreign-owned MNCs in Germany have revealed their reluctance to recognize trade unions (Beaumont et al., 1990; Guest and Hoque, 1995). More generally, survey evidence has shown that foreign-owned MNCs in Britain are less likely than British-owned MNCs and in particular than British domestic companies to recognize trade unions of bargaining purposes, and where they do engage in collective bargaining, this takes place primarily at the level of the individual establishment (Purcell, 1995). There is a dearth of research into the collective bargaining practices of foreign-owned MNCs in Germany. Müller's (1996, 1998) research of American and British-owned MNCs in Germany discovered that of the four British-owned companies researched, three were covered by industry-level collective bargaining and one by a company agreement. In contrast, five of the nine American-owned MNCs did not participate in collective bargaining at all whilst three were covered by industry level agreements and one by a company agreement.

Against this background, the investigation of pay determination practices of the German and British MNCs researched in the present study concerned firstly the position of corporate headquarters of both nationality towards collective bargaining in their home country operations and the extent to which they influence decisions concerning collective bargaining in their foreign subsidiaries. The investigation of the German MNCs in Britain focused particularly on the extent to which trade unions are recognized for collective bargaining, the level and method of pay determination and the extent to which performance-related pay has been adopted. For the British MNCs in Germany, the research was conducted in terms of whether they comply with multi-level collective bargaining, have opted out of this level to conclude company level agreements or are not covered by collective bargaining at all. Moreover, the extent of pressure exerted by corporate headquarters on subsidiary management to introduce performance-related pay systems was investigated.

In terms of employee representation, the British industrial relations system is marked by the absence of statutorily regulated employee representation at plant level (Kahn Freund, 1983; Mueckenberger, 1988). This has led to a fluctuation in the importance of information and consultation mechanisms over time and a multitude of different employee representation bodies and practices (EIRO, 1999). The British system of single channel representation is based on trade unions and with the loss of trade union power, a significant 'representation gap' has opened up (Towers, 1997). According to the 1998 Workplace Industrial Relations Survey, almost three in five workplaces have no worker representatives whether union or non-union (Cully et al., 1999).

In Germany, comprehensive and detailed legal provisions of the Works Constitution Act have the potential to subject all workplaces with more than five employees to uniform regulation of the employer–employee relationship at plant level. Works councils have a range of different representation rights ranging from information and consultation to co-determination rights, their rights being strongest in relation to social policy, weaker in relation to personnel issues and weakest in financial and economic matters (Wächter, 1983). The Works Constitution Act is however an 'enabling' law (Lane, 1989). Studies have shown the different strengths of works councils in practice (Kotthoff, 1981, 1994) and the significant decline in the coverage of works councils in German workplaces, particularly in small- and medium-sized companies (Hassel, 1999). Moreover, with the decentralization of collective bargaining, works councils are experiencing increased pressure due the reduction in support of multi-employer agreements.

Concerning the employee representation practices of foreign-owned MNCs in Britain and Germany, Beaumont et al. (1990), Guest and Hoque (1995) and Ferner and Varul (1999) found a tendency amongst German-owned MNCs towards reluctance to transfer works councils to their subsidiaries in Britain. In his investigation, Müller (1996) found works councils in five of the nine American-owned and all four of the British-owned subsidiaries in Germany.

On the basis of case study research into American-owned MNCs in Germany, Royle (1998) has proposed a typology of possible strategies adopted by foreign-owned MNCs to 'avoid' the German system of employee representation. These include the re-classification of jobs to dilute employee representation, illegal measures such as unfair dismissal, refusing payment and facilities for works councils and non-compliance with the Works Council Act, and the 'buying out' of employee representation rights. Further strategies include the bypassing of works councils through the setting up of alternative representation bodies and mechanisms and coercive comparisons, playing works councils off against each other to ensure that management strategies are adhered to.

Against this background, a key question in the investigation of the employee representation practices of German MNCs in Britain concerned the extent to which they attempt to introduce works councils or functional equivalents or prefer to adapt to local practices. Regarding British MNCs in Germany, in the light of the representation gap and the limited depth of employee representation in British, the main points of focus for investigation concerned the position of headquarters management concerning works councils and the evidence of strategies to avoid or undermine works councils.

The empirical evidence

German Divisional Pharma[2] is the pharmaceutical division of a German chemicals company. It employs 13,000 people, 28 per cent of whom are located in Germany. In 1995, the company acquired the pharmaceutical operations of a British MNC and employs over 1000 employees in that country in research and development, production and sales activities.

In Germany, the company is covered by industry-level collective bargaining and, as part of the chemicals parent company, recognizes the importance of its role in collective bargaining in the chemical industry and the benefits for large companies of retaining industry-level collective agreements, particularly in terms of their function of taking wages out of competition. It regards the representation of its foreign subsidiaries in collective bargaining as a matter to be regulated locally.

Its British subsidiary does not recognize trade unions for the purposes of collective bargaining. When the British operations of German Divisional Pharma were acquired in 1995, there were full recognition agreements for trade unions. However, with the introduction of a performance management system designed to apply to all hierarchical levels, the subsidiary has moved from collective bargaining agreements to recognition agreements, recognizing trade unions for health and safety, grievance and discipline but not for wage negotiations. Since the acquisition, pay determination in German Divisional Pharma's British subsidiary has been transformed from being based on collective agreements and an elaborate system of job grading to a system of performance management which underpins all aspects of HRM in the operations.

The decision to withdraw from collective agreements was made at local level with no direct involvement of corporate headquarters, although the developments were observed with interest at that level. Indeed, the British subsidiary has become an important source of learning for the company in terms of change management and its performance management system. For this purpose, a member of the British subsidiary HRM management was transferred to corporate headquarters with the aim of learning from his experience and knowledge.

In respect of employee representation, German Divisional Pharma has not attempted to set up works councils or functional equivalents in its British subsidiary. British employees are represented through trade unions and a system of staff councils which links into the chemical parent company's European Works Council.

The lack of legally-based representation in German Divisional Pharma's British subsidiary compared to the company's German operations has had very important implications for the British workforce. When German Divisional Pharma acquired its British subsidiary, it had two research and development centers in Europe alone and thus sought to realize synergies by undertaking a comparison of its research and development activities in Britain and Germany, focusing primarily on qualifications levels, costs, in particular labor costs, and motivation levels. Whilst the comparison showed the British operations to be more favorable, 'the decisions made were in favor of the German operations' (HQ respondent) and over 200 jobs were lost in the British subsidiary on the grounds that:

> British labor law makes it easier to make people redundant there. It's not a matter of labor law as a whole but simply the requirements for a [social plan] (Sozialplan) in Germany. It is very time consuming and expensive to reach agreement on a Sozialplan in Germany. In Britain it is a lot easier and cheaper to make people redundant.
>
> (HQ respondent)

The Works Constitution Act regulates that in the event of a substantial alteration to an establishment, the works council is entitled to enforce a social plan, a special form of works agreement to compensate for or reduce the economic disadvantages incurred by employees. The social plan resembles a special form of redundancy program and covers not only financial compensation but may also include re-training programs and the transfer of workers to other parts of the enterprise (Weiss, 1992):

> There is one eye looking with envy towards Britain, how flexible we can be in terms of our labor relations laws and the other part says we are just becoming the poor relation because of the fact that we are so flexible...when the company has needed to cut overheads, because of the flexibility in our labor laws, it has been easy for the parent company to say do we really want the fuss in Germany or is it easier to let the UK sort it out because it is easier there.
>
> (Subsidiary respondent)

The decision made by German Divisional Pharma was however shaped not only by the ease with which redundancies can be made in the British environment, but also in order to protect its home country workforce and operations: 'securing the future of the German operations played a major role' (HQ respondent). Indeed, in the same year as the redundancies were made in the company's British operations, an agreement to secure the future of its German operations was signed between company management and works councils. Employee representatives in Germany had campaigned for the agreement in order to 'gain clear commitment from company management to the German operations...and to make them fit to face future competition – competition not only from external competitors but from the company's other plants throughout the world' (internal company newsletter).

The decision of German Divisional Pharma to protect its country-of-origin workforce to the detriment of the workforce in its British operations in spite of the favorable light in which the comparison of the research and development centers put the British subsidiary, was described by British HRM management as demonstrating the internal battle which the company faces as to whether it is 'really a global organization or a German company with a number of subsidiaries' (subsidiary respondent). The company's utilization of the permissive nature of the British industrial relations environment to protect its home country workforce reflects the deep embeddedness of the company in its home country environment.

German Family Pharma is a family-owned company employing 25,000 people, 32 per cent of whom are in Germany. Its production and sales activities in Britain were set up in 1969 and employ 500 people.

The company is covered by industry-level collective bargaining in Germany and plays an active role in collective bargaining in the chemicals industry. Although it does not have an explicit policy towards collective bargaining and the recognition of trade unions in its foreign subsidiaries, regarding these as matters for local decision-making, German Family Pharma does give 'an important message to all subsidiaries that the company wants partnership relationships with employee representatives and respects local regulations' (HQ respondent). This message is not however reflected in its British operations where there is no trade union recognition for collective bargaining purposes, or indeed for consultation and information on any matters. This has evolved from the time of the establishment and 'is not a reflection of union avoidance' (subsidiary respondent). However, subsidiary management sees itself as employing individuals and 'we do everything we can do to reinforce that' (subsidiary respondent).

In respect of employee representation, the company has not encouraged the setting up of works councils or functional equivalents in its British subsidiary. The lack of formal employee representation structures in German Family Pharma is shaped by the subsidiary's philosophy of employing individuals:

> we have ad-hoc ways of consulting with people as and when we need to. Next year for example, we will have to cut back on the size of our factory so we are going through a process of consultation with employees and ask them if they want to elect representatives to talk to us during this period. Otherwise we see it as our responsibility to talk to everybody all of the time on an equal basis.
>
> (Subsidiary respondent)

German Family Pharma's British subsidiary stands in contrast to the company's other European subsidiaries in being the only plant in Europe in which there is no trade union recognition for collective bargaining purposes and no works council or similar formal body of representation. The British subsidiary is also unique in Europe in being the only plant in which a continuous production system is in operation, subsidiary management arguing that its ability to run such a system is strongly influenced by its industrial relations practices.

British Pharma was formerly part of a large British-owned chemicals company until it demerged in 1993. Of its 32,000 employees, 40 per cent are located in Britain. The company employs 1200 people in Germany in production and sales operations which were acquired in 1973. It has not formulated specific policies regarding collective bargaining in its subsidiaries, although it does not specifically encourage it and sees it as a matter for local decision-making according to local customs and regulations. In its country-of-origin operations, British Pharma has recognition agreements on collective bargaining with a number of trade unions for its blue-collar workers but withdrew trade union recognition rights in respect of white-collar workers in 1993 in order to link pay to individual performance. Performance-related payment for blue-collar workers has been resisted by trade unions and employees.

The company's German subsidiary is covered by the chemical industry's collective agreements. Opting out of collective bargaining has never been considered and the parent company has at no time attempted to influence collective bargaining in its German subsidiary. A performance-related payment system applicable for all hierarchical levels is in operation in the subsidiary. Far from reflecting parent company influence, the system was developed at local level and has led to the German HR manager being selected as chairman of the company's reward and recognition project group.

Concerning employee representation in its foreign operations, British Pharma respects local laws and regards it as beneficial to have a process through which employees can be heard, whilst preferring information and consultation on a voluntary rather than legal basis. In terms of the employee representation structures in its German subsidiaries, there are three plant-level works councils and a group works council in the German operations of British Pharma. Whilst, therefore, there has been no attempt on the part of British Pharma to influence employee representation structures in its German operations, corporate HRM policies have come into conflict with employee representation structures in the German subsidiary and with German labor law. Policies on the part of the parent company to encourage outsourcing, teleworking and the implementation of a standardized employee attitude survey were blocked in the German subsidiary: 'I am happy to be able to decline to introduce concepts which come from the parent company because German employment law does not permit them' (subsidiary respondent).

There are indications that such parent company influence was not only blocked by the nature of the host country environment but also by the willingness of the German HRM manager to utilize German labor law and his expert knowledge of it as sources of power to bargain with corporate headquarters and ultimately to resist country-of-origin influence: 'I am happy that I am able to say no to such influence...the last defense is always German employment law' (subsidiary respondent).

British Chemical employs over 67,000 people world-wide, 25 per cent of whom are located in Britain. It employs over 1000 people in various sites in Germany, the oldest of which was established in 1867. The company has not formulated specific policies regarding collective bargaining, which it does not encourage, but does respect local customs and legislation. In its country-of-origin operations, it has a series of collective bargaining relationships with trade unions but was considering the decentralization of collective bargaining to business division or plant level at the time of the investigation.

In the German operations of British Chemical, there is a mixture of industry-level and company-level collective agreements, the latter of which have been inherited in acquisitions. Opting out of industry-level agreements was considered by German HRM management to be too dangerous in terms of the increased involvement of trade unions at company level. Corporate HRM policies, termed the company 'Way in HR,' stipulate that performance-related payment is mandatory for senior management and is encouraged for managerial and non-managerial employees throughout the company. The company Way in HR is reinforced by management performance reviews and a best practice system. At the time of research, performance-related payment in the German operations applied to senior management only. German HRM management had in the past been able to resist parent company impulses to introduce performance-related pay for other hierarchical levels. The full effect of the company Way in HR had however not been felt at subsidiary level as it had recently been implemented in the company. There are indications that the pressures on the German operations to acquiesce to parent company influence are mounting as the Way in HR becomes more widely disseminated and reinforced by management performance reviews and the best practice system.

British Chemical has a strong commitment to representative consultation in its country-of-origin operations, expressed in its willingness to voluntarily set up a Business and General Committee in the 1970s following the recommendations of the Bullock Committee on Inquiry on Industrial Democracy and its comprehensive system of joint regulation with employee representatives and trade unions at all levels. In terms of employee representation in its foreign operations, it respects local laws and regards information and consultation as beneficial, whilst preferring it to be on a voluntary rather than legal basis.

In the company's German operations, there is employee representation on the supervisory board, a group works council and plant-level works councils in the majority of its operations. Plants where works councils are absent have been recently acquired. Conflict between corporate HRM policies and employee representation structures in the company's

German operations and with German labor law is much clearer than in British Pharma. Corporate and division level management are clearly dissatisfied and frustrated with works council power in the company's German operations. The introduction of a range of HRM practices including performance-related payment and standard bonus systems in its German operations have been prevented by works council power:

> reasonable concepts and ideas and generic HR approaches will be delayed or may not be implemented because they become part of this semi-perpetual bargaining relationship that can develop with the works council...if there is a list of 20 things to be done, and number 17 is a good idea, it just won't get done because there aren't enough trade-offs.
>
> (HQ respondent)

The institutionalized nature of works council rights are seen by corporate management as creating a business disadvantage because of the powers of works councils in delaying decision-making and blocking changes, leading to the German operations being 'behind the times, in some cases they are up to years slower on a number of items which could and should be introduced to improve the business' (HQ respondent).

At the same time, the negative view of the institutionalized system of employee representation in Germany on the part of British Chemical does not reflect a corporate policy against employee representation and trade union involvement, but rather against the blocking of policies and practices seen as necessary for an improvement in business performance by bargaining and legally granted representation rights. Indeed, the support of the company for information and consultation mechanisms has been felt in the German operations of the company. Examples were cited by German HRM management where the parent company positively influenced the way in which restructuring and plant closures were handled:

> the company was extremely fair in its treatment of employees who were affected by restructuring or closures. Our 'social plans' were above average in Germany and a number of managers were put aside purely for the outplacement of affected employees. In this respect the parent company strongly influenced German management – we were not nearly as 'social' as the British.
>
> (subsidiary respondent)

However, the dissatisfaction of the company with what it sees as the negative aspects of the legally-based system of employee representation in Germany is reflected in its investment strategy. A planned joint venture between British Chemical and a German company was abandoned because of the inflexibility of the latter and its inability to introduce change because of works council resistance. Moreover, the inflexibility and slowness of the German operations in introducing change were compared to the situation in the company's other European operations, in particular those in Holland, which were awarded investment on the basis of an international comparison because of their flexibility:

> in Holland, the businesses were having a real problem not being able to compete. They reached some quite creative agreements with the local unions which enabled them to deliver improved productivity... and they got some reinvestment which wouldn't otherwise have happened.

> (HQ respondent)

The dissatisfaction and frustration of corporate management with works council power in the German environment and the importance of internal competition for investment in the company may therefore have important implications for British Chemical's German operations in the future.

The case of British Chemical seems to depict an MNC which has become increasingly denationalized. In the 1990s, the company undertook major restructuring, selling off less profitable businesses and acquiring new businesses in expanding areas of the chemicals sector. It has actively sought to move towards a transnational structure and strategy in which the home country environment plays a decreasing role in the company and centers of strategic importance are spread throughout the company in different national environments. In 1979, 70 per cent of the company's workforce were located in Britain, compared to 25 per cent in 1998. The company now has more employees and company assets in North America than in any other location and the majority of its business division headquarters are located outside of Britain. This, coupled with its dissatisfaction with the constraints posed by German industrial relations institutions on its business activities and its diversion of investment to other European subsidiaries reflect the company's willingness to invest in environments which are favorable to business strategy without loyalty to any particular national business system.

In summary, in the face of the strategic choice offered by the British environment, the two German-owned MNCs have made no attempts to encourage collective bargaining or to set up works councils or functional equivalents in their British subsidiaries, but have rather adapted their HRM practices to the British environment. The British subsidiaries of the two companies stand in stark contrast to their parent companies' other European operations: German Divisional Pharma's British subsidiary has come to be seen as the 'rebel of Europe' (subsidiary respondent) in its industrial relations practices and German Family Pharma's British subsidiary is unique among the company's European plants in terms of the absence of collective bargaining and formal employee representation which has enabled it to operate a continuous production system. The behaviour of German Divisional Pharma has gone beyond adaptation to utilization of the permissiveness of the British industrial relations environment in order to avoid costs, protect the home country workforce and avoid confrontation with works councils in its country-of-origin operations.

The German subsidiaries of the two British-owned MNCs also behave largely as local companies in their industrial relations practices, being covered by industry-wide collective agreements and complying with the indigenous system of employee representation. However, attempts by both companies to transfer practices to their German subsidiaries have been blocked by the German environment. In the case of British Pharma, this is attributable not only to the nature of the host country environment but also to the ability of subsidiary management to use German labor law and its expert local knowledge as power resources to resist country-of-origin influence. In the past, British Chemical's attempts to encourage performance-related payment practices have been blocked by the constraining German environment. There are however indications that the pressure on subsidiary management to acquiesce to parent company influence is mounting and that British Chemical is circumventing the constraints of the German system by shying away from the German environment in its investment policies.

Conclusions

Against the background of the debate around the denationalization versus embeddedness of MNCs, this chapter has focused on the influence of MNCs on industrial relations practices in their foreign subsidiaries. Investigating the extent to which MNCs are informed by their country-of-origin national business systems, it has presented research into the behaviour of MNCs originating in and operating in contrasting institutional environments. German MNCs in Britain were chosen to investigate the extent to which MNCs, faced with the strategic choice offered by a permissive host country environment, transfer practices which have proven successful in their country-of-origin operations or adapt to host country practices. British MNCs in Germany were selected to research the extent to which MNCs operating in a constraining environment are prevented from transferring country-of-origin practices and attempt to develop strategies to circumvent such constraints.

The case study research has shown that the German MNCs have chosen to adapt to the permissive nature of the British environment, adopting industrial relations practices which are very different to those in their country-of-origin and other European operations. One of the companies has however gone further than adaptation to utilizing the permissiveness of the British environment compared to the German environment in order to save costs and to protect its country-of-origin workforce and operations.

The investigation of the behaviour of British MNCs in Germany has highlighted the restrictions which MNCs can face in transferring country-of-origin practices to constraining environments. It has revealed that this can result not only from the constraining nature of institutions themselves but from the ability of subsidiary management to use such institutions and its expert knowledge of them as a power resource to resist parent company influence. Moreover, it has shown that faced with constraining industrial relations institutions, one of the companies has begun to circumvent the German environment, investing in other European countries with less constraining industrial relations institutions.

The contrasting cases of German Divisional Pharma and British Chemical highlight three important debates concerning MNCs and institutional environments. Firstly, the two cases highlight different ways in which MNCs are able to utilize differences in institutional environments to their advantage, German Divisional Pharma using the permissive British environment to protect its home country workforce and British Chemical voting with its feet by shying away from constraining environments and investing in environments more congenial to its business strategies.

Secondly, they reflect the debate concerning the embeddedness versus denationalization of MNCs outlined in the introduction. German Divisional Pharma's restructuring decisions seem to reflect a deep embeddedness of the company in its country-of-origin national business system. In contrast, British Chemical's investment policy seems to indicate that it has become denationalized, without loyalty to any particular national environment.

Finally, the behaviour of the two companies fuel the debate about the significance of regulation in investment and divestment decisions of MNCs. The decision of German Divisional Pharma to reduce the British workforce because of the lack of legally-based employee representation structures in Britain compared to Germany reflects concerns that foreign-owned MNCs, recognizing the ease with which workers can be made redundant in Britain, have chosen to make workforce reductions in Britain rather than in other European countries where the cost of dismissal is higher and highlights the importance for British workers of the much debated European Directive establishing a general framework for informing and consulting employees in the European Community (EIRO, 2002). The dissatisfaction and frustration of British Chemical with the institutionalized rights and bargaining strategies of the works councils in its German operations, its circumvention of the German environment and its awarding of investment to other European countries with less restrictive industrial relations institutions reflects the discussions about the effects of detailed regulation of industrial relations on the attractiveness of Germany as a location for foreign investment, particularly in the light of the reforms made to the Works Constitution Act in 2001 (EIRO, 2001b).

This investigation of the country-of-origin effect on industrial relations practices has been limited to MNCs from two countries of origin and their behaviour in two host countries. In order to gain a deeper understanding of the interactions of institutional environments and industrial relations practices in MNCs, further research is needed which firstly studies the behaviour of MNCs of different countries of origin operating in the same host country in order to discover more about the ways and extent to which MNCs are informed by their countries of origin. Secondly, studies of the behaviour of MNCs originating in one institutional environment in several host country institutional environments enforcing different degrees of constraint on HRM practices would aid in revealing more about the impact of host country environments on the behaviour of MNCs.

Notes

1 The results presented in this chapter are part of a larger investigation into the industrial relations and human resource practices of German and British MNCs. The complete investigation was carried out in five MNCs, the fifth being of German origin and researched not only pay determination and employee representation but also employee development. Moreover, the complete investigation researched not only the extent to which MNCs attempt to transfer practices from their country-of-origin to their host country subsidiaries ('forward diffusion' (Edwards, 1998)) but also the extent to which they attempt to learn from the practices of their subsidiaries ('reverse diffusion' (Edwards, 1998)).

2 For reasons of confidentiality, the companies have been given pseudonyms.

References

Artus, I., Schmidt, R. and Sterkel, G. (2000) *Brüchige Tarifrealität: der schleichende Bedeutungsverlust tariflicher Normen in der ostdeutschen Industrie*, Berlin: Sigma.

Beaumont, P. B., Cressey, P. and Jakobsen, P. (1990) 'Key industrial relations: West German subsidiaries in Britain', *Employee Relations*, 12, 6, pp. 3–7.

Bispinck, R. (1997) 'Deregulierung, Differenzierung und Dezentralisierung des Flächentarifvertrages: Eine Bestandsaufnahme neuerer Entwicklungstendenzen der Tarifpolitik', *WSI-Mitteilungen*, 8, pp. 551–61.

Brown, W., Deakin, S. and Ryan, P. (1997) 'The effects of British industrial relations legislation 1979–97', *National Institute Economic Review*, 38, 3, pp. 69–83.

Brown, W., Deakin, S., Hudson, M., Pratten, C. and Ryan, P. (1998) *The individualisation of employment contracts in Britain*, Research Paper for the Department of Trade and Industry.

Coller, X. (1996) 'Managing flexibility in the food industry: A cross-national comparative case study in European multinational companies', *European Journal of Industrial Relations*, 2, pp. 153–72.

Coller, X. and Marginson, P. (1998) 'Channels of influence over changing employment practice in multinational companies a case from the food industry', *Industrial Relations Journal*, 29, 1, pp. 4–17.

Cully, M., Woodland, S., O'Reilly, A. and Dix, G. (1999) *Britain at work*. London: Routledge.

Dickens, L. and Hall, M. (1995) 'The state: labour law and industrial relations', in Edwards, P. K. (ed.) *Industrial relations. Theory and practice in Britain*, Oxford: Blackwell, pp. 255–303.

Dickmann, M. (1999) *Balancing global, parent and local influences: International human resource management of German multinational companies*. D. Phil thesis, Birkbeck College, University of London.

Dörre, K. (1996) 'Globalisierungsstrategien von Unternehmen – ein Desintegrationsphänomen? Zu den Auswirkungen grenzüberschreitender Unternehmensaktivitäten auf die industriellen Beziehungen', *SOFI-Mitteilungen*, 24, pp. 15–28.

Dörre, K. (1997) 'Globalisierung – eine strategische Option. Internationalisierung von Unternehmen und industrielle Beziehungen in der Bundesrepublik', *Industrielle Beziehungen*, 4, 4, pp. 265–90.

Economist, The (1995) 'A survey of multinationals', 24th June, pp. 3–30.

Edwards, P. K., Ferner, A. and Sisson, K. (1993) 'People and the Process of Management in the Multinational Company: A Review and Some Illustrations', *Warwick Papers in Industrial Relations*, No. 43.

Edwards, P. K., Hall, M., Hyman, R., Marginson, P., Sisson, K., Waddington, J. and Winchester, D. (1998) 'Great Britain: from partial collectivism to neo-liberalism to where?', in Ferner, A. and Hyman, R. (eds) *Changing industrial relations in Europe*, Oxford: Blackwell, pp. 1–54.

Edwards, T. (1998) 'Multinationals, work organisation and the process of diffusion: A case study', *International Journal of Human Resource Management*, 5, 4, pp. 696–709.

EIRO (European Industrial Relations Online) (1997) 'Ford case highlights the costs of inward and outward investment', *www.eiro.eurofound.ie*, February 1997.

EIRO (1999) 'Information and consultation in the UK: an alien imposition?', *www.eiro.eurofound.ie*, April 1999.

EIRO (2001a) 'Corus announces large-scale redundancies', *www.eiro.eurofound.ie*, February 2001.

EIRO (2001b) 'Works Constitution Act reform adopted', *www.eiro.eurofound.ie*, July 2001.

EIRO (2002) 'UK reaction to agreement on EU employee consultation Directive', *www.eiro.eurofound.ie*, January 2002.

EIRR (1994) 'Labour costs and international competitiveness', *European Industrial Relations Review*, 241, February, pp. 13–17.

EIRR (2000) 'Unrest at Peugeot', *European Industrial Relations Review*, 320/12.

Ferner, A. (1997a) 'Country of origin effects and HRM in multinational companies', *Human Resource Management Journal*, 7, 1, pp. 19–37.

Ferner, A. (1997b) 'Multinationals, relocation and employment in Europe', in Gual, J. (ed.) *Job creation: the role of labour market institutions*, Aldershot: Edward Elgar, pp. 164–96.

Ferner, A. and Varul, M. (1999) *The German way: German multinationals and the management of human resources in their UK subsidiaries*. London: Anglo-German Foundation for the Study of Industrial Society.

Ferner, A., Quintanilla, X. and Varul, M. (2001) 'Country-of-origin effects, host-country effects and the management of HR in multinationals: German companies in Britain and Spain', *Journal of World Business*, 36, 2, pp. 107–28.

Grant, W. and Paterson, W. (1994) 'The chemical industry: a study of internationalisation' in Hollingsworth, J. R., Schmitter, P. C. and Streeck, W. (eds) *Governing Capitalist Economies. Performance and Control of Economic Sectors*, Oxford: Oxford University Press, pp. 129–55.

Guest, D. and Hoque, K. (1995) 'National ownership and HR practices in UK greenfield sites', *Human Resource Management Journal*, 6, 4, pp. 50–74.

Hassel, A. (1999) 'The erosion of the German system of industrial relations', *British Journal of Industrial Relations*, 37, 3, pp. 483–505.

Hirst, P. and Thompson, G. (1996) *Globalization in question*, Oxford: Blackwell.

Hu, Y.-S. (1992) 'Global or stateless corporations are national firms with international operations', *California Management Review*, Winter, pp. 107–26.

Jacobi, O., Keller, B. and Müller-Jentsch, W. (1998) 'Germany: facing new challenges' in Ferner, A. and Hyman, R. (eds) *Changing industrial relations in Europe*, Oxford: Blackwell, pp. 190–238.

Jungnickel, R. (1996) 'Globalisierung: Wandert die deutsche Wirtschaft aus?', *Wirtschaftsdienst*, 6, pp. 309–16.

Kahn-Freund, O. (1983) 'Labour law and industrial relations in Great Britain and West Germany', in Wedderburn, K. W., Lewis, R. and Clark, J. (eds) *Labour law and industrial relations: building on Kahn-Freund*, Oxford: Clarendon Press, pp. 1–13.

Kohaut, S. and Schnabel, C. (1998) 'Flächentarifvertrag im Westen viel weiter verbreitet als im Osten', *Institut für Arbeitsmarkt- und Berufsforschung Kurzbericht* Nr. 19.

Kohaut, S. and Schnabel, C. (1999) 'Tarifbindung im Wandel', *IW-Trends*, Vol. 26, No. 2.

Kotthoff, H. (1981) *Betriebsräte und Betriebliche Herrschaft. Eine Typologie von Partizipationsmustern im Industriebetrieb*, Frankfurt: Campus Verlag.

Kotthoff, H. (1994) *Betriebsräte und Bürgerstatus. Wandel und Kontinuität betrieblicher Mitbestimmung*, Munich: Hampp Verlag.

Kurdelbusch, A. (2001) 'The rise of variable pay in Germany: evidence and explanations', Paper presented at the conference Multinational Companies and Human Resource Management: Between Globalisation and National Business Systems, De Montfort University, Leicester, 12th–14th July.

Lane, C. (1989) *Management and labour in Europe. The industrial enterprise in Germany, Britain and France*, Aldershot: Edward Elgar.

Lane, C. (1995) *Industry and society in Europe. Stability and change in Britain, Germany and France*, Aldershot: Edward Elgar.

Lane, C. (1997) 'European companies between globalisation and localisation – a comparison of internationalisation strategies of British and German MNCs', *Economy and Society*, 27, 4, pp. 462–85.

Lawrence, P. (1991) 'The personnel function. An Anglo-German comparison', in Brewster, C. and Tyson, S. (eds) *International comparisons in human resource management*. London: Pitman, pp.131–44.

Lohr, K., Röbenach, S. and Schmidt, E. (1995) 'Industrielle Beziehungen im Wandel', in Schmidt, R. (ed.) *Chancen und Risiken der industriellen Restrukturierung in Ostdeutschland*, Berlin: Akademie-Verlag, pp. 183–215.

Marginson, P. (1994) 'Multinational Britain: employment and work in an internationalised economy', *Human Resource Management Journal*, 4, 4, pp. 63–80.

Marginson, P., Buitendam, A., Deutschmann, C. and Perulli, P. (1993) 'The emergence of the Euro-company: towards a European industrial relations?', *Industrial Relations Journal*, 24, 3, pp. 182–90.

Marginson, P. and Sisson, K. (1994) 'The structure of transnational capital in Europe: the emerging Euro-Company and its implications for industrial relations', in Hyman, R. and Ferner, A. (eds) *New frontiers in European industrial relations*, Oxford: Blackwell, pp. 15–51.

Mendez, A. (1995) 'Stratégie des entreprises et intégration sociale européenne' *Quint-Essenzen*, no. 43, January, Institut für Arbeitsrecht und Arbeitsbeziehungen in der Europäischen Gemeinschaft, Trier.

Mueckenberger, U. (1988) 'Juridification of industrial relations: A German-British comparison', *Comparative Labour Law Journal*, 9, pp. 526–56.

Mueller, F. (1996) 'National stakeholders in the global contest for corporate investment', *European Journal of Industrial Relations*, 2, 3, pp. 345–68.

Mueller, F. and Purcell, J. (1992) 'The Europeanisation of manufacturing and the decentralisation of bargaining: multinational management strategies in the European automobile industry', *International Journal of Human Resource Management*, 3, 1, pp. 15–34.

Müller, M. (1996) Unitarism, pluralism and human resource management in Germany: A comparison of foreign and German-owned companies. D. Phil Thesis, Birkbeck College, University of London.

Müller, M. (1997) 'Institutional resilience in an changing world economy? The case of the German banking and chemical industries', *British Journal of Industrial Relations*, 35, 4, pp. 609–26.

Müller, M. (1998) 'Human resource and industrial relations practices of UK and US multinationals in Germany', *International Journal of Human Resource Management*, 9, 4, pp. 732–49.

Ohmae, K. (1990) *The borderless world*, London, New York: Collins.

Ohmae, K. (1993) 'The rise of the region state', *Foreign Affairs*, Spring: 78–87.

Porter, M. (1990) *The competitive advantage of nations*, London, Basingstoke: Macmillan.

Purcell, J. (1993) 'The end of industrial relations institutions', *Political Quarterly*, 64, 1, pp. 6–23.

Purcell, J. (1995) 'Ideology and the end of institutional industrial relations: evidence from the UK', in Crouch, C. and Traxler, F. (eds) *Organized industrial relations in Europe: what future?* Aldershot: Avebury, pp. 101–20.

Royle, T. (1998) Avoidance strategies and the German system of co-determination, *International Journal of Human Resource Management*, 9, 6, pp. 1026–47.

Ruigrok, W. and van Tulder, R. (1995) *The logic of international restructuring*, London: Routledge.

Schmidt, R. (1998) 'The transformation of industrial relations in Eastern Germany', in Hoffmann, R. and Jacobi, O. (eds) *The German model of industrial relations between adaptation and erosion*, Düsseldorf: Hans-Böckler-Stiftung, pp. 51–60.

Smith, C. and Meiksins, P. (1995) 'System, society *and dominance effects in cross-national organisational analysis'*, Work, Employment and Society 9, 2, pp. 241–67.

Sparrow, P. and Hiltrop, J.-M. (1994) *European human resource management in transition*, Hemel Hemptstead: Prentice Hall.

Strange, S. (1997) 'The future of global capitalism; or will divergence persist forever?', in Crouch, C. and Streeck, W. (eds) *Political economy of modern capitalism. Mapping convergence and diversity*, London: Sage, pp. 182–91.

Streeck, W. (1987) 'The uncertainties of management in the management of uncertainty: employers, labor relations and industrial adjustment in the 1980s', *Work, Employment and Society*, 1, 3, pp. 281–308.

Tempel, A. (2001) *The cross-national transfer of human resource management practices in German and British multinational companies*, Mering: Hampp.

Towers, B. (1997) *The representation gap: change and reform in the British and American workplace*, Oxford: Oxford University Press.

TUC Press Release (2000) 'The media shouldn't learn of job losses before workers, says TUC', *www.tuc.org.uk*, 19th December 2000.

Tüselmann, H-J. (1998) 'Deutsche Auslandsinvestitionen in den neunziger Jahren: Abwanderung der deutschen Industrie und Abbau von Arbeitsplätzen?' *WSI-Mitteilungen*, 5, pp. 292–302.

Tüselmann, H.-J., McDonald, F. and Heise, A. (2001) Die Globalisierung der deutschen Wirtschaft: Deutsche Direktinviestitionen in Nordwestengland, *WSI Mitteilungen*, 1, pp. 13–19.

Wächter, H. (1983) *Mitbestimmung*, Politische Forderung und betriebliche Reaktion. München: Verlag Vahlen.

Weiss, M. (ed.) (1992) *European employment and industrial relations glossary: Germany*, London: Sweet and Maxwell.

Whitley, R. (1992) 'Societies, firms and markets: the social structuring of business systems' in Whitley, R. (ed.) *European business systems. Firms and markets in their national contexts*, London: Sage, pp. 5–45.

Whitley, R. (1994) 'Dominant forms of economic organization in market economies', *Organization Studies*, 15, 2, pp. 153–82.

7
Middle Managers: Differences between Britain and Germany

Hans-Dieter Ganter and Peter Walgenbach

Introduction

For a long time, proponents of a structuralist approach have assumed that the division of economic actors within firms into the groups of owners, managers and workers allows an explanation of their actions and behaviour. Roles, according to this approach, are, above all, contingent on economic categories such as ownership or the control of means of production, which are assumed not to differ between cultural settings (that is, the culture-free thesis). Members within each of these three groups are believed to act in a similar way, no matter where the firm is located. Interaction between members within each of these groups should therefore pose no obstacles for conducting business internationally: there would seem to be no need to think about peculiarities within specific countries.

Empirical studies on managerial work and behaviour, many of them originating in the US and Britain (for a critical overview, see Hales, 1986), have produced convergent results. According to these studies, there are similar patterns in the working day of all managers. The manager's working day is highly fragmented, consists of many short episodes and the manager is often reacting to unscheduled events rather than actively shaping his or her work. Looking more closely, however, one can detect significant differences between the behaviour patterns of managers on different hierarchical levels or in different functions. However, none of these studies on management behaviour takes into consideration factors of influence outside the organization: cultural and societal institutions are not seen as relevant factors. In contrast to this, cross-national organizational research shows us significant differences in organization structures and value systems of organization members in different countries. A number of cross-cultural studies have pointed out existing differences in, for example, hierarchical levels between basically comparable organizations in different cultures (Sorge and Warner, 1986; Lane, 1989). Lane (1989) emphasized that German firms usually have fewer hierarchical levels and are much more functionally integrated than comparable British firms. For German managers, this implies different sets of tasks than for their British counterparts. Hofstede (1991) shows in his study that German and British managers have different underlying 'implicit models of organization': German managers view their organization as a 'well-oiled machine', while British managers describe their organization as a 'village market'. It is, therefore, much more common for German managers to resort to structure when solving problems than for their British colleagues, who prefer meetings to coordinate activities. This implies, in the German case, the establishment of procedures or organizational routines and a strong emphasis on them due to the strong tendency to avoid uncertainty. In Britain, neither hierarchy nor organizational routines are considered to be as important as in Germany: instead, according to Hofstede, the demands of the situation determine what will happen.

This leads us to the question of whether there are differences in the work behaviour of managers from different countries. Astonishingly, there is little empirical work on inter-cultural differences in managerial behaviour: we know very little about the differences between managers operating in different cultures, such as Britain and Germany, although in the 1990s some researchers did start to investigate the attitudes of British and German top managers (Eberwein and Tholen, 1993). This chapter aims to illuminate differences in behaviour and work patterns of managers in selected industries in Britain and Germany and to propose explanations for these differences. It will present findings from a cross-cultural study on managerial jobs and behaviour (Stewart et al., 1994, 1996), which looked at different understandings of management, different career patterns and different forms of qualification of managers in Britain and Germany.

A joint team of British and German researchers conducted the study. It deliberately focused on middle managers for two reasons. The first was, quite simply, because they are still a species of managers we know very little about. Often it is assumed that middle managers are just a miniature version of top managers, that they perform more or less the same functions and behave similarly to their bosses (Torrington et al., 1989). But a few authors (for example, Petit, 1975) insist that the role of middle managers as economic actors is, in general, quite different and that they have special tasks or functions, acting as repositories of prevailing organizational knowledge (Walgenbach, 1993, 1994) and as a buffer (Thompson, 1967) against internal and external problems that the organization may face. The second reason for the focus on middle managers is that the roles and behaviour of middle managers are more likely to be affected than those of CEOs by factors such as organization structure and are, therefore, more open to cultural influences.

Methodology

Due to the lack of theoretical and empirical studies on the influence of national culture and institutions on managerial beliefs and behaviour, we decided to analyse the jobs and working strategies of 30 middle managers in both Britain and Germany. Two of the research questions we addressed in our study were: What are the differences in the understanding of management and work behaviour between British and German middle managers? And, what influence do management education and career paths have on these differences?

The companies in each country were chosen in order to achieve the best possible equivalence between the German and British cases (pair-matching). Industries, as well as companies, were therefore roughly the same size within the national economy and the firms selected were comparable in terms of their performance. Also, in order to rule out the possibility of organizational structure or managerial behaviour being influenced by the nature of the parent company, the firms selected were not foreign-owned. We selected companies from the brewing industry, the insurance industry and the construction industry. The brewing industry was chosen as a representative of the manufacturing industry: it produces a simple product and applies process production as its core technology. The insurance industry was chosen as a representative of the service sector because of the standardized contracts and highly automated (computerized) administrative procedures in life assurance, the operations and, therefore, the core technology are akin to that of mass production. The construction industry was chosen as a second representative of the manufacturing sector: it is project-driven and applies a unit production system of technology. We also tried to match, as far as possible, the jobs of the middle managers studied. In all the companies, we selected jobs from the production and administrative departments and in each company we conducted semi-structured interviews with ten middle managers. The British research team carried out the interviews with the British managers, and the German team interviewed the German managers. The interview guideline was based on Stewart's 'demands, constraints, choices approach' for analysing managerial jobs (Table 7.1) (Stewart 1976, 1982) and was designed jointly by both research teams, to ensure that the questions probed the same issues in both countries. The interviews were recorded then transcribed for analysis.

Nearly half the managers interviewed in each country were observed for two to three days. In some cases, we made joint observations to avoid an ethnocentric bias in the collection of the data: thus, a member of the British team and a member of the German research team observed the activities of the managers together. A semi-structured observation schedule was used for the observation. Our intention was not only to record the kinds of activity that managers are involved in, for example, face-to-face contacts, scheduled and unscheduled meetings and so on, as in many of the earlier studies on managerial behaviour, but to record the way they actually carried out their jobs: how they fulfilled their tasks and duties and how they handled their subordinates or colleagues.

Furthermore, the direct superiors of the middle managers were also interviewed, because they could be regarded as important communicators of role expectations. Another reason for the interview with the direct superiors was to enhance the reliability of the middle managers' answers. Additionally, we collected information on the backgrounds of the middle managers and their bosses, for example their formal qualifications and their career paths. This was accomplished by using a structured questionnaire (Table 7.2 gives an overview of the methods we used to collect the data of our study).

Table 7.1   The interview schedule for the interview with middle managers

Issues	Items
Tasks and responsibilities	Perceived responsibilities and priorities; how the managers feel about their jobs and where they see the difficulties
Work pattern	How much work time is spent doing what kinds of work and what scope there is to change the pattern
Contacts	Networks and relationships; the nature of contacts vertically and horizontally, internally and externally
Understanding of management	What managers expect of others and what they feel is expected of them; what they regard as effective and ineffective management

Table 7.2 Summary of methods used to collect information

Method	Information targeted
Library search	Background information on industry and news clippings on the company
Preliminary interview with senior manager	More detailed background information about the company and its various systems; collection of organization charts and job descriptions
Pre-interview questionnaire	Factual information about the jobs to be studied and the jobholder's background
Semi-structured interview (manager)	Designed to get a deeper understanding of the job and the manager's perception of it
Semi-structured interview (boss)	Designed to get a fuller picture of the subordinate's job: the level of choice, the boss's demands and expectations
Observation (sole and joint)	Provides a cross-check on the answers given in interviews, provides tangible evidence and raises unexpected issues

Source: Stewart et al. (1994: 38).

While aiming to make the study as representative as possible, we are aware of the fact that the size of the sample (60 middle managers and 26 bosses) is not statistically meaningful. But, if the differences between British and German managers' behaviour and attitude prevail in spite of differences in the personalities of jobholders, the specific technologies used by the companies, their organization or industry structure, we have every reason to assume that our findings are reliable and would not diverge fundamentally even if we had chosen other companies from the same or different industries.

Findings

The findings reported in this section will be restricted to those factors which are relevant for the managers' roles and behaviour, as well as their understanding of management. Therefore, we deliberately dispense with reporting the study as a whole and look only into which variables, in the light of our study, may help to account for cultural differences. Firstly, we will present the findings from our study concerning work behaviour and how British and German middle managers understand management. Then we will analyse the findings by drawing on explanatory factors, such as management education and career systems in the respective countries (for a more detailed presentation of the study, see Stewart et al., 1994).

Differences in the understanding of management and work behaviour of British and German middle managers

The German middle managers' understanding of management was mainly characterized by a strong technical orientation. They viewed their responsibilities and the most important aspects of their jobs to be, first and foremost, the technical duties of their departments; whereas less than half the German managers in our study mentioned leadership or management responsibilities. Twenty managers mentioned specific aspects of their technical tasks and some of them gave detailed descriptions of their job responsibilities. Quite often they only brought up managerial responsibilities after being prompted by the interviewer.

Management by 'expert knowledge' (*Führung durch Fachwissen*) seems to be the dominant way in which German middle managers understand their job (cf. Lane, 1989). Handy's (1988: 7) earlier assumption about the understanding of management in Germany still seems to be correct: 'Management as a concept of its own, divorced from what is to be managed, is not widely understood or accepted.' German middle managers' understanding of management does not seem to reflect the role of the manager outlined in the Anglo-American literature on management. According to their replies, German managers considered technical responsibilities and managerial duties to be integrated and not separable.

> Actually, the most important aspect would be managerial responsibility. But if I don't participate in any job-related tasks, I don't get the overall picture. And, therefore, I perform technical tasks so that, on the other hand, I don't lose the overall picture concerning my managerial responsibilities. (commercial branch operations manager, construction)

The British managers did not dwell on technical responsibilities to the same extent. They considered their main responsibilities to be the managerial tasks of their position. They perceived their management role to be that of a generalist and believed effective management was the ability to run departments with a hands-off approach, using management information systems to keep the overall picture.

It is interesting to note here that there are also different views on organizational structures in Germany and Britain. Some of the German middle managers explicitly stated that structures are an important key to successful management. For them, it seemed necessary to have clear-cut structures, in which every single jobholder knows what his or her and the other jobholders' tasks and responsibilities are. In Germany, the emphasis was on getting the structure right to start with, then filling the jobs with the right people.

The British middle managers interviewed were mostly of the opinion that a department should be built around individual strengths rather than insisting on filling pre-arranged slots. Their answers were more people-focused than structure-oriented: the onus was on the creative input of the individual manager, on his or her ability to put together a team.

This difference in German and British middle managers' understanding of management became even more obvious in relation to the tasks they considered to be the (most) important. Here, the British middle managers gave first priority to managerial tasks and a large number emphasized the activities of people management. The general idea was that making people feel part of the team is the precursor to getting the best out of them.

German middle managers' focus on technical expertise was also important for another reason: it was the means by which they legitimized their authority, rather than through their position in the organizational hierarchy. This finding appears not to be limited only to middle managers in Germany. In their study of top German managers, Eberwein and Tholen (1990: 102) also identify technical expertise as the basis of their authority. The notion of a hierarchically superior position as a basis of authority was even rejected by the middle managers in Germany. They preferred to be regarded by their subordinates as peers rather than managers:

I want to be viewed as a normal employee, not as a superior. (accounting manager, insurance)

It is actually more important to me to be viewed as a colleague who supervises, but not necessarily as a superior. (maintenance manager, brewery)

The German middle managers not only viewed themselves as colleagues who supervise, they also tried to live up to this role. It was important for them to be a 'good example' and a 'role model' for their employees. In accordance with this belief, they often consciously gave up managerial privileges: for example they punched their time cards, even when they did not have to. This rejection of the role of the superior shows a certain self-confidence, based on technical probity. The German middle managers did not have to distance themselves artificially from their subordinates in order to be respected by them; they earned their respect simply by being better at doing their jobs or being able to perform a greater number of tasks more proficiently than their subordinates. The German emphasis was on being *an* authority rather than being *in* authority.

The managers in Britain, on the other hand, clearly viewed their roles differently and this difference was evident in their behaviour. They emphasized their supervisory role by setting their own work schedule and break periods, by organizing their departments and introducing new task areas.

> Management is 'I know a man who does'. A manager cannot do everything. He is a fool to himself if he believes he can. But he must know a man who does – for every single subject. (director of finance, insurance)

When the British middle managers referred to the technical side of their job, they tended to relate it to managerial considerations for the department as a whole:

> Another important aspect is the accuracy of the work that goes out of this department, which determines the credibility of the department. (administration manager, brewery)

The British managers understood themselves to be man-managers and they saw their ability as man-managers as the key to advancing to a higher managerial position. Managerial status was seen as deriving from skills in handling people, not so much from technical expertise or demonstrable professionalism: 'The engineering niceties go over my head' (brewing and fermenting manager, brewery).

The middle managers in Germany were involved to a much greater extent than their British counterparts in the technical tasks of their department, and their bosses expected this of them. Technical duties could take up a large proportion of a German middle manager's day and the German managers were, in a way, very proud of their ability to perform these tasks. The British managers preferred a 'hands-off' approach, in that they tried not to get involved in the technical details of their subordinates' work. Although the role of managers in both countries was viewed as running their department smoothly, this was accomplished in different ways in the two cultural settings. The British middle managers, as well as the Germans, saw themselves as being responsible for fulfilling the duties of their department, but the British managers did not want to become personally involved. Instead they saw their duties much more as getting their subordinates to accomplish the tasks necessary for achieving departmental goals. Managerial work and technical work were not seen as two sides of the same coin but as a hierarchical threshold. Therefore, British and German middle managers viewed their actual roles quite differently (Figure 7.1).

Therefore, it is not surprising that this difference could be observed in their daily work behaviour. For instance, we found noticeable differences in the way in which German and British middle managers checked their employees' work. German middle managers generally applied formalized control instruments to examine the work of their subordinates. They also made use of qualitative controls, such as feedback from other departments or customers to judge their subordinates' effectiveness. Where they had to intervene directly, they employed specific controls or spot checks to review each individual case of their subordinates' work in detail. Such control requires an exact understanding of the work and the work processes of their subordinates, which German middle managers possess due to their training and career paths, as we will later show. British middle managers, on the other hand, utilized such controls on a much smaller scale. They often did not have

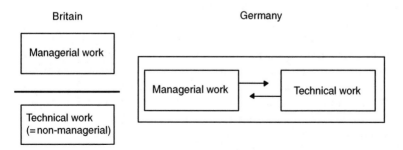

Figure 7.1 Different conceptions of management in Britain and Germany.

the necessary detailed knowledge of their subordinates' duties and work processes to do so. This finding underlines the assertion made by Torrington and Weightman (1987: 78) that a certain amount of technical expertise and activity is central to a manager's effectiveness, but that middle managers in Great Britain often do not possess this ability.

It was not only within the framework of German managers' control duties that technical tasks played an important role, in their daily work they were also occupied with a large number of technical duties. The reasons for this have various origins. The performance of technical tasks provides the job incumbent with both choices and demands, which must be met. Due to the lack of personnel in the German middle managers' departments, a fact they often criticized in the interviews, the managers often had to complete work themselves which they normally should have been able to delegate. The middle managers were not able to put off these tasks because their superiors expected them to ensure that everything was 'running smoothly' in their departments. How can we explain the differences in the understanding of management and in the work behaviour of British and German middle managers? In the following section, we will consider two factors which seem critical to us: the different systems of management education and management careers in the two countries (for a more detailed analysis, see Stewart et al., 1994).

Explaining the differences

Management education

When looking at management education, the system of general education within a particular country cannot be ignored. In this chapter, however, due to lack of space, we shall concentrate on vocational training and pre-entry management education.

In Germany, the 'dual system' of vocational training influences managerial careers and behaviour even at the highest management levels. This system comprises both in-company training and general education in vocational schools (*Berufsschulen*). Apprenticeship courses are at the heart of the German vocational training system and are also regarded as a key entrance qualification, particularly for middle management positions. Such courses last two or three years, depending on the vocation and the prior education of the candidates. Most school leavers in Germany sign apprenticeship contracts with companies. This applies not only to vocations in the manufacturing sector, but also to those in the service sector. Nor does it apply only to certain lower levels of general education; even those who want to go on to university sometimes elect to serve an apprenticeship, for example in insurance companies or banks, prior to studying subjects such as business administration.

Whilst the practical part of an apprenticeship takes place within a company under the supervision of a qualified instructor, theoretical instruction is given in the vocational schools, where about half the apprentices' time is devoted not only to the specific trade, but also to classes in maths, German and general studies. German vocations have their own training programmes, which are the result of negotiation between various partners, including, of course, employers' associations and unions. All companies employing apprentices must conform to them; it is a tightly regulated system. Instructors are accredited by local chambers of commerce, which organize the standardized exams which every trainee must pass in order to qualify. This guarantees that all apprentices passing the exam are trained according to a similar pattern.

In cross-cultural comparative studies, the 'dual training system' is often seen as operating only at the level of production worker and foremen (*Meister*). For two reasons this view is too narrow. Firstly, the principles of the dual training system, which are based on training in a business environment and theoretical education in a school environment, are also adopted by the technical colleges (*Fachhochschulen*), which are roughly comparable to the British polytechnics. Secondly, an apprenticeship is also an important component of vocational training at higher management levels, especially in commercial functions. Eberwein and Tholen (1990) found in their study that 55 per cent of the managers on the first and second hierarchical levels of German companies had completed an apprenticeship.

In Britain, the apprenticeship has little influence on the education or training of aspiring managers; it is rather the provision of management training at pre-entry level that has flourished in Britain for a number of years now. Business may be studied at college or university and a wide variety of certificates and degrees are available, for example, the sub-degree certificates of BTEC and the Higher National Diploma or one- and two-year postgraduate MBAs.

Professional institutions, although they exist in Germany, are primarily concerned with organizing conferences and disseminating information. In contrast to Britain, membership does not help in job applications. In Britain, however, membership of such institutions is status enhancing. In the professional approach found in Britain, tutored work experience is combined with formal study. 'There is a graded series of qualifications in the different professional bodies corresponding to varying levels of membership, culminating with full membership of such an institution' (Stewart et al., 1994: 50). This applies particularly to the accountancy associations: 'Accountancy is considered to be a well-worn path into general management jobs in Britain. And this profession is larger and more organised in the UK than in Germany' (Stewart et al., 1994: 50). But other professional associations have also prospered, either by being attached to a particular industry, such as the Institute of Bankers or the Institute of Brewers, or by cutting across industries, such as the Institute of Marketing or the Institute of Personnel Management (now Chartered Institute of Personnel and Development).

Comparing the two systems of management education and training, there seems to be a more consistent pattern in the German model of education, training and development, whilst the British model seems to offer a wider number of routes into managerial posts, without a dominant philosophy about how management can best be learnt, taught or developed.

These general remarks on the different roads to managerial competence were reflected, to a large extent, in our sample (Tables 7.3, 7.4 and 7.5). Twenty-four of the German middle managers in our project had completed either a commercial or technical apprenticeship (Table 7.3); 13 of the German middle managers had studied a subject which was closely linked to their actual tasks and responsibilities within the company at a professional academy (*Berufsakademie*), a polytechnic institute or university (see Table 7.4).

In Britain, the situation seems to be quite different. The British middle managers had either no or very little direct work-related vocational or professional training and the qualification patterns of the middle managers in Britain were less standardized than those of their German counterparts. There was a wide variety of certificates and degrees, ranging from the sub-degree certificates and the Higher National Diploma through to one- and two-year postgraduate MBAs (see Table 7.5). But among the British middle managers studied, widespread membership of professional associations was found.

Table 7.3   Vocational training of the German middle managers

Vocational training level	Total	Percentage of total
No vocational training	6	20.0
Commercial training	20	66.7
Technical training	4	13.3
Total	30	100.0

Source: Stewart et al. (1994: 52).

Table 7.4 Academic degrees received by German middle managers

Academic degree	Total	Percentage of total
None	17	56.6
Professional academy (*Berufsakademie*)	2	6.7
Polytechnic (*Fachhochschule*)	5	16.7
University	6	20.0
Total	30	100.0

Source: Stewart et al. (1994: 53).

Furthermore, there is also a remarkable difference between middle managers in Britain and Germany when we compare the formal qualifications they hold and the relationship these qualifications have to the tasks to be performed in the incumbents' departments. All the vocational and academic training which German managers have received, is directly related to the tasks of the positions they now occupy. All the middle managers studied in the insurance company, for instance, were insurance agents: 'German companies perceive the management task in strictly functional terms, especially for middle and lower managers. Hence, the direct relationship between vocational training or studies and the job to be done is of utmost significance.' (Randlesome, 1988: 139).

With regard to the qualification levels of the middle managers studied and those of senior executives, significant differences can be found. According to studies of senior executives in Germany (Hartmann, 1958; Zapf, 1965; Kruk, 1972; Poensgen, 1982; Wuppermann, 1989), top and

Table 7.5 Highest qualification attained by British middle managers

Qualification	Total	Percentage of total
First higher degree	6	20.0
Member of professional institute	11	36.6
HNC/HND	0	0.0
Apprenticeship	2	6.7
ONC/OND, City and Guilds, A levels	5	16.7
O levels or equivalent	3	10.0
CSEs	1	3.3
None	2	6.7
Total	30	100.0

Source: Stewart et al. (1994: 53).

senior managers have a high level of formal qualifications, which is, on average, considerably higher than that of the middle managers we studied (cf. Tables 7.3 and 7.4). Eberwein and Tholen in their study (1990: 35) found only 18 per cent of their sample had not completed any form of higher education, while 16.2 per cent had completed studies at a polytechnic and 65.7 per cent at a university. Moreover, 24.3 per cent of these senior executives had received a doctorate degree. Other studies, which are not restricted to the highest levels of management, provide evidence that the level of formal education increases, the higher they move up the hierarchical ladder. This tendency was also confirmed in our study. Only six of the middle managers we studied had successfully completed a university degree, five had received their degree from a polytechnic and two others had received further training at a vocational academy after having completed an apprenticeship. On the other hand, the qualification level of their superiors was considerably higher: ten of them had completed a university degree, and two of them had even received their doctorates, one had completed studies at a polytechnic and only two had not acquired any further formal qualification prior to completing a commercial apprenticeship.

The difference between senior and middle management qualifications in Britain had no real influence on the hierarchical position held by a person. Hence, there is not the same sense of predestination for British managers. They are not condemned to the lower ranks by a lack of formal qualifications, nor are graduates guaranteed to climb further than middle management level. From this, it becomes evident that German firms can rely on a pool of human resources with extensively standardized vocational qualification profiles. Managers who wish to obtain a certain rank have to acquire specific vocational or professional qualifications. There is another consequence for the organization of the firm resulting from the qualifications of both managers and workers: since managers can rely on their qualifications, they derive pride in their jobs and their managerial authority is based on their technical expertise rather than their status. Furthermore, they can rely on a fairly stable qualification structure, which shapes both their own behaviour as well as that of their subordinates.

In Britain, on the other hand, the professional substance of a position has more to do with the individual manager and his or her negotiating skills than in Germany. This is also reflected in job descriptions for middle managers, such as that of the British brewery: 'Desirable to be educated to degree standard'. The widely varying vocational and professional qualifications of British middle managers may be an important reason why frequent reorganization occurs in British companies when a 'new' person takes over a managerial function in a department. It also plays a principal part in British middle managers' interpretation of the right way of obtaining or keeping a position. They are mostly of the opinion that a department should be built around individual strengths rather than on filling prearranged slots. There is evidence that the demand is, above all, for man-management skills: 'Essential to have experience of man-management' (job description, brewery).

Career paths of German and British middle managers

A career can be described as all the consecutive positions or jobs held by a person within the organizational structure of a business. This concept is not limited to one single firm; it also refers to changing positions between firms (Berthel, 1987). Careers are made up of a combination of business activities, which are dependent on certain decisions and situations, as well as the individual behaviour and characteristics of an organization member. The term 'career' is to be understood not only as the achievements of a single individual but also reflects the goals set within the career systems of all firms within a business system – particularly in its aggregated form. Important demands and expectations, which the firms within a business system have of their managers, are reflected in the careers observed.

The typical career of a German manager still usually takes place entirely within a single company, even if this pattern is eroding to some extent due to the application of management concepts such as lean management or downsizing. The careers of 76 per cent of the senior executives studied by Zapf (1965) and 53 per cent of those managers studied by Eberwein and Tholen (1990) showed a maximum of one change of employer. In our study, we found the same pattern of career path for middle managers: two-thirds of them had spent all their working life in one company, while only four of the ten 'switchers' had changed employers more than once. Furthermore, with one exception, each move was between companies operating in the same industry, and these moves had generally taken place ten or more years before the time of the study. Our findings also show, again except for one manager, that each of the managers studied had held at least two, but no more than three, positions before he was promoted to his current one. Once the middle managers in Germany reached their position, they stayed in it for a long time. For example, two-thirds of the managers studied had held their current post for more than five years.

Table 7.6 Length of time in current position of middle managers

Time in current position	German managers	British managers
Less than 2 years	3	13
2–4 years	7	12
5–9 years	8	4
10–19 years	6	1
20 and more years	6	0
Total	30	30

Source: Stewart et al. (1994: 60).

Twelve of them had even held it for more than ten years and six for more than twenty years (Table 7.6).

But in spite of the lengthy stay of German middle managers in their posts relative to their British counterparts (cf. also Nicholson and West, 1988), there are considerable differences in the rate at which German managers had changed their previous positions. Those middle managers in our study, who had achieved a higher level of formal qualification, had changed their previous positions more quickly than their peers. Those who had completed a university degree held their posts for an average of only four years. This rate of movement between jobs also coincides with Bröcker's (1991) findings on German senior executives: those managers who had 'only' a commercial or technical training qualification had held their previous posts for an average of eight years. It becomes quite clear, bearing in mind that the type of education received by the manager is directly related to the types of task which must be performed within the department, that emphasis is placed on the level of occupational qualification in German firms.

Another similarity in the careers of the middle managers in Germany is that, with only one exception, each of them has worked in only one functional area within their current company. The only middle manager, who has not remained in the same department under his present employer, had moved horizontally from the marketing department to the sales department. This underlines the idea of a chimney career (*Kaminkarriere*), where middle managers remain in the same functional area of a firm throughout their entire career. In line with their German counterparts, the British middle managers studied tended to have been with their firms for several years, generally more than ten. However, about one-third (9 of the 30) had worked in other industries. This finding of low inter-company mobility contradicts the results of many other studies, which generally indicate that British managers not only change positions more often than German ones but also have worked for more than two companies (cf. Nicholson and West, 1988). Quite often, these companies operate in completely different industries. Lane (1992: 90) states that 'management promotion in Britain is more often gained by movement between firms. The generalist education...among top managers and the more diversified nature of British firms makes movement between companies and even industries relatively easy, and more frequent movement between firms gives British managers a wider industrial perspective.' Two possible explanations are available for the deviating findings in our study. Firstly, the low inter-company mobility may be related to the specific industries chosen for the study, which require a relatively high level of specialized vocational qualifications according to British standards, thus reducing the probability of movement between firms or industries. Secondly, this finding may also be explained by the fact that the high level of inter-company mobility in Britain only applies if managers have reached higher management levels. Evidence for this hypothesis can be found, for instance, in the British insurance company studied. Within this company, many posts on the hierarchical level above middle management were held by people who had gained their management experience in completely different industries.

With respect to the duration of both previous and current positions, the career paths of British managers differed completely from those of the Germans. In Britain, the middle managers studied changed positions within their current firm much more often than their German counterparts. Whilst in Germany, the job incumbents have, in general, been in their current position more than five years, in Britain, this length of time in one post is the exception (see Table 7.6). One of the managers in the insurance company, for instance, had changed jobs nine times within eight years, with the longest time in one position being 20 months. It seems as though such frequent changes of positions are not uncommon within British firms (cf. Nicholson and West, 1988).

There is also a remarkable difference with respect to the movement between functional areas. British middle managers, except for those in construction industry, move more often between functional areas, which are not directly related, whilst their German colleagues stay within the same function once chosen (see Figure 7.2).

Looking at these differences in the careers of middle managers, it becomes evident that the objectives within the career systems of the companies in the two business systems diverge considerably from each other. By their long process of socialization within a particular firm and

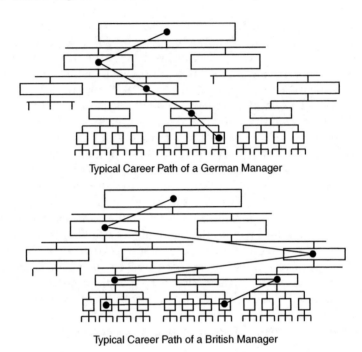

Figure 7.2   Different career systems in Britain and Germany.
Source: Walgenbach and Kieser (1995: 280).

a particular functional area, German managers gain experience in technical matters. It is exactly this which helps them to run the work processes in their department smoothly. In the case of problems, they are able to intervene on all levels thus functioning as organizational buffers. For the firm, the managers' long experience can be regarded as a sort of organizational data bank, which can be relied upon. In this respect, it is the middle managers' task to pass on their specific organizational knowledge, as well as their technical expertise, to future generations (Walgenbach, 1994). So, whereas in Germany the objective is apparently to gain comprehensive technical experience, British managers within their career system are confronted at an early stage with the need for general management capabilities, which are not related to technical qualification. The aim behind this is to prepare them for a general management position. Thus, the technical orientation, which to a large extent characterizes German middle managers' understanding of management, may be traced back to the direct relationship between the vocational and academic education of the managers and the tasks of the departments which they are responsible for. But it may also be explained by the typical career paths of German managers, while the man-management orientation of the British managers can be traced back to their respective education and career systems.

The fundamental differences between the two career systems might be explained by the fact that the historical development of British companies differs significantly from that of Germany: British companies have often taken on the form of a holding, in which a small number of central staff controls a large number of divisions, which often operate in highly diverse industries. In Germany there is also a much higher degree of vertical integration and a functional 'hyper-specialization' at the company level of management (Lane, 1992; Horovitz, 1978; Dyas and Thanheiser, 1976), even if this seems to be on the decline in Germany at the moment due to the influence of the debate on new concepts of organization.

Differences in management education and, consequently, differing career systems between the two countries may be expected to have an impact on the organization of firms. If we consider middle managers as part of the hierarchy in their organization, different notions of hierarchy in Britain and Germany emerge. While middle managers in the German companies were deeply embedded in their function within the firm, both as the result of their formal qualification and career, this was not the case in Britain. This means that middle managers in Germany are, in the first place, members of their occupational community and thus belong to a hierarchy of skills and qualifications within their field. Only secondly, and in this particular capacity, are they members of the managerial team of a firm. This has a strong impact on the content and form of control over their subordinates' performance, which differs significantly from their British colleagues. British managers view themselves, first and foremost, as managers with no particular inclination to the technical aspects of their department. Consequently, their actual behaviour and understanding of management differ from that of their German counterparts.

Discussion

The findings of our comparative study show that the roles, work and behaviour, as well as the understanding of management, vary considerably between the two samples. Let us summarize the main differences:

- British middle managers prefer a 'hands-off' approach. Their German colleagues tend to deal with the technical details of their departments to a large extent. This is also reflected in the qualifications middle managers hold in the two settings: there is a strong emphasis on technically qualified managers in the German context, while in the British there is not.

- German middle managers view themselves as peers rather than as superiors and try to live up to this, while British managers stress their superior role more often.

- British middle managers move more often from a managerial job in one function to another and do not normally stay in their job of managing one particular department for more than three years. German middle managers, on the contrary, stay in their job as a manager for a long time and usually do not move from one function to another. Both inter- and intra-company mobility were lower in the German setting than in the British one.

Many of the existing empirical studies (cf. the overview of Hales, 1986) on managerial work and behaviour do not reflect such differences but have produced convergent results. In the light of the findings reported, but also those of other recent cross-cultural studies (Eberwein and Tholen, 1993), such convergence is not confirmed. There appears to be an Anglo-American bias in the literature on management, in which nearly all the concepts and theories for understanding management emanate from an Anglo-American context. These concepts have thus been developed in highly individualistic countries and reflect this value orientation. The question of what managers do can, however, only be answered if we take into account the cultural setting within which managers act. This leads to a number of research requirements, which partly relate back to other cross-cultural studies carried out in other areas.

In our view, the differences in managerial work and behaviour seem to be interdependent with the different forms of organizational structures in the two countries. Organizational structures are also influenced by cultural factors, such as institutions or values, as demonstrated by a number of previous cross-cultural studies (for example, Child and Kieser, 1979; Sorge and Warner, 1986; Lane, 1989). Most of the previous Anglo-German comparisons found, for instance, that the span of control in German companies was wider than in comparable British ones, which translates itself into hierarchies with fewer levels. In British companies, organization seems to have grown more laterally than in German ones, since jobs incorporating specialized knowledge were created more often than in Germany, where companies tend to incorporate such jobs into the line (Lawrence, 1980). Comparative studies have also showed that the degree of formalization is higher in British companies than in German ones, at least in relation to the use of job descriptions, organization charts and written procedures. Our findings correspond to most of those reported in previous Anglo-German comparisons.

Job descriptions, for example, were present in all British companies, while only one of the companies studied in Germany had them. However, in Britain they were not usually binding and were sometimes ignored. In Germany, on the other hand, in spite of the lack of job descriptions, there was always a clear understanding of the formal qualifications a manager should possess for his job.

Differences in organization structure have a strong impact on the coordination of activities in the firm. For example, at the time of the study, none of the German companies had a separate department or unit for quality functions, while this was the case in all the British firms studied. The simple fact that quality departments launched activities or conducted audits meant that British middle managers spent much more time in meetings than their German counterparts. In the German case, quality control was integrated into the line functions, which reduced coordination requirements in this respect. In the meantime, as a result of the diffusion of quality systems, such as ISO 9000, many German companies have now created positions for quality managers. However, the quality systems often remain largely decoupled from the work activities within the departments of the organization (see Walgenbach, 2000, 2001). This stronger integration of functions within German companies and the decoupling of parts of the quality system from the work activities in the functional departments can, at least partly, be explained by the higher occupational qualifications of German workers and managers and the experience they gain due to the length of time they stay in their positions. This enables them to gain a broad and detailed expert knowledge of the technical tasks and problem-solving procedures within their own departments.

The impact of culture, that is, management education and career systems, could also be clearly seen in the meetings we observed, particularly in their duration. Whilst in German firms, meetings tended to focus strictly on subjects to do with the coordination of departments and technical problems, in Britain, meetings were viewed as a general exchange of information. They went beyond the simple process of communication, coordination and problem-solving and had a motivational and developmental function. This may be explained by the broader approach to management in Britain, while in Germany, management is closely linked to the technical aspects of the job. As a result, the meetings of

British managers in general lasted much longer than the meetings of their German counterparts.

The way managers check their subordinate's work is influenced to a large extent by the skills and career movements presented in the sections above. Middle managers, in particular, are expected to implement decisions taken by others. They are, therefore, responsible for 'keeping the show on the road' (Stewart et al., 1994: 116). In Germany, middle managers tended to have a technical approach to control and were often engaged in detailed technical problems of their subordinates. This type of control is only possible if the manager has the formal qualifications and career experience to do it. In the British case, this method of checking subordinates' performance was far less usual. Most of the British managers studied did not possess the detailed knowledge required to control their subordinates in this way. When the British managers checked their subordinates' work, they asked short, open-ended questions to find out whether they were on top of the situation. Intervention in the actual work itself, so common for German middle managers, was the exception in the British case. Hence, they were not checking on the technical problems but on the human problems of motivation and development. Despite the many differences that we found between British and German middle managers, they have one important task in common and it is this task or function which distinguishes their job from that of top management: they have to 'keep the show on the road'. However, the way middle managers in the two countries fulfil this task is very different.

The patterns we found in our study seem to be consistent in the two respective countries. Nevertheless, further research is required to address the following questions in a broader survey. In what way is the cultural setting reflected in the organizational setting and how does this influence the actual behaviour of managers and workers in the respective culture? Thus, what is needed is a broader database to make the findings more representative and 'harder'. Further research on a longitudinal basis should address the question of whether cultural differences will decline as a result of globalization. However, from our point of view, it appears unlikely that the globalization of business (Yip, 1992) will lead to a convergence of managerial work and behaviour – at least not in the short run.

References

Berthel, J. (1987) 'Karriere und Karrieremuster von Führungskräften', in Kieser, A., Reber, G. and Wunderer, R. (eds) *Handwörterbuch der Führung*, Stuttgart: Poeschel, pp. 1183–95.

Bröcker, H. F. (1991) *Managementkarrieren in Europa – Eine vergleichende Analyse der Merkmale, Mobilitätsprofile und kohortenspezifischen Verlaufsmuster der Karrieren europäischer Führungskräfte*, Stuttgart.

Child, J. and Kieser, A. (1979) 'Organisational and managerial roles in British and West German companies: An examination of the culture-free thesis', in Lammers, C. J. and Hickson D. J. (eds) *Organizations Alike and Unlike – International and Interinstitutional Studies in the Sociologies of Organizations*, London: Routledge & Kegan Paul, pp. 251–71.

Dyas, G. and Thanheiser, H. (1976) *The Emerging European Enterprise*, London: Macmillan.

Eberwein, W. and Tholen, J. (1990) *Managermentalität – Industrielle Unternehmensleitung als Beruf und Politik*, Frankfurt a.M.: Frankfurter Allgemeine Zeitung.

Eberwein, W. and Tholen, J. (1993) *Euro-Manager or Splendid Isolation? International Management – An Anglo-German Comparison*, Berlin: De Gruyter.

Hales, C. (1986) 'What do managers do? A critical review of the evidence', *Journal of Management Studies*, 23, pp. 88–115.

Handy, C. (1988) 'The quest', in Handy, C., Gordon, C., Gow, I. and Randlesome, C. (eds) *Making Managers*, London: Pitman.

Hartmann, H. (1958) *Unternehmer-Ausbildung – Die Rolle der deutschen Hochschulen*, München: Hanser.

Hofstede, G. (1991) *Cultures and Organizations – Software of the Mind*, Maidenhead: McGraw-Hill.

Horovitz, J. H. (1978) 'Management control in France, Great Britain and Germany', *Columbia Journal of World Business* (Summer 1978), pp. 16–22.

Kruk, M. (1972) *Die großen Unternehmer – Woher sie kommen, wer sie sind, wie sie aufsteigen*, Frankfurt a. M: Societäts.

Lane, C. (1989) *Management and Labour in Europe: The Industrial Enterprise in Germany, Britain and France*, Aldershot: Edward Elgar.

Lane, C. (1992) 'European business systems: Britain and Germany compared', in Whitley, R. (ed.) *European Business Systems – Firms and Markets in their National Contexts*, London: Sage, pp. 64–97.

Lawrence, P. (1980) *Managers and Management in West Germany*, London: Croom Helm.

Nicholson, N. and West, M. A. (1988) *Managerial Job Change: Men and Women in Transition*, Cambridge: Cambridge University Press.

Petit, T. A. (1975) *Fundamentals of Management Coordination: Supervisors, Middle Managers, and Executives*, New York: Wiley.

Poensgen, O. H. (1982) 'Der Weg in den Vorstand – Die Charakteristika der Vorstandsmitglieder der Aktiengesellschaften des Verarbeitenden Gewerbes', *Die Betriebswirtschaft*, 42, pp. 3–25.

Randlesome, C. (1988) 'West Germany', in Handy, C., Gorden, C., Gow, I. and Randlesome, C. (eds) *Making Managers*, London: Pitman.

Sorge, A. and Warner, M. (1986) *Comparative Factory Organization – An Anglo-German Comparison of Management and Manpower in Manufacturing*, Aldershot: Gower.

Stewart, R. (1976) *Contrasts in Management – A Study of Different Types of Managers' Jobs: Their Demands and Choices*, Maidenhead, Berkshire: McGraw-Hill.

Stewart, R. (1982) *Choices for the Manager*, Englewood Cliffs, NJ: Prentice Hall.

Stewart, R., Barsoux, J.-L., Kieser, A., Ganter, H.-D. and Walgenbach, P. (1994) *Managing in Britain and Germany*, London: Macmillan.

Stewart, R., Barsoux, J.-L., Kieser, A., Ganter, H.-D. and Walgenbach, P. (1996) 'A comparison of British and German managerial roles, perceptions and behaviour', in Joynt, P. and Warner, M. (eds) *Managing across Cultures: Issues and Perspectives*, London: International Thomson Business Press, pp. 202–11.

Thompson, J. D. (1967) *Organizations in Action*, New York: McGraw-Hill.

Torrington, D. and Weightman, J. (1987) 'Middle Management Work', *Journal of General Management*, 13 (2), pp. 74–89.

Torrington, D., Weightman, J. and Johns, K. (1989) *Effective Management: People and Organization*, London: IPM and Gower.

Walgenbach, P. (1993) 'Mittlere Manager', in Ganter, H.-D. and Schienstock, G. (eds) *Management aus soziologischer Sicht – Unternehmensführung, Industrie- und Organisationssoziologie*, Wiesbaden: Gabler, pp. 190–215.

Walgenbach, P. (1994) *Mittleres Management – Aufgaben, Funktionen, Arbeitsverhalten*, Wiebaden: Gabler.

Walgenbach, P. (2000) *Die normgerechte Organisation – Eine Studie über die Entstehung, Verbreitung und Nutzung der DIN EN ISO 9000er Normenreihe*, Stuttgart: Schäffer-Poeschel.

Walgenbach, P. (2001) 'The production of distrust by means of producing trust', *Organization Studies*, 22, pp. 693–714.

Walgenbach, P. and Kieser, A. (1995) 'Mittlere Manager in Deutschland und Großbritannien', in Schreyögg, G. and Sydow, J. (eds) *Managementforschung 5*, Berlin: De Gruyter, pp. 259–309.

Wuppermann, M. (1989) *Geschäftsführer in Deutschland*, Frankkfurt a. M.: Campus.

Yip, G. S. (1992) *Total Global Strategy: Managing for Worldwide Competitive Advantage*, Englewood Cliffs: Prentice Hall.

Zapf, W. (1965) 'Die deutschen Manager – Sozialprofil und Karriereweg', in Zapf, W. (ed.) *Beiträge zur Analyse der deutschen Oberschicht*, München: Piper, pp. 136–149.

8
Resistance is Useless! The Problems of Trade Union Organization in the European Fast-food Industry: The Case of McDonald's

Tony Royle

Introduction

This chapter is based on a comparative case study which examines the employee relations practices of the American multinational the McDonald's Corporation in several European countries. It focuses on the problems of union organization in the European fast-food industry and the implications of these trends for employee rights to representation, pay and conditions of employment.

The European fast-food industry is becoming increasingly dominated by a small number of MNCs. The largest seven employers employ well over 500,000 people in the European Union (EU) alone, and this figure is steadily increasing. McDonald's is the biggest of these employers and market leader in most European countries. It is a truly global operator; by 2002 McDonald's employed around 2 million people in over 30,000 restaurants worldwide. It is the largest food service operation in the world and worth well over $40 billion. By the end of 2002, McDonald's employed over 200,000 people in the 17 countries of the European Economic Area (EEA) in approximately 4000 restaurants. McDonald's first came to Europe in 1971, it opened its first restaurant in Holland and then in Germany later in the same year. Restaurants were then opened in Sweden in 1973, the UK in 1974, Austria and Ireland in 1977, Belgium in 1978, France in 1979, Denmark in 1981, Spain in 1982, Norway in 1983, Finland in 1984 and Italy in 1985.

The McDonald's corporation has a well-documented and long history of anti-unionism (Love, 1995; Vidal, 1997; Royle, 2000; Royle and Towers, 2002). Until the mid-1970s, it routinely used lie detector tests in its recruitment procedures to weed out union sympathisers and even used them on existing employees on some occasions (Love, 1995; Vidal, 1997). John Cooke, McDonald's US labour relations chief in the 1970s, was technically employed to 'educate' US employees about unions, however, in practice, his job was to keep the unions out. He organized 'flying squads' of experienced McDonald's restaurant managers, who were dispatched to a restaurant the same day that word came in of an attempt to organize it. He also trained managers on how to deal with employees and union representatives. As Cooke himself made clear (Love, 1995: 397): '...unions are inimical to what we stand for and how we operate'. Similar union busting techniques are still in use today, although McDonald's had to drop lie detector tests when it ran into trouble in the American courts in the mid-1970s (Royle, 2000). In 1991, Michael Quinlan, Chief Executive of the McDonald's Corporation until 1998, stated (BNA, 1991: 66):

> McDonald's is basically a non-union company and intends to stay that way... I do not feel unionisation has interfered with employees' loyalty to McDonald's, or to the company's philosophy of service and employee motivation...unions do not bring much to the equation.

Despite a number of union organization attempts over the years, McDonald's restaurants in the USA have remained strictly non-union. For example, in Macedonia, Ohio, some McDonald's workers staged a five-day strike in April 1998. The workers behind the union organization effort were later dismissed and little was achieved. Similar efforts have surfaced over the years in Detroit, Chicago and San Francisco, but none were successful. In fact, attempts by unions to organize workers in the US fast-food industry as a whole have also met with little success (Leidner, 2002; Royle and Towers, 2002). Of course, this reflects wider trends in the USA, where union membership is reckoned to be the lowest in the western world and is still declining (Bamber and Whitehouse, 1998). In addition, anti-unionism is commonplace: US employers are increasingly investing in coercion against trade unionists, particularly in the private sector. In recent years, this has reached endemic proportions in the USA, with thousands of people being fired or suffering reprisals when seeking to exercise their rights to union representation (Human Rights Watch, 2000).

In what appeared to be a softening of the approach towards trade unions in 1991, the then McDonald's Chairman, Quinlan, suggested that McDonald's must adapt to local conditions where labour relations are concerned and that the corporation had 'learnt its lesson' from labour disputes of the past (BNA, 1991: 66): 'McDonald's has had some horrible union fights around the world,... do it their way not your own.' But how has McDonald's approached its employee relations policies in practice in its European operations? As the following sections suggest, far from 'adapting', McDonald's has continued to try to impose its non-union system of employment relations wherever possible and has only made some adaptation where this is absolutely unavoidable. We begin by providing a brief summary of the research methods used in the study.

Research methods

The data is derived from an ongoing comparative case study examining the employment relations policy of the McDonald's Corporation in Europe. The study has now become part of a broader study examining labour relations in the fast-food sector in general. It covers a period of eight years and has utilized a variety of research methods, including, for example, a period of participant observation (working in McDonald's restaurants in Germany and the UK), the distribution of questionnaires, a large number of qualitative interviews and documentary analysis. The study originally focused on Germany and the UK, but it has since been extended and developed to cover 13 European countries. These countries are Austria, Belgium, Denmark, Finland, France, Holland, Ireland, Italy, Norway, Spain and Sweden. The bulk of the data draws on over 150 interviews and an analysis of documentary materials. The interviews have included trade unions, trade union federations, international trade union organizations, national and international employers' associations, McDonald's senior management, restaurant management, franchise operators and a large number of employees, including works councillors and trade unions representatives in the restaurants.

McDonald's and union organization in Europe

Although European trade unions still enjoy a relatively strong position in a number of European countries, they have also come under pressure. In the 1990s, there were problems of rising and high unemployment, issues associated with job restructuring and increased international competition. These factors have arguably all led to a decrease in union bargaining power and lower levels of union membership. In particular, Germany, with the added pressure of reunification, has experienced a sharp fall in trade union membership, which has fallen from 12 million in 1991 to 8.6 million by the end of 1997 (Bowley, 1998). As a whole, European trade unions lost nearly 11 per cent of their membership between 1990 and 1995 (Visser, 1998). Nevertheless, in 1995, unioniza-tion in Western Europe, at 31 per cent, was more than twice that of the USA at only 14 per cent. However, the decline in European membership has been twice as fast as in the USA during the 1990s. European trade unions have, however, made some gains in membership in some coun-tries and retained their influence through national-level involvement in social pacts and the reform of regulatory regimes (Waddington, 2001). European unions are most underrepresented in the 'most flexible' seg-ment of the labour market, where temporary contracts and part-time work abound. This may be partly explained by the declining and low levels of union membership amongst younger workers (Visser, 1998), precisely the kind of employee found in the fast-food sector.

Table 8.1 sets out the numbers of employees and restaurants and compares the union density rates per country, in the private sector and in McDonald's. The levels of union membership provide some indication of the ability of unions to organize McDonald's workers, but they are not necessarily representative of the real influence that unions have on pay and conditions. Even where unions have been relatively successful in some countries, union density figures in McDonald's are much lower than the national average. This is not entirely surprising, as union density figures are usually lower in the private sector and lower still in the hotel and restaurant sector than in other industries, but union density is lower again in the fast-food sec-tor. For example, the figure for union density in the UK hotel and restaurant sector in general in 1995 is only 8 per cent, in Finland it is around 65 per cent but with density in the fast-food sector estimated at around 8 per cent (LFS, 1996). In most European countries, the union density figures at McDonald's appear to be lower than in the hotel and restaurant sector in general and often lower even than in the broader fast-food sector itself (Royle and Towers, 2002). One might have expected that the Scandinavian countries, especially Sweden, Denmark, Finland and Norway with the highest union dens-ity rates in Europe, would also have the highest union membership rates at McDonald's. But this is not the case. It is actually Italy

Table 8.1 Union density in McDonald's European operations

Country	McDonald's restaurants	McDonald's workers	Union density country (1995)	Union density private sector	McDonald's union density (1999)
North					
Denmark	80	4,000	79.1	68.0	6.0
Finland	85	4,250	78.4	65.0	7.0
Norway	44	2,200	57.7	45.0	3.5
Sweden	151	7,500	87.6	78.0	15.0
West					
Ireland	25	1,250	46.2	37.0	0.0
UK	900	55,000	32.1	21.0	0.0
Centre					
Austria	80	4,000	40.3	–	20.0
Belgium	62	3,250	51.9	–	1.5
Germany	930	51,000	29.0	25.0	4.0
Netherlands	180	13,000	25.7	19.0	4.0
South					
France	720	35,000	10.1	6.0	1.5
Italy	220	10,000	37.7	32.0	20.0
Spain	161	8,000	18.6	–	1.0

and Austria that have the highest union density within McDonald's European operations.

The following sections examine the distinct experiences of unionization and union recognition or derecognition in each country and try to unravel the reasons for the low levels of membership and the variations in trade union density across countries.

'Do it your own way': the UK and Ireland

McDonald's first restaurant was opened in the UK in 1974, but it was not until the early 1980s that the corporation really began to employ any significant numbers of employees. By that time, the British trade unions were finding life difficult under the new neo-liberal government of Mrs Thatcher. Up until that time, the UK industrial relations system had had a long history of voluntarism and, in comparison with most European countries, was weakly regulated (Edwards et al., 1998). In a context of huge increases in unemployment and a government actively undermining the position of the unions, it is hardly surprising that McDonald's had few problems in operating its usual non-union system. In fact, as Table 8.1 indicates, union membership in the UK is at zero or close to it. The three main trade unions, who have some interest in representing workers in the UK fast-food industry, are the Union of Shop Distributive and Allied Workers (USDAW), the Transport and General Workers Union (TGWU) and the General Municipal and Boilermakers Union (GMB), with the GMB probably the largest of the three unions in the fast-food industry (TICL, 1987). Despite the fact that these unions have been trying to target part-time workers and students in recent years, none of them has had any real success in organizing McDonald's workers in the UK. As the following sections will indicate, the new 'Fairness at Work' legislation is also unlikely to achieve union recognition for McDonald's UK workers. While it may be welcome in that it halts the tide of anti-union legislation introduced by successive Conservative governments from 1980 to 1993, it has serious weaknesses as far as the unions are concerned, with the new procedures still being heavily in favour of companies (LRD, 1999; Towers, 1999). It seems likely that the new statutory recognition procedure envisaged in the Act is unlikely to trigger recognition in an aggressively non-union industry of this kind.

A lack of supportive legislation has led to a similar situation in Ireland. McDonald's opened its first restaurant in Dublin in early 1977. Over the next two years, the Irish ITGWU (now SIPTU) union managed to recruit a few McDonald's workers (between six and eight) and issued a claim for improvement in wages and conditions. The company did not respond. Union officials point out that as soon as somebody joined or showed interest in joining the union, they were put under pressure by management and often dismissed. In March 1979, the union balloted its then six members for strike action. The company was given one week's notice of the strike action. Three more workers joined the union and the strike took place, with the Bakery Workers Union stopping bread supplies in a sympathy action and mass pickets outside the two restaurants. By now the union had recruited 30 members but McDonald's managed to get a High Court injunction to limit the number of pickets to three per restaurant. The strike went on for six months until, finally, the Labour Court issued a recommendation in favour of union recognition. Some of the pickets who had returned to work were dismissed not long afterwards and union members were not allowed to wear union badges or put up union notices in the restaurants. Union officials claimed that management continued to harass their members and that, by the end of 1981, nearly all the union members had been removed. Later attempts to organize restaurants simply ended in failure: union members were dismissed and, although the union won a number of cases taken to the courts in the mid-1980s and compensation was paid, it was to no avail. Once the union members were 'eradicated', the union effectively lost its right to recognition. Union officials state that McDonald's are now willing to meet them in joint labour management catering committees, but only together with other employers. Since that time, McDonald's in Ireland has remained totally non-union and SIPTU officials believe that the new legal compromise on union recognition procedures (EIRR, 1999) is unlikely to achieve union recognition or have any effect on union membership.

Unions in the centre: Germany, Austria, Belgium and the Netherlands

As we suggested earlier, the industrial relations systems and unions of mainland Europe arguably pose a more serious challenge for McDonald's non-union policy than in the UK and Ireland. Germany is a good example as it has a highly juridified industrial relations system and a small number of relatively strong, well-organized unions. McDonald's first German restaurant was opened in 1971 and initially encountered little 'opposition'. However, as more restaurants were opened, McDonald's found itself increasingly in conflict with the German unions. By the early 1980s, McDonald's was facing a major public relations crisis over its employment policies. The German union, the NGG (*Gewerkschaft Nahrung Genuss Gaststätten*), was increasingly critical of the company in the press over its pay and conditions of employment, with one article describing conditions in the restaurants as being like the 'Wild West' (*Der Spiegel*, 1981). Things probably came to a head with the publication of Walraff's book *Ganz Unten* (1985). Walraff reported a McDonald's memo that detailed the recommended recruitment procedure for restaurant managers. This explicitly instructed that the recruitment procedure should ascertain whether or not the applicant had any membership or interest in a trade union. If this was found to be the case, the interview was to be quickly terminated and, as Walraff (1985: 80) puts it, '...of course the applicant should in no circumstances be employed' (all translations by the author). The company later distanced itself from this statement, stating that its source had been one overzealous manager and in no way represented company policy. After the continuing build-up of bad publicity, however, the corporation apparently decided on a shift in policy. After 15 years of struggle, the company finally entered into negotiations, which resulted in the first collective agreement with the unions some three years later (Royle, 1999a, 2000). This might suggest that anti-unionism would now be a thing of the past, however, in most European countries McDonald's are still in ongoing conflicts and disputes with the unions. In Germany, union officials of the NGG are adamant that the collective agreements, while welcome, were merely a pragmatic decision to improve the organization's image and did not represent any change in the underlying non-union stance of the corporation. In particular, they argue that McDonald's activities as regards both the German works councils and the European works council clearly highlight the corporation's unwillingness to enter into any meaningful dialogue with the unions. A considerable amount of conflict over the existence and operation of German works councils in McDonald's is still ongoing (Royle, 1998, 1999b, 2000). More ominously, it appears that, in the last few months, McDonald's has been trying to establish its own 'enterprise' union.

A similar pattern also emerges in Austria. Union officials at the HGPD described the first 17 years of the 'relationship' with McDonald's as 'open warfare'. However, in 1994, the corporation softened its approach to allow the unions to recruit; union membership levels have increased considerably since that time and, on the surface, relations have improved. However, union officials report that they are unable to establish any codetermination rights through works councils or a supervisory board, although works councils play a key role in 'policing' individual restaurants to ensure that collective agreements are not infringed.

In Belgium, union officials from both the CCVD and CCAS state that it has been impossible to have any kind of meaningful dialogue with the corporation. Although collective agreements are automatically imposed on the corporation, unions have been unable to negotiate a company-level agreement. Union membership is a big problem and there is very little effective union representation in the restaurants. They have been unable to establish works councils and there are only a small number of union delegates in the restaurants. Unions report problems of collective agreement infringements and unfair dismissals. Overall, the unions conclude that McDonald's is essentially anti-union in its approach but will respond quickly if its image is threatened. In such a situation, it is very difficult to establish effective union representation in the restaurants.

According to union officials at the FNV-affiliated HORECABOND in the Netherlands, the relationship between McDonald's and the union was also very poor from when it entered the Dutch market in 1971 until the mid-1980s; 13 to 14 years went by before McDonald's 'toned-down' its outspokenly anti-union policies. As it increasingly came into conflict with the unions during that time, it faced more and more bad publicity. After losing a number of court cases involving infringements of the national collective agreement, McDonald's made public pronouncements that it would thereafter agree to recognize the trade unions and take part in and adhere to collective agreements. Since that time, the public image of the corporation in the Netherlands has improved a good deal. The unions also confirm that their relationship with the corporation has improved. Union officials state that in 1997, of the approximately 13,000 McDonald's employees, only 80 were union members. After a six-month campaign ending in early 1998, the union successfully increased its membership to what are now around 500 members. This is still a small proportion of the total workforce and, because there is such high labour turnover, this figure may not remain static for long. Despite some cooperation with McDonald's management, however, union officials state that problems still exist, such as issues relating to unfair dismissals, inadequate notice of working hours, late payment of wages, managers asking workers to work longer hours than agreed in their contracts and incorrect sick pay calculations. In particular, there is also a major problem of McDonald's classifying some workers into a lower pay group called 'apprentice fast-food worker'. According to union officials, this grade does not exist and it therefore violates the collective agreement. This problem has been particularly marked in the franchise operations that run nearly 90 per cent of the 180 Dutch restaurants. Up to now, the union has been unable to establish any significant number of union representatives or works councils in the restaurants. However, it is optimistic that, with the 1998 changes in Dutch works council legislation, they will now be able to establish a proper structure of works councils (Royle, 2000).

Unions in the south: France, Spain and Italy

Only three years after Quinlan's statement about 'doing it their way', McDonald's French management appeared to be doing just the opposite. In France, 12 McDonald's managers were arrested at their place of work and put under judicial investigation, accused of denying unions and staff their rights (Sage, 1994; Royle, 2000). As one CFDT official remarked (Sage, 1994: 16): 'The company has a resistance to unions that is incredible.' Although the corporation signed a union recognition agreement and a company-level agreement with the French unions in 1996, they only cover the 10 per cent of the corporation's wholly owned restaurants and not its joint venture and franchise operations. Union officials describe the corporation's 'change' of employment relations policy as little more than a public relations exercise. Indeed, there was a long-running strike in a McDonald's restaurant in Paris in the winter of 2000 over the unfair dismissal of union representatives, management interference in works council elections and poor working conditions.

McDonald's first came to Spain in 1982 and since that time it has refused to recognize the trade unions. The corporation has to abide by a national sectoral agreement for the wider hotel and restaurant sector but there are wage disparities between the restaurants owned by McDonald's and the majority of franchise outlets. McDonald's has been able to capture Spanish works councils for a managerially sponsored agenda and, in some cases, management has used the works council to negotiate a franchise-level agreement and actively prevent union involvement (Royle, 2000). Union (FECOHT) officials state that there are frequent cases of unfair dismissals and infringements of collective agreements in McDonald's.

The situation in Italy, however, is somewhat different. The Italian unions have, together with Austria, the highest union density rate in McDonald's restaurants in Europe. Part of the explanation for this is that many of McDonald's restaurants were previously owned by national food chains and were already unionized. A second explanation is that labour turnover is not so high because unemployment levels have remained high, especially in the south of Italy. Thirdly, representative unions have the right to enter premises and, in this way, have managed to establish a fair number of union delegates and some works councils. McDonald's is automatically covered by a sectoral collective agreement, but union attempts to negotiate a company-level collective agreement have so far failed. Union officials and McDonald's workers complain that 20 per cent of workers are not paid in accordance with the correct pay grouping and allege that union delegates face regular harassment and poorer working conditions than non-union workers. Typically, there are many more problems in the franchise restaurants than in the restaurants owned by McDonald's and, in particular, workers complain of unsatisfactory health and safety procedures and working conditions. Even as recently as May 1999, McDonald's Italian workers went on strike, shutting restaurants on consecutive Saturdays in a number of Italian towns and cities, including Milan and Bologna. As in the other countries, union membership is much higher where works councils or union delegates are in place.

Unions in the north: Denmark, Finland, Iceland, Norway and Sweden

The history of the relationship between McDonald's and the unions is somewhat mixed in the north. In Denmark, Iceland and Norway, McDonald's had initially refused to recognize unions or sign collective agreements; in Sweden and Finland, McDonald's appeared to be more union friendly in its approach. In Denmark, the dispute between the unions and McDonald's was rather acrimonious and long running. From the time McDonald's opened its first restaurant in 1981, they would not come to an agreement with the unions. The conflict really came to a head in 1988, when, according to Danish (RBF) union officials, a McDonald's spokesman confidently stated in 'Dalek-like' tones that union resistance would be useless:

> McDonald's has as much money as there is water in the sea, we will not give in to an agreement, industrial action is useless.

Nevertheless, the Danish unions still went ahead with strike action and boycotts were organized. There was frequent and extensive coverage in the newspapers and daily demonstrations outside the restaurants. The Danish graphics workers refused to deal with their advertising material, brewery workers refused to deliver beer and construction workers refused to build any new McDonald's. The unions were particularly pleased with a poster designed for them by a Danish graphics worker, which portrayed a dog urinating on the McDonald's 'M' symbol; this illustration was used on all their placards and posters. In February 1989, the Finnish unions also organized sympathy action with the intention of providing as much media coverage as possible. They organized reports in the newspapers, radio advertising, large-scale information campaigns in Finnish schools and students and youth organizations distributed leaflets asking people to boycott McDonald's. In May 1989, McDonald's finally caved in and joined the Danish employers' association for the hotel and restaurant sector. However, Danish union officials claim that the relationship has not really changed and that McDonald's frequently break the collective agreement, particularly in the area of working hours and overtime payments. It has also been very difficult to establish union delegates in the restaurants, union membership is still very low and cooperation committees simply do not exist (Royle, 2000).

Arriving in Finland in 1984, three years later than in Denmark, McDonald's joined the Finnish employers' association and agreed a collective agreement with the Finnish trade unions. The unions are, however, not entirely satisfied with the current agreement because it covers the whole hotel and restaurant sector and does not adequately deal with some of the issues in the fast-food sector. In addition, there is little in the way of a 'relationship' between McDonald's and the unions. Union officials point out that McDonald's has tried to hinder the election of union representatives and will not negotiate directly with the unions. There are no workers committees or councils but there is a health and safety committee and a supervisory board without, however, union representation. Overall, there are problems with the establishment of union representatives in the restaurants and a number of concerns about infringements of the collective agreements.

In a similar approach to that adopted in Denmark, the opening of the first McDonald's restaurant in Iceland in 1993 coincided with the owners' announcement that they would not join the employers' association nor conclude any collective agreements with the trade unions. McDonald's eventually gave way on some general principles but union officials still report workers being dismissed for having contact with the trade unions and regular infringements of the sectoral collective agreement.

McDonald's came to Norway in 1983 and, once again, ran into trouble with the unions. McDonald's was automatically covered by a broad framework collective agreement for the hotel and restaurant sector, which was originally established in the 1930s. The Norwegian union (HRAF) has been trying to negotiate plant-level agreements with groups of franchisees and company restaurants but to do this they must have union members in the restaurants. This has proved to be very problematic, partly because of the high level of labour turnover, but also because of McDonald's anti-union stance. For example, in 1992, a previous union campaign for an agreement covering three franchise restaurants in Oslo collapsed when the unionized workers left McDonald's for other jobs. In 1993, when 12 cleaners joined the union, the union demanded a company-level collective agreement and McDonald's responded by dismissing all 12 workers. After an appeal and negotiations, the workers were reinstated, but after only a few months they once again came under pressure to leave the company. Only after strike action was threatened, and there had been considerable coverage of the conflict in the press, did McDonald's finally concede an agreement. Problems still remain, however: HRAF officials state that collective agreements are not properly adhered to, there are problems with young workers working illegally and an unwillingness to provide adequate notice of work schedules.

Sweden was the first Scandinavian country to experience McDonald's in 1973. The initial reaction to the company was extremely hostile: Lederhausen, the Swedish businessman who opened the first franchises, received regular hate mail and his restaurants were smoke bombed by left-wing groups complaining of what they termed 'creeping American imperialism' (Vidal, 1997: 41). Despite admiring the American way of doing things (Love, 1995), Lederhausen decided that taking on the Swedish unions, who have the highest union membership rates in Europe, would not be a wise move. In any case, the restaurants would automatically be covered by a sectoral collective agreement. As a result, the relationship with the Swedish unions is probably the best in Europe. Collective agreements are in place and a union delegate works full-time on union matters in the McDonald's head office in Stockholm. However, problems still remain: union membership levels are extremely low compared to Swedish norms, there is also a serious problem with establishing union representation in the restaurants and some question marks about the effectiveness of the head office union representative. Where restaurant representatives do exist, union awareness is much higher as is union membership; where there is no representative, there are often no union members and serious problems with the application of collective agreements.

Explaining low union membership in general

Union organization is made very difficult by the nature of the jobs in the wider hospitality industry, which are often geographically dispersed, small unit, temporary, part-time, with a low skills base and largely reliant on youth and female employment with high levels of labour turnover. However, unions themselves may also be somewhat to blame, as they have not always been willing to focus adequate resources on recruitment in this industry. From a UK and US perspective, union organization in the wider hospitality industry has always been low (Lowery and Scott, 1996). The industry often reflects the 'Bleak House' scenario of industrial relations (Sisson, 1993), with its highly 'individualized' employee relations, high dismissal rates, high levels of accidents and absenteeism, high labour turnover, a large number of grievances and low pay (Lucas, 1996). The fast-food area of this sector is at the vanguard in respect of these poor employment conditions. The previous sections also suggest that, despite the normally high levels of union and state involvement in most European countries, the same kinds of problems are surfacing. In most cases, unions have not been able to recruit sufficient members or establish adequate numbers of union representatives and works councils. Without these mechanisms in place, European systems of collective bargaining lose their efficacy. The following sections attempt to unravel, in more detail, the particular problems of union recruitment in the European fast-food industry by examining the typical responses of workers and managers towards unions in Germany and the UK.

Management attitudes towards unions

Marginson and Sisson (1994) suggest that industrial relations issues are deeply rooted in societal frameworks and are particularly impervious to the transmission of employee relations practices by MNCs. One might, therefore, expect that there would be significant differences in the responses of German and UK management regarding the issue of trade unions. However, responses from management in McDonald's German and UK operations were remarkably similar. A senior UK manager stated:

> Unionisation has risen its ugly head over the years, but you know, we feel that we don't need unions. I think we've seen that the unions' power within business has been eroded quite considerably over the last 15 years, we've managed to get rid of them.

Whilst a senior German manager commented:

> We don't see the need for unions. McDonald's has shown that it's not necessary in this industry. We already have a good system of communications. Unions are less important than they used to be.

From the previous analysis, the basic assumptions (Schein, 1984) of the McDonald's corporate culture remain strongly grounded in anti-unionism. But to what extent are these assumptions transmitted and internalized by restaurant management in different countries? Interviews with German and UK management suggest that the non-union message is transmitted to management at restaurant level in both countries. A German restaurant manager commented:

> Of course unions play an important role in society, but they are unnecessary in the McDonald's system, we don't need them here.

UK managers made similar comments, such as:

> I think unions have an important role to play, but in the restaurant, where it's only one on one, there's no need for them. I've never thought of joining a union, never been in a union, my initial feeling is, it's not worth bothering.

Salaried management in Germany were more likely to have had some experience of unions and were generally better informed than their UK counterparts. UK salaried managers usually had had no personal experience of unions and appeared to be poorly informed about their current strength relative to employers and their wider role in society. They also seemed to have little concrete knowledge of the changes in union legislation introduced in the 1980s and 90s. The following comment by a young UK salaried manager was typical:

> I think they are more political than they used to be. I think they lobby for a lot more than their predecessors did. I think they are a lot stronger than they were. They've got all these lawyers looking for loopholes now, that they never used to and outside help. They've got a lot of money and a lot of backing, so they can do a lot of damage, that's the main reason why I'm against them, well not against them, but I think they can do a lot of unnecessary damage.

A majority of German managers in the interview sample also had a negative attitude to the unions, as a German floor manager commented: 'With good management it is possible that there will not be unions in the future.' This notion was also strongly reflected in comments from UK respondents; one UK restaurant manager commented:

> Well, we must take on the role of the trade union and protect the employees. It comes back to the motivation thing, if we protect them and look after their interests, they are going to be motivated, there's no need for trade unions at McDonald's because we are two organisations in one. I can't see a problem with having no unions in society if each business had a philosophy of looking after their employees like McDonald's, but then, that's Utopia isn't it?

These responses suggest that, regardless of societal differences, the McDonald's corporate culture is quite effective in moulding the required responses of management to the unions. Willmott (1993) argues that strong corporate cultures 'exclude and eliminate' other values, such as, in this case, the acceptance of unions. The emphasis placed on the importance of 'good' management suggests a moral tone. Willmott (1993) suggests that the extent to which individuals may be willing to internalize these norms and values may depend on their assessment of its moral character. The McDonald's 'culture' appears to be one that encourages managers to see unions as an unwarranted interference, who will 'destroy' the corporation and the 'good' management practice already in place.

Franchisees: the benefits of small operations

One might assume that McDonald's ability to ensure behavioural consistency across societies would be complicated by franchising. In Europe, some 65 per cent of its restaurants are operated as franchises and, in some European countries, this figure is as high as 90 per cent. However, as we have already argued elsewhere (Royle, 2000), franchisees are so tightly controlled by the corporation that McDonald's franchises are more like subsidiaries than truly independent operations. Legally separate but economically tied, franchisees are motivated by profits not wages. They pay much more attention to the fine details of the operation and are much better at eradicating waste and keeping labour costs low. In this sense, franchisees provide the corporation with highly motivated 'managers' of small business operations. Franchisees also foster paternalistic relations with their employees and are able to keep a very close eye on their activities. As one UK franchisee stated:

> I like people to tell me every little incident in detail that goes on, because, if there is a problem, I can react to it.

Abbott (1993) makes the point that large organizations find it more difficult to stop unionization because of the distance between senior managers and employees, whilst small operations make it more difficult for unions to recruit members. The majority of small business owners in the UK often comment that they do see the need for unions in society in general, but see no need for unions in *their* businesses. Typically, Abbott suggests, this was because they believe that they are good employers and would interpret any interest in union involvement by their employees as a failure of *their* management style. This was also strongly reflected in responses from franchisees in this study. One German and one UK franchisee made the following comments:

> If they wanted a union here I would take it personally, I'd feel a little bit insulted and think, well, why do they want one?

> I don't think they are necessary. If the crew wanted to join a union, I would feel disappointed, because it would mean that I had failed in my efforts to look after them. I'd feel I'd not been doing my job properly. I think because of the damage other employers have done

to some employees, unions will stay popular, I don't think they will die off overnight in those old industries. Fast-food is a new breed.

In addition, franchisees are well aware that inviting unions into restaurants would not fit well with the values of the corporation, especially as it would be likely to increase labour costs. Franchises are unlikely to do anything that might attract the corporation's criticism and risk losing their franchise or the chance to run additional restaurants in the future. McDonald's, therefore, have the best of both worlds, with willing 'partners' in sharing the costs and risks of development and highly obedient and motivated operators spreading the corporate message and leaving little room for union involvement.

General workforce characteristics and workers' attitudes

The reason for the low union organization rates in McDonald's European operations is not entirely due to its anti-union corporate culture and close monitoring of employees. The characteristics of the workforce itself are also an important factor. In most European countries, the majority of McDonald's workers are very young, many are still at school and a considerable number are students. Young workers tend to have very little previous job experience; if they have worked before, it often in similar types of low-skilled work (Royle, 2000). Many of the young workers are only there for 'pocket money' and therefore tend to have highly instrumental attitudes; after all, they may not work at McDonald's for very long. In addition, they tend to have very little idea about trade unions and often do not see their relevance. Coupled with the frequently hostile management attitudes towards unions, this makes union recruitment of young workers extremely difficult. The following comment from a young German worker in McDonald's is typical of responses from young McDonald's workers in other European countries:

Unions are not important for me personally at the moment, here at McDonald's, but maybe later when I get a better job.

In the UK, in particular, a majority of the young workers were simply not well informed about the current status of unions, union roles and priorities or what services unions may be able to provide for them. Not one of the UK interview respondents within the restaurants, at any level, could say which union was responsible for the fast-food industry or knew which union they should approach if they had wanted to. The following comments from UK workers were typical:

I just don't know enough about them, I tend to associate unions with strikes, but I don't know a lot about it.

I don't know, I've never really thought about unions, it's not something I think about. I don't know really, don't know what they do. I've never been told or given anything about unions.

In the Scandinavian countries, the unions enjoy much better access to McDonald's workers, but still find it very difficult to recruit young workers. Danish and Finnish union officials suggest that McDonald's restaurant management would often try to persuade young employees that the reasonably good pay and conditions they enjoyed, which had been established by collective agreement, had nothing to do with the trade unions, 'who were only troublemakers', but were down to McDonald's being a benign and generous employer. Finnish union representatives pointed out that workers often had more than one part-time job and were unwilling to pay the union membership fee, in some cases, because collective agreements automatically applied or because they did not intend to stay with the company.

Older workers' and foreign workers' attitudes

However, it would be a mistake to think that McDonald's workforce was only made up of young workers. In Italy, the average age of the workforce is older than in the UK. Italian McDonald's workers claim that this is simply because of the problem of high unemployment. These older workers cannot get jobs elsewhere and this problem is particularly acute in the south of Italy. In Germany, many McDonald's employees are economic migrants (*Aussiedler*) from the Eastern European countries, such as Poland, Albania and Russia. In addition, there are a large number of workers from ethnic minorities; in some of the big cities, for example, many of the workers are of Turkish descent. This means that the average age of the German and Austrian McDonald's workforce is older than in other countries such as the UK and Denmark. These workers are likely to find it difficult to find work elsewhere, partly because of problems with the language and partly because of problems with the recognition of their qualifications.

In some cases, foreign workers had had some contact with unions in their previous jobs, but this was no longer seen as a possibility while working at McDonald's, either because of obvious management hostility or, simply, because they did not know who to contact. Very few foreign workers in Germany seemed to have any knowledge of what the German unions had already achieved for them by way of collective agreements and no idea that a union had actually negotiated on their behalf. This was particularly acute in restaurants, where there were no union representatives or works councils in the restaurant. For example, only ten per cent of the hourly-paid employees interviewed in the German restaurants, where no works council existed (that is, the majority of German restaurants), knew that a union had negotiated on their behalf and only three per cent knew the name of the union concerned. This comment made by an economic migrant in a German restaurant was typical:

> There are no unions at McDonald's, I don't know why we don't have them here, you hear so little about unions in this industry.

This was despite the fact that a copy of the collective agreement was supposed to be available to every German employee. In practice, the restaurant manager would usually have a copy but it would rarely be made available to employees unless they specifically asked for it or there was a union representative in the restaurant. Management often claimed that it was 'unnecessary' for the crew to see the collective agreement, because employees could always ask managers if they wanted to know something about it. Only where union-supported works councils were established were copies of the collective agreement freely available. Despite the lack of knowledge about unions amongst workers interviewed in Germany and the UK, a majority of those interviewed seemed to have a positive view of them:

> Unions are important, they play an important role in limiting the power of employers and stop employees being exploited.

> Unions are really too important, it's really a pity that McDonald's are not involved with the unions.

> I hope there will always be unions, but there's no information about them here.

The attitudes of long-term employees

Even in the UK, where approximately 70 per cent of the workforce is under 21, there is often a core of older workers, who tend to stay with the company in the long term, in some cases, five years or more. In the UK, those who stay longer with the company tend to fall into two categories. Firstly, those who have been 'washed-up' in the labour market because of poor qualifications and a lack of other opportunities. Secondly, those I have termed 'coasters', who could find better work elsewhere, but are undecided and stay with the company because they are unsure of what to do with their lives (Royle, 2000). In other countries, such as Finland, Spain and Italy, workers tend to stay longer because of high unemployment, especially amongst younger workers. Many Italian workers pointed out that 'there are no other jobs'. Young Finnish workers also reported that it was very difficult to find work elsewhere and that, once they had worked at McDonald's, other employers would not take them seriously when they applied for other kinds of work:

> There are so many young people without a job, it is hard to get other jobs, when you go and they ask if you have any experience and you say 'Oh, I worked at McDonald's', they say, 'Go back there and make some burgers!' I've tried, I know.

Of course, McDonald's may also offer an opportunity for some to make a real career with the company, especially while the company continues to expand at such a fast rate. A Norwegian union official described these workers as 'career collaborators'. Although there are clearly differences in the profiles of the workers in different countries, we can discern a common thread: McDonald's appears to be able to take advantage of weak or marginalized sectors of the labour market in each country in which they operate. Such workers can be described as 'acquiescent' (Royle, 2000): in other words, they are difficult for the unions to recruit because they really need the job and are not likely to go against managerial will and join the union if they think their job will be threatened. In many cases, workers just do not know about their rights or that a union is there for them. For many young workers, the union does not seem relevant or worth the effort or the membership fees.

Explaining different levels of union membership in the EU

How then can we explain the different levels of union membership in the different McDonald's operations in Europe? Both Austria and Italy have achieved far higher levels of union membership than the Scandinavian countries, which are normally associated with the highest union density rates in Europe. There seems little doubt that the role of the union representative and/or the works council is an important factor. This is not only due to their role of raising workers' awareness of their rights and the importance of the union, but also their recruitment of union members. Where unions have been able to establish a union representative and/or some form of works council, then union membership levels within those restaurants often increase dramatically; in some cases, from zero to anything up to 50 per cent or more. For example, virtually all of the 2,000 German union members in McDonald's are in restaurants, where there are union-supported works councils. However, workforce characteristics also appear to have some impact. In the Scandinavian countries, the workforce tends to be similar to that in the UK with a high proportion of young workers. Unions in these countries have found it very difficult to recruit members and to establish union representatives in the restaurants. This is partly because, in many cases, young workers are only there for a short time, partly because the unions are perceived as old fashioned or 'irrelevant' and partly because management are often hostile to union activity in the restaurants. Although the Swedish HRF union has a union representative working full time on union business in the McDonald's headquarters in Stockholm, they do not have union representative working in every restaurant, in fact there appear to be very few in the restaurants themselves. The Swedish union appears to be placing most of its faith in the full-time union representative, whereas representatives in the restaurants suggest that this is not really adequate. In Denmark, the unions only have one representative working in one restaurant and nobody at all working at the head office.

With the exception of Germany and Austria, the average age of the workforce in Italy is higher than in most other European countries. In Italy, McDonald's took over a number of existing businesses during its expansion and these units already had unionized workforces. In addition, in comparison with Germany, the UK and Ireland, the Italian unions have a legal right to enter the workplace and the right to hold meetings on the premises, wherever there are 30 or more employees. In Austria, union membership has increased considerably, largely due to the recognition agreement signed in the mid-1990s but this was apparently at the expense of establishing works councils. In Spain, the unions have only been able to recruit a small percentage of the McDonald's workforce because the corporation refuses to recognize the unions and the works councils have been 'captured' by management-supported candidates (Royle, 2000).

Comparing union membership statistics across different countries is not a straightforward matter, as high levels of membership in some countries, for example, can be explained by the fact that their unions administer and distribute unemployment benefits. In any case, unionization rates do not of themselves necessarily reflect the strength or influence of trade unions in the bargaining process. For example, McDonald's Denmark 'offered' the Danish unions 100 per cent union membership in their restaurants if the union would renegotiate its collective agreements to allow lower pay and conditions; the union, of course, refused. There may, therefore, be no direct correlation between employer attitudes and levels of union membership in organizations in different countries. Nevertheless, union density rates are likely to have some impact on the employer–employee relationship and comparisons of union membership levels across countries do raise some interesting issues regarding effective employee interest representation in the face of 'new' forms of employment, especially where these trends are driven by MNCs.

Conclusion

Even though there are some relative successes in different countries, union membership at McDonald's is still low when compared to the wider hotel and restaurant sector and even the broader fast-food sector in some countries (Royle and Towers, 2002). This appears to be due to a number of reasons. Firstly, a sophisticated and consistent management strategy that aims to keep unions, if not out of sectoral collective bargaining arrangements, then at least out of its restaurants. Secondly, the nature of the work itself, which is part-time, low skilled and temporary and usually associated with high levels of labour turnover. Thirdly, the 'acquiescent' nature of the workforce (Royle, 1999c, 2000), which allows McDonald's to take advantage of marginalized and 'weak' segments of the labour market such as ethnic minorities, young, inexperienced, low-skilled and foreign workers. These workers do not join unions, partly because, in many cases, they do not intend to stay very long with the company and partly because they do not want to pay union fees. In addition, in many European countries, a large proportion of employees have little or no knowledge of unions, being, in many cases, unaware that a union even exists, let alone what it can do, or has been doing, for them; younger workers, in particular, tend to be particularly poorly informed. Furthermore, those with career aspirations will not join a union, because they are concerned that it will negatively affect their job prospects.

A further reason for the low level of union membership is McDonald's use of the franchise, which enhances the corporation's ability to undermine collective bargaining arrangements and avoid national and supranational works councils and plant-level union representatives (Royle, 1998, 1999b, 2000). Without works councils and union representatives, union membership is often non-existent. Furthermore, franchises also operate as 'small firms' and this allows for paternalistic relations and the close monitoring of employees, recreating the problems for union organization which are typical in other small operations (Rainnie, 1989; Abbott, 1993; Holliday, 1995; Dundon et al., 1999).

Some European unions have achieved higher levels of union membership than others, but this does *not* necessarily correlate with general membership trends in the countries concerned. Instead, it appears to depend, in part, on the stringency of the collective bargaining arrangements in place and the 'activating' legislation for institutions such as works councils, as well as plant-level union representatives, the right, or otherwise, of unions to enter premises to talk to workers and the particular 'strategies' adopted by unions themselves. The implications of these findings for union membership as a whole do not look very positive. Fast food is now a global industry and is one of the few industries which is still expanding rapidly and creating a significant number of new jobs: for example, in the USA, over 10 per cent of all workers had their first job at McDonald's (Love, 1995) and a study by Disney et al. (1998) suggests that, in the UK at least, when workers begin life in non-union firms, they are more likely to stay non-union in later jobs.

As yet, there appears to be no easy way in which unions can respond to the situation in the fast-food industry. In the UK, where unions face a multitude of problems, they appear to have given up the struggle in the fast-food sector and the advent of the 1999 Employment Act has done nothing to change this situation. Union membership itself may not be such a problem in some other countries, because bargaining power is already buttressed by sectoral agreements and other forms of state intervention. However, without works councils and/or union representatives in the restaurants, there is no way to ensure that collective agreements are properly enforced. The implications of this for workers' rights and conditions are, therefore, considerable and this raises a number of questions about the efficacy of contemporary industrial relations systems, questions that may become of increasing significance for the future regulation of European labour markets.

These findings support the notion of a growing diversity *within* national industrial relations systems. Marginson and Sisson (1994) have already suggested that MNCs may be increasingly focusing on employer-based employment policies, which may or may not conform to host societal frameworks depending on organizational need. Similarly, Locke's (1995) analysis of cross-national changes in employment relations suggests that, while national institutions and traditions continue to be important in shaping employment relations, there is significant variation within national systems and that these variations are being driven by the competitive strategies of firms. The findings from this study support the view put forward by Marginson and Sisson (1998) that some MNCs are establishing corporate frameworks which parallel or even undermine existing national frameworks. This does not necessarily mean that national systems are becoming redundant, but that there is a dynamic relationship between these systems and the needs of MNCs.

This analysis also reminds us that static models of national industrial relations systems and institutional arrangements do not provide an adequate explanation of industrial relations in practice. It is evident that more cross-national case studies of this kind will be required if we are to gain a more realistic picture of the way in which MNCs actually manage their employees across national boundaries.

References

Abbott, B. (1993) 'Small firms and trade unions in services in 1990s', *Industrial Relations Journal*, 24, 4: 308–17.

Bamber, G. J. and Whitehouse, G. (1998) 'International data on economic, employment and human resource issues', *International Journal of Human Resource Management*, 3, 2: 364.

BNA Bureau of National Affairs (USA) (1991) *Bulletin to Management*, 7 March: 66–71.

Bowley, G. (1998) 'German unions seek safety in numbers', *Financial Times*, 10 March, 3.

Disney, R., Gosling, A., Machin, S. and McCrae, J. (1998) *The Dynamics of Union Membership in Britain: A Study Using the Family and Working Lives Survey.* Employment Relations Research Series, 3, London: Department of Trade and Industry.

Dundon, T., Grugulis, I. and Wilkinson, A. (1999) 'Looking out of the black hole: non-union relations in an SME', *Employee Relations*, 21, 3: 251–66.

Edwards, P. K., Hall, M., Hyman, R., Marginson, P., Sisson, K., Waddington, J. and Winchester, D. (1998) 'Great Britain: From Partial Collectivism to Neo-Liberalism to Where?', in Ferner, A. and Hyman, R. (eds) *Changing Industrial Relations in Europe*, Oxford: Basil Blackwell.

EIRR (1999) 'Unions and employers agree compromise on union recognition', *European Industrial Relations Review*, May, 304: 27–30.

Holliday, R. (1995) *Investigating Small Firms: Nice Work?*, London: Routledge.

Human Rights Watch (2000) *Unfair Advantage: Workers' Freedom of Association in the United States under International Human Rights Standards*, London: Human Rights Watch.

Leidner, R. (2002) 'Fast-food work in the United States', in Royle, T. and Towers, B. (eds) Labour Relations in the Global Fast-food Industry, London: Routledge.

LFS Labour Force Survey (1996) *Labour Market Trends*, May: 215–25.

Locke, R. (1995) The Transformation of Industrial Relations? A Cross-National Review, in Wever, S. and Turner, L. (eds) *The Political Economy of Industrial Relations*, Industrial Relations Research Association Series, Madison: Wisconsin.

Love, J. F. (1995) *McDonald's Behind the Arches*, London: Bantam Press.

Lowery, C. M. and Scott, C. (1996) 'Union organizing amongst hospitality workers', *Hospitality Research Journal*, 19, 4: 3–16.

LRD (1999) *Employment Relations Bill: A Trade Unionists Guide*, London: Labour Research Department Publications.

Lucas, R. (1996) 'Industrial Relations in Hotels and Catering: Neglect and paradox?', *British Journal of Industrial Relations*.

Marginson, P. and Sisson, K. (1994) 'The Structure of Transnational Capital in Europe: The Emerging Euro-Company and its Implications for Industrial Relations', in Hyman, R. and Ferner, A. (eds) *New Frontiers in European Industrial Relations*, Oxford: Basil Blackwell.

Marginson, P. and Sisson, K. (1998) 'European collective bargaining: a virtual prospect?' *Journal of Common Market Studies*, December, 36, 4: 505–28.

Ramsay, H. (1991) 'The Community, the multinational, its workers and their charter: a modern tale of industrial democracy?', *Work, Employment and Society*, 5, 4: 541–66.

Rainnie, A. (1989) *Industrial Relations in the Small Firm: Small Isn't Beautiful*, London: Routledge.

Royle, T. (1998) 'Avoidance strategies and the German system of co-determination', *The International Journal of Human Resource Management*, December, 9, 6: 1026–47.

Royle, T. (1999a) 'The reluctant bargainers? McDonald's, unions and pay determination in Germany and the UK', *Industrial Relations Journal*, June, 30, 2: 135–50.

Royle, T. (1999b) 'Where's the beef? McDonald's and the European works council', *European Journal of Industrial Relations*, November, 5, 3: 327–47.

Royle, T. (1999c) Recruiting the acquiescent workforce: a comparative analysis of McDonald's in Germany and the UK, *Employee Relations*, 21, 6: 540–55.

Royle, T. (2000) *Working for McDonald's in Europe: the Unequal Struggle?*, London: Routledge.

Royle, T. and Towers, B. (eds) (2002) *Labour Relations in the Global Fast-food Industry*, London: Routledge.

Sage, A. (1994) 'France puts bite on Big Mac', *The Observer*, 10 July: 16.

Schein, E. H. (1994) 'Coming to a new awareness of organizational culture', *Sloan Management Review*, Winter, 3–16.

Der Spiegel (1981) 'Land des Lächelns', 22: 72–5.

Towers, B. (1999) 'Editorial: "the most lightly regulated labour market" the UK's third statutory recognition procedure', *Industrial Relations Journal*, June, 30, 2: 82–95.

TICL (Transnational Information Centre London) (1987) *McDonald's: From Local Store to Transnational*, London: Calverts Press.

Vidal, J. (1997) *McLibel: Burger Culture on Trial*, London: Macmillan.

Visser, J. (1998) 'European trade unions in the mid-1990s', in Towers, B. and Terry, M. (eds) *Industrial Relations Journal: European Annual Review 1997*, Oxford: Blackwell.

Waddington, J. (2001) 'Articulating trade union organisation for the new Europe?', *Industrial Relations Journal Annual Review*, December, 32, 5: 449–63.

Walraff, G. (1985) *Ganz Unten*, London: Methuen.

Willmott, H. (1993) 'Strength is ignorance; slavery is freedom: managing culture in modern organisations', *Journal of Management Studies*, 30, 4: 515–52.

9
Global Market Pressures in a Regional Context: Experiences from Field Research in the Industrial Region of South Wales, UK

Jean J. Boggis

Introduction

In the globalized marketplace, it is generally acknowledged that manufacturing in developed economies is under severe pressure, and the UK Trade and Industry Secretary recently conceded that the sector in Britain as a whole is currently 'in recession' (*Financial Times*, 06.11.01: 4). All too frequently, discussion of global industrial restructuring is conducted on the basis of corporate policy and its economic ramifications, in a reified debate that effectively ignores or devalues the existence and contribution of the human actors within workplaces, who are actually engaged in the task of creating corporate wealth. This chapter offers a less depersonalized view of the pressures on the actors involved in industrial relations in manufacturing workplaces, who are located within a particular region of a developed economy, namely the UK. It aims to illustrate how globalization has been used as a powerful managerial rationale for changes to working practice by focusing workplace trade union representatives' minds on their members' vulnerability in the global marketplace for labour and thereby enlisting their cooperation and negating any form of overt protest against change. (See also Tempel in this volume for the effect of globalization on collective bargaining relationships). The chapter will first describe the regional context of the research and the case study factories prior to discussing the use of globalization as a managerial rationale for change.

Regional context of the research and the case study factories

In the course of this research, factory studies were undertaken in plants across a range of manufacturing sectors located within the industrial region of South Wales in the UK. The geographical boundaries of the area, currently termed the 'industrial region', correspond with what was once the South Wales coalfield. This is a region characterized by widespread industrial restructuring and a continuing move away from its traditional reliance on the primary sector and heavy manufacturing industry. Despite facing serious challenges and exhibiting a 4.8 per cent decline in employment in the year to March 2001, manufacturing industry in Wales remains a major contributor to the economy and currently accounts for 198,000 employees (Roberts et al., 2001: 21). The industrial region has historically been home to the bulk of Wales's industrial base and, in 2001, 61 per cent of Welsh manufacturing jobs were still in the South (*Digest of Welsh Local Area Statistics*, 2001: 176).

UK business has exhibited a marked trend towards internationalization since 1980, with significant increases in inward investment in manufacturing and an increasing incidence of British multinationals (Millward et al., 2000: 32). This trend is even more marked in South Wales, where there is strong reliance on investment from outside the region, particularly from the USA and Japan, and thus the region offers particular opportunities for examining global market pressures on industrial relations in manufacturing workplaces. The following sections will introduce the case study factories prior to discussing the influence of regional policy and inward investment, the relevance of the subsidiary factory status and a brief review of the incidence of industrial conflict in regional manufacturing in Wales.

The case study factories

The plants studied occupy different manufacturing sectors, making products ranging from women's trousers to electronic heat inductors for the car industry. Factory studies were undertaken in each of these units based on non-participant observation, but it should be noted that access varied in degree from one unit to another. The nature of access requested was that the researcher should be allowed to conduct semi-structured interviews with representatives of management, trade unions and the general factory floor workforce, to observe the work process on the factory floor itself and to have access to company documentation and collective agreements with a view to assessing changes in the climate of industrial relations. In general, there was little problem

Table 9.1 Case study factories – ownership and plant characteristics

Manufacturing industry by product	Location of ownership
Light electronics	Japan
	USA since 1990 (originally
Upholstered furniture	founded
Factory 1	under British ownership)
Factory 2	
(Owned by same parent company)	
Automotive industry – manufacture of components	USA
Metal manufacture – Plant 1	USA since the 1960s (originally British)
Metal manufacture – Plant 2	Netherlands
Engineering company – manufacturing electronic heat inductors for the automotive industry	USA since 1998 (originally British)
Four clothing factories	England
White goods plant	Italy since 1998 (originally USA)
Small electrical goods plant	Germany since 1998 (founded under joint British and German ownership)

in gaining access to managers and trade union representatives but there was greater difficulty in gaining access to ordinary employees and company documentation was variable in both content and quality of information on collective agreements.

Brief profiles of the factories studied are outlined in Table 9.1. From this it becomes immediately apparent that ownership is internationalized and all the factories take the form of a subsidiary or 'branch' factory, although this was not as a result of specific selection by the researcher.

Regional policy and inward investment

The ownership of the case study factories illustrates a major feature of Welsh manufacturing employment, namely its reliance on inward investors to the region. It has been argued by Thomas that 'the major forces which have shaped the growth of the Welsh economy have been international' due to its reliance, past and present, on inward investment and the export trade (1962: 1). This tradition continues and exhibits a tendency to grow rather than to diminish: in 1976, 13.1 per cent of Welsh plants were foreign owned and employed 41,500 people, but by

Table 9.2 Employment in overseas owned manufacturing plants by country of ownership, 2000

Country of ownership	Number of plants	Number of companies	Employment (thousands)	Employment as % of total in overseas owned plants in Wales
USA	134	118	30.7	41.6
Canada	13	12	2.6	3.5
Japan	41	30	14.3	19.3
EC (excluding UK) of which:	131	113	19.6	26.6
Germany	37	30	6.8	9.2
France	21	19	3.1	4.2
Sweden	10	8	1.4	1.9
Asia	7	6	3.2	4.4
Other European	16	13	2.0	2.7
Other countries	14	12	1.4	1.9
Total overseas-owned plants	356	304	73.8	100.0

Source: *Digest of Welsh Statistics* (2001: 224).

1996 that figure had risen to 36.5 per cent of plants, employing an approximate total of 75,000 workers, that is, around one-third of current manufacturing employment (Williams, 1998: 35). Table 9.2 illustrates the current breakdown of employment in overseas-owned manufacturing plants in Wales.

Traditionally, the biggest investors in South Wales were companies from North America but, since the late 1980s, there has been an increase in the incidence of investment from countries such as Japan and Korea. US investment in British manufacturing has a history going back to the last quarter of the nineteenth century, but the years between 1939 and 1955 provided conditions that markedly stimulated the expansion of American business interests in Britain. American producers set up in the UK in order to sell their goods in sterling and thereby avoid the constraints of the post-war 'shortage of dollars' that limited their sales outlets; there was also a growing demand for and acceptance of American products in the UK; and new industries desired by the post-war UK government, such as petrochemicals, pharmaceuticals and electronics, demanded American expertise (Dunning, 1998: 8–31). South Wales had been a favoured location for the relocation of industry away from areas in England that were vulnerable to air attacks during the

Second World War (Thomas, 1962: 30) and, as American investment in the UK generally followed established geographical patterns of British industrialization, the region was a beneficiary, made even more attractive by its development policy (Dunning, 1998: 60–1).

Regional development grants have clearly helped to stimulate inward investment. The three main foci of regional assistance to inward investors in the UK were factory building, financial incentives and planning regulations, which encouraged investors to locate in disadvantaged areas rather than elsewhere. Over the years, the levels of public expenditure on regional development have varied according to political will and priorities and the terminology used to describe the region has similarly varied, with the industrial area of South Wales being designated a 'Special Area', then an 'Assisted Area' and now has 'Objective One' status conferred by the European Union. The key goal of regional policy has, however, always been to take 'work to the workers' (McKenna and Thomas, 1988: 263).

The US post-war investment was primarily focused in technologically advanced sectors of manufacturing, where it already held some degree of competitive advantage. This can be contrasted with a new wave of investment from Japan in the 1970s, which concentrated on labour-intensive, standardized production with limited need or potential for technological research. Japan has become an increasingly important source of investment in Wales since the late 1980s and is now the second largest investor in the region. Early trail-blazing Japanese investors in South Wales, such as Sony, were influential in providing a powerful example to compatriot firms that Japanese firms could succeed in the region (Morris et al., 1993: 4–11). The greenfield jobs created in this process were welcomed in South Wales, but there were concerns that the type of employment being offered by Japanese investors was low skill and primarily focused on female workers (Morris et al., 1993: 23). Undoubtedly, the work is very different from that which had prevailed in the traditional South Wales industrial region, and it has been argued that 'highly skilled, well paid, mainly male jobs are being replaced by de-skilled, low paid, mainly female jobs' in industries, which are either non-union or governed by single-union agreements (George and Mainwaring, 1988: 9). This raises concerns about future skill levels as forecasts predict that, as manufacturing faces further challenges in the coming years, indigenous producers will decline more rapidly than inward investors in the region, with the anticipated result that by 2010 foreign-owned manufacturing could account for around 50 per cent of manufacturing employment in Wales (Roberts et al., 2001: 25).

The Third Report of the Select Committee on Trade and Industry (2001) to the British Parliament notes that the UK has much to recommend it as a location for manufacturing, in particular, a 'stable macroeconomic environment' and 'workforce flexibility' (see Chapter IV, para. 86), but that the developed nature of this economy brings with it costs which may outweigh the limited adaptability and attractiveness of relatively low-skilled workers which are anyway plentiful in the global labour market. During the research process, it was noted that acceptance of the realities of market pressures across the sectors pervaded the attitudes of workers and managers alike. Their concern with levels of productivity was frequently voiced, but in discussions about new company outlets in other locations, there was, in general, a clear perception that overseas outlets would not be able to match Welsh standards of skill and quality. While this is still true of the clothing plants at the present time, for British manufacturing in general this is a long outdated perception. Lane has pointed to the predominance of accountants in British management, the voluntarist institutional framework, and the focus on short-term returns on capital investment contributing to underinvestment in training and an 'inclination to compete on price rather than on skill based quality' (1994: 172). This does not bode well either for the survival of the British manufacturing sector in general, or for the case study factories in particular, where even current low levels of skill are being effectively eroded by the implementation of new technologies.

The subsidiary or 'branch' factory

A further feature highlighted by the case study factories is Welsh manufacturing's 'heavy reliance' on the subsidiary, or branch factory, a status that is seen to make establishments vulnerable to closure if market conditions change (George and Mainwaring, 1988: 188–97). Whilst the relationship between branch factory status and ease of closure may not be straightforward or inevitable, the role played by the factory within the parent company and the absence of managerial functions such as research and development and marketing are clearly factors taken into account when selecting a plant for closure (Fothergill and Guy, 1990: 99–137; see also Geppert et al., this volume). In Welsh plants, it has been reported that amongst inward investors in general the incidence and level of research and development is low, with Japanese ventures establishing sites with the greatest limitations (Young, 1989: 59–63). This has implications for the skill levels of workers and the quality of the involvement of subsidiary factories within the parent company, and, ultimately, impacts upon their dispensability (Morris et al., 1993: 54).

All the plants studied had devolved budgets and a degree of autonomy about how to achieve their financial targets in line with 'divisionalized' structures associated originally with Anglo-American companies (Marginson and Sisson, 1994: 26; see also Mayer and Whittington, this volume). Centralized control of business units is, however, increased due to the transparency of their accounting systems and the increasingly common practice of pitting subsidiary factories against one another in the competition for business, which is seen as a means of driving up standards of performance in individual plants (Sisson, 1995: 56–80). In this competition, the strongest units will survive to enhance the prosperity of the parent company and weaker units will be sold, or, alternatively, their functions contracted out to cheaper providers. This focus on the individual plants has the effect of moving industrial relations bargaining down to the individual workplace and away from the national or industry level ((Marginson and Sisson, 1994: 27).

Industrial conflict

In 1998, there were no reported industrial stoppages of work within the manufacturing sector in Wales (Statistical Directorate of the National Assembly for Wales), reflecting the pattern of strike activity elsewhere in British manufacturing, which declined after 1979–80 and dipped significantly between 1984–85 (Lyddon, 1994: 12–16). This decline coincided in the UK with the first term in office in the 1980s of the Conservative government, when manufacturing was hit by recession and there were 'drastic cutbacks' in manufacturing employment, a process repeated in 1990–92 (Kessler and Bayliss 1998: 50). Tables 9.3 and 9.4 outline the incidence of industrial stoppages at work in Wales from 1985 onwards. The classification of 'manufacturing' changed in 1994; hence the statistics are split between two tables.

In analysing the fall in industrial action, managerial literature frequently attributes it to a transformation in the nature of industrial relations (McLoughlin and Gourlay, 1994: 2). There is an underlying managerial assumption here that harmony has replaced the outmoded concept of a conflict of interests within the employment relationship and has moved the conduct of industrial relations 'away from adversarial approaches towards the generation of commitment' (Edwards, 1992: 359). However, within the asymmetrical power relations of the employment contract, it can be erroneous to equate the absence of overt collective industrial action with employee contentment. Many factors inhibit collective action, not least the 'demonstration effect' of the failure of other workers to secure their objectives by using strike action (Hyman,

Table 9.3 Number of industrial stoppages in Wales 1985–94

Manufacturing industry	1985	1986	1987	1988	1989	1990	1991	1992	1993	1994
Metals, engineering and vehicles	14	8	15	8	11	14	5	–	1	1
All other manufacturing industries	13	12	10	8	6	4	2	3	1	2
Total	27	20	25	16	17	18	7	3	2	3

Source: Digest of Welsh Statistics (2001).

Table 9.4 Number of labour disputes in Wales 1994–2000

Industry	1994	1995	1996	1997	1998	1999	2000
Manufacturing	3	3	5	2	-	2	-

Source: *Digest of Welsh Statistics* (2001).

1989: 226). In addition, in the UK context, where a legal right to strike does not exist and striking workers may be dismissed for being in breach of their employment contract, there may be the real fear of unemployment and legal penalties to take into account (Edwards, 1991: 27).

Having considered the regional context of the case studies, the next section of the chapter will discuss some empirical results from the case study factories. Despite the varied product range, there were some marked similarities which can be related to a central feature of managerial strategy, namely the use of the concept of 'globalization' as a rationale to justify change in the workplace.

Globalization as a managerial rationale for workplace change

As the fieldwork progressed, it became apparent that the language of human resource management and flexibility, along with the fear of competitive pressure, was ubiquitous. Factory practices based upon teamwork, just-in-time initiatives, the elimination of job demarcation, high performance, new technology and a central focus on employees 'with the right attitude' had become well established as the perceived route to greater global competitiveness. This chapter cannot discuss the fieldwork in detail for each plant studied, so discussion is limited to plants, which exhibit the clearest, or the most extreme, examples of these practices. The more general results will be briefly tabulated for reference. The discussion of the findings will focus on the fear of unemployment, the role of the trade union and the likelihood of success in preserving manufacturing employment.

Fear of unemployment

Writing in 1989 about productivity gains in UK manufacturing industry, Metcalf reviewed the various rationales behind the changes and concluded that 'Fear must be what matters here' (Metcalf, 1989: 19). He was referring to the fear of business collapse on the part of employers and the fear of unemployment on the part of employees – in his view, it was this that had galvanized managers and workers into making changes to work practices and thereby raising output. Referring particularly to the region currently under review in this chapter, Danford has described the use of managerial 'manipulation of the perpetual fear of unemployment in South Wales' in order to increase managerial discretion (Danford, 1999: 177). Any threat must, however, be credible to have an effect, and empirical findings from the case studies highlight actions taken by parent companies that have demonstrated the vulnerability of each plant to closure. Table 9.5 gives details of the numbers employed at the various plants prior, during and following the introduction of new working practices. In every case, redundancies and threats of closure preceded a change in working practice which was often associated with the introduction of new technology. Table 9.5 shows that some redundancies were declared as the research progressed, despite the successful introduction of changes to working practices in the plants concerned.

The regional context of industrial restructuring further focuses workers' minds upon the consequences of failure to compete in world

Table 9.5 Triggers for change and numbers employed in the case study factories

Manufacturing unit	Nos employed
Light electronics	2200 in 1999/2000 700 permanent redundancies + 500 temps Terminated 2001
Upholstered furniture factories 1 and 2	Factory 1: 300 in 1999/2000 Winding down 2001 Factory 2: 300 in 1999/2000 Still in production
Auto components plant	Originally 1800 in 1970s, now reduced to 250
Metal manufacture 1	Steady fall – tens of thousands Latest reduction – 3,000 in 2001
Metal manufacture 2	Reduced from 1400 in 1960s to 400 today
Specialist engineering	From 300 in 1970s to 100 in 1990, reduced to 45 in 2000
Clothing factories	Factory 1: 300 Factory 2: 300 Factory 3: 190 – Closed 2001 Factory 4: 200 – under notice of closure 2001
White goods	Reduced from 5000 in 1960s to 400 workers today
Small electrical goods	Redundancies in 1990s halved workforce to 45. Aims to grow again

markets. South Wales has acquired a reputation for 'militancy' in its industrial relations but this is related more to the coal industry rather than general manufacturing or other occupations. The consequences of this reputation for redundant miners and steelworkers have been considerable. Stereotyped as 'antagonistic' and 'difficult to manage', redundant miners and steelworkers have found it difficult to find alternative employment after pit closures and steel redundancies in the 1980s and 1990s, according to a Coalfields Communities Campaign official interviewed. A local study reported that, after one pit closure, 70 per cent of those made redundant did not work again; this was felt to be representative of the experience of miners elsewhere in the coalfield as well as steelworkers due to the depressed labour markets (Wass, 1988: 14–15). Thus the fate of some of the most well-organized and best-paid workers in the industrial region provide contemporary workers with an unenviable example of long-term unemployment. This came after being made redundant from industries where industrial relations were classed as 'adversarial' and the cost of their products was seen as uncompetitive.

The potential for plant closure is enhanced by the UK's national institutions and its essentially voluntarist framework (Whitley, 2000; see also Tempel, and Royle, this volume). For example, employment legislation on redundancy is less rigorous than elsewhere in Europe. In the early months of 2001, the British Trade and Industry Commons Select Committee heard evidence from senior trade unionists that British workers are losing jobs in the global market for labour because 'it is easier to sack them than their European counterparts', due to shorter statutory periods of consultation, lower statutory minimum redundancy payments and the absence of any requirement on an employer in the UK to fund a social plan in the event of a mass redundancy. The Select Committee's response to this allegation was to agree, saying that 'the suggestion that it is easier and cheaper to dispose of employees in the UK than elsewhere seems to us to have been shown to be factually correct' (Third Report, 2001, Chapter IV, paras 87–91).

Thus, the highly credible threat of job loss or factory closure in the UK has a dual effect of stirring up the fear of unemployment and providing an incentive for the acceptance of change, as the logic behind managerial action is presented as being for the common good (Terry, 1989: 194). In this context, the managerial ideology of unitarism, that is, 'we're all in this together', can be legitimized and acts as a very powerful agent of change, particularly in terms of bringing trade union representatives on board. In this way, the balance of bargaining power between the parties to the employment contract is shifted significantly in management's favour, and presents trade union representatives with a real dilemma in relation to the representation of their members' interests. It is to an examination of the role of trade union representatives that we now turn.

The role of the trade union

The relative lack of state regulation and the demise of national bargaining structures in the UK allow great scope for variation in trade union activity in different workplaces (Cully et al., 1999: 84). The research unearthed individual idiosyncrasies in some of the sites, but perhaps a more interesting feature was the degree of uniformity in the behaviour of the lay workplace representatives across the various manufacturing sectors. Findings from the case study companies suggest that trade union representatives have largely moved towards strategies of workplace partnership with employers in order to protect manufacturing jobs in the highly competitive global market for work. In the process, workplace union representatives have facilitated, and even championed, changes to working practices, which managers have argued are essential to the continued survival of their business (see also Tempel, this volume). However, these 'partnerships' for change cannot be compared with the forms of strategic social partnership found elsewhere in Europe, as they are essentially defensive, localized, workplace-centred, operational partnerships founded on the relative weakness of trade unions in the current UK labour market, rather than on their strength (Tailby and Whitston, 1989: 1–21).

Table 9.6 illustrates the different roles played by trade unions in the case study factories. All plants except two were unionized and the union's current role in each plant was described in terms of being 'reasonable' or 'constructive' by management. There was frequently reference to workplace union representatives having obstructed change initially, but in several plants, for example light electronics, clothing, auto components, metal manufacture and white goods, previous union representatives had either stood aside or been voted out in workforce ballots and had been replaced by individuals described by managers as 'reasonable' in their approach.

The association of traditional, now exhausted industries, such as coal, with high levels of unemployment allows managers to blame adversarial industrial relations as being partly responsible for their decline, since it is said to have led to their products being priced out of the market. They then argue that current trade union strategies need to

Table 9.6 Manufacturing units and the trade union role

Manufacturing unit	Union role
Light electronics	Single union – conciliatory
Upholstered furniture factories 1 and 2	Factory 1: Single union – well organized and engaged in continuous improvement with management Factory 2: Single union – traditional bargaining stance but amenable to changes
Auto components plant	Single union – strong partnership agreement
Metal manufacture 1	Multi-union but dominated by one union, now collaborating in changes to traditional working practice
Metal manufacture 2	Multi-union but dominated by one union – partnership relations
Specialist engineering	No union recognition
Clothing factories	Varies from union incorporation to traditionally adversarial but rarely challenges the right to manage
White goods	On site reluctant partnership
Small electrical goods	No union recognized

focus on the competitive realities. However, the resultant ('fear of the dole and fear of the customer') (Danford, 1999: 180) can undermine the rhetoric of commitment and empowerment in use in all the plants surveyed and adversely affect plant performance, unless trade union representatives and workers have some avenue of hope. In the case studies, this was provided by managerial assertions that the battle for survival was a common struggle for (everyone) – managers, trade unions and workers alike – and that there was a real possibility of success if targets were achieved.

For example, in the auto components plant, which was the clearest example of a workplace partnership between management and the trade union, great attention had been paid to encouraging the trade union representative and workers to 'identify the enemy'. The workforce in this plant faces a multifaceted challenge to its survival from alternative products and alternative labour from within the parent company, as well as from external producers. The effect of this was to draw plant management and the union steward into a very strong partnership. Kelly argues that 'employers are increasingly aware of the role played by language in framing the way employees think about issues'

(1998: 55), and this was particularly well demonstrated in this plant. The idea of being an 'embattled' site united against 'the competition' meant that anyone outside the plant, be it a member of the trade union hierarchy or a representative of senior management within the parent company, qualified for the epithet of potential 'enemy'.

Walton and McKersie, in their study of the behavioural theory of negotiations, point out that in the 1990s union negotiators frequently found themselves

> operating in a negative bargaining range, between, on the one hand, the demands of the employer to meet competitive realities and, on the other hand, the unwillingness of union members to accept changes they perceive as a 'step backward' (1991: xx).

This tension was present in all the factories with union representation and manifested itself in many forms, from mild expressions of discontent with the actions of union representatives in, for example the auto components plant, to spontaneous short-lived industrial action without reference to the trade unions by shop-floor workers in one clothing plant and the white goods plant.

The issues raised by the new working practices, the role played by the trade union and the tensions generated are very evident in the situation at the light electronics plant. Here, the handling of the introduction of annualized hours highlights the issues of power, managerial prerogative, the union role and worker response. A system of annualized hours was introduced to employees in 1994. Savings accrued to the firm as overtime premia were eradicated and they felt they were better able to manage output. The workforce accepted annualized hours as an alternative to redundancies, but over time the working patterns have become stressful and are the cause of great shop-floor resentment, which is focused as much on the workplace union representatives as it is towards the plant management. The chief union negotiator described himself as a committed trade unionist and a firm negotiator and managers described him as 'reasonable'; however, in the workers' view, he was seen as 'too soft with management' and 'in management's pocket'. Uppermost in his mind was the consideration that the company had just opened a plant in the Czech Republic, where wages were in the region of £100 per month, a fraction of the earnings of production line workers in South Wales, many of whom earned around £300 per week. Some lower level work was already being transferred from the plant overseas and, in his opinion, industrial action to enforce a change in the annualized hours arrangements simply could not be countenanced in these circumstances. The restraining influence of the union representative in this example was typical of shop steward behaviour in the other unionized case study plants and has resonance with the findings of the Donovan Commission on British Industrial Relations, which reported in 1968 that shop stewards were more often than not a 'moderating influence' in British workplace relations (1968: 29, para. 110).

Influential trade union representatives offer a powerful avenue of communication with the workforce. In general, empirical findings from this research suggest that in highly organized plants such as metals manufacture and the auto components plant, the nature of the changes to working practices was more coherent and comprehensive than in factories where unions had traditionally had less influence. In the case of well-organized industries, factors such as job demarcation and so-called 'restrictive' practices gave managers a greater incentive to introduce change and here the appeal to the logic of change had been made very forcibly to trade union representatives, who had frequently responded by championing the changes themselves. In one of the metals plants, a senior union representative asserted with some pride that 'they [management] couldn't have done it without us [the trade union] – the men just wouldn't have accepted the changes'. This result is in line with the 1998 Workplace Employee Relations Survey that reported a positive correlation between the introduction of high commitment management practices and high union density in UK workplaces (Cully et al., 1999: 111). Contrastingly, in factories where the trade union had achieved a lower level of formal regulation of employment, for example in the clothing plants, workplace change was characterized by a more ad hoc and reactive managerial approach. Here, there were fewer rigid demarcations of work to break down and it was easier for management to enforce their decisions unilaterally, based on traditional hierarchical relations of authority with workers, without the need to enlist the help of trade union representatives.

In adopting strategies of cooperation with management, frequently regarded as 'collaboration' by their members, workplace union representatives in the case study factories are not alone. The widespread managerial focus on leaner, more flexible methods of production crosses national and sectoral boundaries, and many trade unions have cooperated in their introduction. This involves their acceptance of the inevitability of the restructuring of the work process in the interests of competitive advantage and their concentration on preserving the employment and terms and conditions of the workers involved, in what has been described as a form of 'global business unionism'. However, it is argued unequivocally by Moody that such policies, wherever in the world they occur, are a 'dead end for workers and their unions' because they are simply unlikely to succeed in their objectives. He asserts that, in the longer term, transnational corporations will move work and/or change terms and conditions in order to best serve their corporate strategy, no matter what short-term concessions are made by workers (Moody, 1997: 2–3). The research findings in the case study plants show that, although, superficially at least, industrial harmony appears to have been achieved by means of union–management policies of partnership in change, the UK's institutional framework and the actions of the employers suggest that the case study factories do not provide secure working futures for manufacturing workers in the global marketplace for labour, despite the conciliatory stance of the majority of workplace representatives.

Prospects of success if factory targets are achieved

Where change has been effected and profits are being generated, are manufacturing workers in the case study companies more secure in their employment prospects? The example of the auto components plant appears to indicate that it does indeed have a long-term future within the parent company, providing its production and quality levels are maintained and new business is secured. In some of the other plants, however, this appeared to be an unlikely scenario and the long-term future of the plants and workers seems precarious, despite the adoption of changes to working practices and the sacrifice of hard-won industrial relations traditions, such as privileges related to 'seniority' in the metals manufacturing and engineering plants.

Although the clothing plants had few such privileges to lose, there had been considerable change in two of the four factories studied as they moved to the use of microelectronically controlled production systems, which allow for the implementation of just-in-time principles and the minimization of inventory. Managers asserted that all the South Wales' factories could maintain their existence if their productivity and quality remained high. However, although their parent company was British, it had extensive manufacturing capacity in Morocco and all its factories in the UK and elsewhere were in competition with one another for the total available work. The phrase frequently on the lips of managers at these plants was 'Our only competitors are ourselves'. The parent company had dispatched most of its labour-intensive work from the

South Wales' plants without microelectronics overseas, and retained only high-volume, simple skill, 'staple' products in these factories. This action was taken despite the currently higher skill levels and efficiency ratings of the plants in South Wales. It can be inferred from this that the low cost of labour in their overseas subsidiaries more than compensated for their weaknesses in these areas. Significant quality problems in the overseas outlets militated against the complete transfer of production, although, in any case, this is something that the parent company had assured the workers in South Wales it did not intend to do. However, in 2001, the factories without microelectronic production systems were targeted: one was closed and the second was given three month's notice of closure. Production from the closed unit was to be transferred to the company's outlets in Morocco. The factory under notice of closure had at that time an overall efficiency rating of 70 per cent, with weekly profits of around £20–30,000. Its counterpart unit in Morocco, with an efficiency rating of 30 per cent was producing weekly profit figures of around £250,000. The unit in South Wales remains on monthly notice of its fate and workers believe that they will be retained only until overseas ratings on quality and performance improve. This is a clear example of a unit which has met all its targets, yet is unlikely to survive. Similarly, in the case of one of the metals manufacturing plants, despite its high productivity and quality and its achievement of targets, it was chosen as the locus for mass redundancies. The reason suggested for this was that it was selected in preference to a large plant in the Netherlands, where statutory regulations on redundancy would have led to higher costs for the parent company.

These are not the only examples where significant challenges have come from manufacturing around the globe. All the plants studied are facing significant challenges from countries with markedly lower labour costs – for example Poland, the Czech Republic, China and India – and several have opened their own plants in these locations. Furniture manufacturers at the lower end of the price market, for example, face enormous competition from cheaper producers in Eastern Europe, where upholsterers are currently earning around £100 per month in comparison with upholsterers in South Wales who earn around £500 per week including productivity bonuses. Managers admitted privately that, although meeting their production targets, they were unlikely to be able to compete in the longer term and, since the research was completed, one furniture factory has been given notice of closure. Table 9.7 illustrates how all the case study plants are investing in manufacturing locations overseas.

Table 9.7   Investment committed to sites of production overseas

Manufacturing unit by product	Focusing investment in other locations
Light electronics	Czech Republic
Upholstered furniture factory 1	Poland, China
Upholstered furniture factory 2	Poland, China
Auto components plant	USA
Metal manufacture 1	Europe
Metal manufacture 2	USA, Australia – internationally
Specialist engineering	India, USA, southern England
Clothing	Morocco
White Goods	Italy, also sourcing components from Eastern Europe, for example Romania
Small electrical goods	Germany

This transfer of investment in taking place despite the fact that Wales, and South Wales in particular, has one of the lowest cost labour markets in the UK. In 2000, Wales had average weekly earnings just £2 higher, at £368 per week, than the northeast of England, which has the lowest average level wages amongst all the UK regions (*New Earnings Survey*, Part E, April 2000). However, as shown earlier, these rates of pay are significantly higher than in manufacturing locations in Eastern Europe and other developing economies around the globe. When the investment plans of parent companies, such as those studied here, are examined, managerial assurances of plant survival in return for changes to working practices, which often amounts to the erosion of working conditions, seem disingenuous to the objective observer.

Conclusion

This paper has focused on empirical research undertaken in a mature industrialized region of the UK, where the threat of unemployment is very real in the minds of workers. Traditional norms of industrial relations within the case study factories have all been challenged by the new global context for competition (see also Tempel, this volume). Massive 'demanning' had taken place in the majority of the companies studied, thereby increasing the credibility of the risk of unemployment and influencing the power relations between the parties to the employment relationship to the advantage of the employer. Resulting trade union and worker fears have been a catalyst for acceptance of changes in working practices, often facilitated or championed by workplace union representatives. Moves towards partnership between managers and unions at plant level are being pursued as a means of enhancing competitiveness, increasing productivity and flexibility and, ultimately, protecting jobs, but empirical evidence suggests that, in the words of Terry, such 'atomised unionism' is 'unlikely to wield effective power' (1994: 247) in pursuit of its objectives. The subsidiary status of the plants in South Wales makes them vulnerable to closure, and the relatively low level of workforce skill and the institutional context of industrial relations in the UK does little to present any obstacles to exit, although the transfer of operations to new factories does take time and involves the addressing of issues of quality and speed of response in some cases.

As product markets expand and change, the global market in labour is a constant threat to the longer term survival of manufacturing in regions such as South Wales, particularly where skill levels are relatively low, as is the case in the majority of the factories studied. Skill levels in clothing, furniture, and light electronics were not high and even in the higher skill areas such as metals industries, the white goods factory and auto component production, the introduction of new computerized automation was eroding traditional skill requirements. This has resonance with the longstanding debate over the gap between the rhetoric and reality of HRM (Lane, 1994; Legge, 1995; Moody, 1997). Despite the prevalence of the language of HRM, the introduction of new working practices in the case study companies was concerned with cost minimization rather than truly empowering or 'up-skilling' the workforce to be able to compete globally. In line with Lane's argument that the response of British unions has been 'poorly developed or mainly defensive' (1994: 181; also Marginson and Sisson, 1994: 30–1), empirical findings in South Wales support the view that the shift in the balance of power away from labour during the 1980s and 1990s has delivered workplace representatives who are nervous of challenging the validity of this cost-focused managerial approach. Products, in the main, continue to be differentiated by low-cost production rather than innovative product design or high levels of research and development in the regional factories and workplace-centred union strategies do not present an effective challenge to the parent company's strategies (Terry, 1994).

As branch plants of multidivisional companies, the subsidiaries in South Wales have limited opportunity to influence the parent companies' investment decisions. The assessment of the success of the multidivisional model of firms tends to centre on the survival of the global company as a whole and some judge the structure to be a robust and successful model of organization in that context (see Mayer and Whittington, this volume). However, the separation of strategy from operational decision-making in the multidivisional company tends to favour systems of corporate governance based on the 'outsider' system. This 'outsider' system is associated with Anglo-American companies and may lead companies to see their employees as 'disposable liabilities' rather than assets (Marginson and Sisson, 1994: 31). The case studies in South Wales illustrate the closures and redundancies faced by several of the plants to ostensibly ensure the survival of the parent company. Simply meeting productivity targets for standardized goods, whose production is associated with lower levels of skill, does not guarantee the continuity of the plants and the jobs involved. The demise of manufacturing capability is something that British managers seem to be able to accept far more easily than their European competitors (see Geppert et al. this volume) and, although senior figures in the British government, employers' organizations and the trade union movement frequently voice concerns about the future of the sector, employer strategies and institutional structures appear to be working against the retention of existing jobs or the promotion of new investment in high-skill manufacturing employment. In the light of these facts and in the context of the global market in labour, the inescapable conclusion is that assurances of secure futures in return for workplace change cannot realistically be made to workers in any of the regional factories studied in connection with this research. Manufacturing industry currently contributes less than 20 per cent to the overall UK economy. It seems clear from this regionally based fieldwork that, unless change occurs at an institutional level to improve the skills and 'marketability' of the UK manufacturing workforce to enable it to compete on a global scale, this contribution of manufacturing is destined to decline still further.

References

Cully, M., Woodland, S., O'Reilly, A. and Dix, G., *Britain At Work – as Depicted by the 1998 Workplace Employee Relations Survey* (London, Routledge 1999).

Danford, A., *Japanese Management Techniques and British Workers* (London, Mansell 1999).

Digest of Welsh Local Area Statistics National Assembly for Wales (2001) Digest of Welsh Statistics, National Assembly for Wales (2001).

Donovan, Lord, *Royal Commission on Trade Unions and Employers' Associations 1965–68 Report* (London, HMSO 1968).

Dunning, J. H., *American Investment in British Manufacturing Industry* (London, Routledge 1998).

Edwards, P. K., 'Will the Giant Wake?' *People Management* September (1991) 26–9.

Edwards, P. K., 'Industrial Conflict: Themes and Issues in Recent Research' *British Journal of Industrial Relations* 30, 3 September (1992) 359–403.

Financial Times 'Blair offers measures to ease business burden' (06.11.01) page 4.

Fothergill, S., Guy, N., *Retreat from the Regions – Corporate Change and the Closure of Factories* (London, Jessica Kingsley and Regional Studies Association 1990).

George, K. D. and Mainwaring, L. (eds) *The Welsh Economy* (Cardiff, University of Wales Press 1988).

Hyman, R., *Strikes* (4th edn) (London, Macmillan 1989).

Kelly, J., *Rethinking Industrial Relations – Mobilization, Collectivism and Long Waves* (London, Routledge 1998).

Kessler, S. and Bayliss, F., *Contemporary British Industrial Relations*, (3rd edn) (London, Macmillan 1998).

Lane, C., 'Industrial Order: Britain, Germany and France' in Hyman, R. and Ferner, A. (eds) *New Frontiers in European Industrial Relations* (Oxford, Basil Blackwell 1994).

Legge, K., *Human Resource Management – Rhetorics and Realities* (London, Macmillan 1995).

Lyddon, D., Recent British Strike Trends: Disaggregation, The Demonstration Effect and 'Turning Points' (1994) Paper to British Universities Industrial Relations Association.

Marginson, P. and Sisson, K., 'The Structure of Transnational Capital in Europe: the Emerging Euro-company and its Implications for Industrial Relations' in Hyman, R. and Ferner, A. (eds) *New Frontiers in European Industrial Relations* (Oxford, Basil Blackwell 1994).

McKenna, C. J. and Thomas, D. R., 'Regional Policy' in George, K. D. and Mainwaring, L. (eds) *The Welsh Economy* (Cardiff, University of Wales Press 1988).

McLoughlin, I. and Gourlay, S., *Enterprise Without Unions – Industrial Relations in the Non-Union Firm* (Buckingham, Open University Press 1994).

Metcalf, D., 'Water Notes Dry Up: The Impact of the Donovan Reform Proposals and Thatcherism At Work on Labour Productivity in British Manufacturing Industry', *British Journal of Industrial Relations* 27, 1 (1989) 1–31.

Millward, N., Bryson, A. and Forth, J., *All Change at Work? British Employment Relations 1980–1998, as portrayed by the Workplace Industrial Relations Survey Series* (London, Routledge 2000).

Moody, K., *Workers In A Lean World* (London, Verso 1997).

Morris, J., Munday, M. and Wilkinson, B., *Working for the Japanese – the Economic and Social Consequences of Japanese Investment in Wales* (London, The Athlone Press 1993).

New Earnings Survey, Part E (2000) Department of Employment, London.

Roberts, A., Bryan, J., Jones, C. and Munday, M., 'Welsh Economic Review' *Cardiff Business School* 13, 2 (2001) 5–25.

Sisson, K., 'Organisational Structure' in Tyson S. (ed.) *Strategic Prospects for HRM* (London, IPD 1995).

Tailby, S. and Whitston, C. (eds) *Manufacturing Change – Industrial Relations and Restructuring* (Oxford, Basil Blackwell 1989).

Terry, M., 'Recontextualising Shopfloor Industrial Relations: Some Case Study Evidence' in Tailby, S. and Whitston, C. (eds) *Manufacturing Change – Industrial Relations and Restructuring* (Oxford, Basil Blackwell 1989).

Terry, M., 'Workplace Unionism: Structures and Objectives' in Hyman, R. and Ferner, A. (eds) *New Frontiers in European Industrial Relations* (Oxford, Basil Blackwell 1994).

Third Report of the British Parliament Trade and Industry Select Committee 2001.

Thomas, B., (ed.) *The Welsh Economy – Studies in Expansion* (Cardiff, University of Wales Press 1962).

Walton, R. E. and McKersie, R. B., *A Behavioral Theory of Labor Negotiations – an Analysis of a Social Interaction System* (2nd edn) (Ithaca, NY, Cornell 1991).

Wass, V. J., 'Redundancy and Re-employment: Effects and Prospects following Colliery Closure' *Coalfield Communities Campaign Working Papers* 5 (1988) 3–23.

Whitley, R., *Divergent Capitalisms: The Social Structuring and Change of Business Systems* (Oxford, Oxford University Press 2000).

Williams, L. J., *Digest of Welsh Historical Statistics 1974–1996* (Government Statistical Service 1998).

Young, S., 'Scotland vs. Wales in the Inward Investment Game' *Quarterly Economic Commentary* 14, 3 (1989), 59-63.

Part III

Globalization and the Institutional and Cultural Framework of Europe: An Outlook

10
The Effects of Globalization on State–Business Relationships: A Conceptual Framework

Ian M. Taplin

> Impersonal forces of world markets, integrated...by private enterprise in finance, industry and trade are more powerful than states to whom ultimate political authority over society and economy is supposed to belong
>
> (Strange, 1996)

> States exhibit considerable adaptability and variety – both in their responses to change and in their capacity to mediate and manage international and domestic linkages, including in particular the government-business relationship
>
> (Weiss, 1998)

Do governments matter anymore? Given the rhetoric on the globalization of business practices, the apparently unstoppable growth of multinational enterprises following transnational mergers and acquisitions and claims by some that state power has been eroded so much as to make centralized decision-making, especially by smaller states, irrelevant, one might think not. When one examines the international spread of financial markets, the interpenetration of industries across borders, the spatial reorganization of production and the growth of supranational trade associations, it is perhaps easy to assume that globalization is ubiquitous and its impact has emasculated the state. Even amongst those who question the one-way causality implicit in many popularizers of global trends (Mittelman, 2000), there is a tendency to adduce a powerful logic to the dynamics of globalization.

With technology given primacy in the almost instantaneous spread of information, the communications revolution has eroded many of the cultural barriers in societies and transformed many aspects of civil society (Hutton and Giddens, 2000). In doing so, states are assumed to have lost much of their potency as arbiters of change and defenders of last resort. Having domesticated the harsher aspects of the market economy (Kuttner, 2000), they have been relegated to the sidelines of a self-regulated global economy of the type that Adam Smith might easily have envisioned.

In this chapter, I critically evaluate these claims, particularly those that relegate the state to a position where its activities are severely delimited. In doing so, I raise questions about what role the state *does* play and how part of its continued legitimacy rests upon its ability to provide an institutional framework that buttresses market activity.

I start by looking at the rise of the nation state and its interdependence with the growth of capitalism. From this, it will be apparent that the state serves multiple functions, which are both indispensable for the continued growth of commerce and trade as well as its own legitimacy. In the next section, I examine the arguments that claim markets as the new masters of states. Looking particularly at the globalization of financial and capital markets, the transnationalization of business activity and the mobility of labour as well as the role of technological change, one can see how globalization might pose a challenge to state sovereignty. This is especially problematic in activist states, where a form of consensual capitalism prevails (for example, Germany) and where any erosion of state capacity to direct economic activities can have serious consequences.

This follows with an examination of the ways in which markets depend upon states to, for example, guarantee stable property rights, provide infrastructural support and legitimize institutional arrangements. These provisions, as can be seen in many of the other chapters in this book, are crucial, even in an interdependent global economy.

Underlying much of the discussion in this chapter is the pervasiveness of economic globalization in an age of political sovereignty. Does growing economic integration, as evidenced by cross-border flows of capital and goods, constrain state governance? Despite fluctuations in business cycles, is there an inexorable logic of growth towards the liberal international order that will eventually produce a convergence of capitalist systems? Or, as some authors in this volume argue, do national capitalist systems retain a distinctiveness that will persist despite growing economic integration?

Capitalism and the nation state

By the fourteenth century, Italy, or, to be more precise, cities such as Venice, Pisa and Genoa were the centre of European and Mediterranean trade. Goods flowed through cities en route from the Middle East to markets in Northern Europe. Italian traders set up benches (*bancos*, from which the word bank is derived) with their scales and coins to exchange currency from different parts of the world and were the first to develop documents (bills of exchange) that provided a means to exchange money and credit in different currencies (Crosby, 1997; Landes, 1998). This greatly expanded the potential for trade and set the stage for the further growth of commerce and, eventually, capitalism.

As a system, capitalism separates the economic and the political (as feudalism did not) and, as a consequence, the last five centuries have been marked by two linked, but conceptually distinguishable, trends. One is economic, the other political. By economic, I refer to the growth of banking and trade, followed by industrialization and, more recently, the growth of globalized production, where components are manufactured in various separate countries then brought together for assembly in another country, together with foreign direct investment (FDI) that facilitates cross-border flows of capital and goods. Initially, capitalism developed as a set of national economies only loosely integrated (mainly through trade) but with quite separate producing and consuming spaces. Increased global economic integration has broken down this de facto autarky, although some argue that, even now, the world economy is still not truly global but is concentrated in a triad of areas (Europe, North America and South-East Asia) (Berger and Dore, 1996; Hirst and Thompson, 1996).

The second, political, trend is associated with the emergence of a system of nation states, the Westphalian system, out of a myriad of territorialities and empires of late feudalism. Sovereignty under this system was based upon a state-centric pattern of governance, in which enhanced domestic authority was predicated upon highly centralized organizational structures and defined, and generally accepted, geographic territoriality (see Held et al., 1999; Scholte, 2000). This process of consolidation took centuries to achieve, since it required the fusion of 'nation' and 'territory', which was only really possible when capitalism provided the economic means for financial and material stability.

The growth of mercantilism in the seventeenth century was the first systematic attempt to consolidate the embryonic nation states, both politically and economically. It saw states attempting to impose their own logic on economic events and, initially, they were somewhat successful. However, when this eventually declined, it pointed to the limitations of keeping capitalism as a purely local phenomenon. After the dynamism of the nineteenth and early twentieth centuries, in which vast individual fortunes were established and states pursued aggressive overseas expansion through imperialism, many assumed that the economic and political had been fused. Pointing to disappearing political boundaries on any map that shows financial flows and industrial activities, global integrationists, such as Ohmae (1990), foresee the withering away of states or, at least, a diminished governance capacity. Others claim that capitalism remains very much a national phenomenon (Rodrik, 1997) and that the state remains the final arbiter of fiscal reliability and the protector of property rights; features crucial for the maintenance of capitalist growth.

If we are to find a way out of this conceptual impasse, it is necessary to examine the functions of the nation state as they emerged under the Westphalian system. This can be used as a background against which one can analyse the globalization of economic activities and determine what effect such activities have had upon state responsibilities.

Responsibilities of states

Defending territory

Any notion of state activity involves some fundamental 'defense of the realm' feature that is central to state responsibility. Protecting its territorial integrity and maintaining control over its domestic geography and, to some extent, the people within it have been longstanding concerns of states and their rulers. While large standing armies are a feature of the twentieth century, even medieval rulers were required to assemble soldiers from time to time to deal with domestic insurgencies and overseas threats. But armies cost money and hence forms of taxation were introduced by states as legitimate ways to pay for such endeavours. States also borrowed heavily to fund their military adventures, furthering the interests of trader/bankers who underwrote such activities. Renaissance Italian princes protected their economic gains with the help of the German merchant Jacob Fugger; Britain fought the Napoleonic War with much financial assistance from the Rothschilds. States were seen by merchants as good investments, since they rarely defaulted and the long-term benefits such as preferred positions and so on were extensive. States, meanwhile, saw defending their territorial integrity as indispensable for their own continued legitimacy.

Maintenance of currency

Ever since the days of Italian merchants who established norms of currency convertibility, a primary function of the state has been to maintain currency stability. Without a stable medium of exchange, as Strange (1996) has argued, the market economy cannot function properly and a reliable savings and investment climate will be jeopardized. States introduce policies to regulate the money supply, adjust interest rates to either stimulate or contain spending and, more generally, regulate to maintain the value of the currency. Such monetary policies are often linked to taxation and fiscal policies, since this interdependence is an important element in national economic growth aims.

Admittedly, recent events associated with the adoption of the euro and the creation of a supranational European Central Bank in the European Union suggest that, perhaps, this is one area of state responsibility that might actually be changing. But it is important to note that admission to the euro zone was contingent upon countries meeting strict fiscal and budget criteria. This entailed member states exercising control of their currency at least prior to admission. I will return to this issue of supraterritorial constituencies, and what it entails in the case of the European Union, later.

Correcting cyclical market tendencies

Even prior to Keynes, states recognized that they had the responsibility to intervene in the marketplace in times of economic downturns. In the latter part of the nineteenth century, recessions were no longer seen as part of capitalism's ineluctable logic, against which states were powerless. Instead, because of their inevitability, states could develop policies to counter the more serious aspects of such recessions. They did this through various stimulus packages to restore confidence in market activities as well as to boost spending. Since Keynes and the Great Depression, the state's role in 'priming the pump of economic activity' (Strange, 1996: 75) has become more systematic, if not, in recent years, always so effective. Whilst it is debatable whether Keynesian counter-cyclical measures could still work in an interdependent global economy, the state nonetheless retains its role, as the body deemed ultimately responsible for intervening when market activities falter.

Welfare function

Since the late nineteenth century, it has been recognized that there will be less privileged individuals in society, for whom the state should assume some responsibility. These include the young and the old, the sick, as well as those who are unwitting victims of the marketplace. The latter include those who are involuntarily unemployed, together with those who, following work dislocation, need new skill sets. This 'cushioning of periodic dislocations', to use Kuttner's (2000: 151) term, and provision of social income have become crucial to the state's role in domesticating the market economy. How extensively the state involves itself in such welfare functions, however, varies greatly across societies (see Coates, 2000). Whereas Northern European states have extensive welfare provisions that offer a wide range of protections, including national health care systems, the United States has a much more limited programme of benefits. Nonetheless, the growth of the welfare function in the twentieth century has spawned the rise of state bureaucracies and, despite efforts in recent years to reduce expenditure, they continue to constitute a high percentage of GDP in most advanced capitalist nations.

States have also increasingly regulated the marketplace in order to protect consumers and workers. In the case of workers, this represents not only efforts to guarantee safety in the workplace, but also attempts to mediate employee–employer relations. For example, the institutional contours of collective bargaining are country specific and demonstrate the ability of states to project themselves into industry or workplace-specific conflict. Thatcher's programme of labour market deregulation in Britain was made possible, in part, by her victory over the miners in the industrial unrest of the 1980s. By essentially emasculating the National Union of Miners (NUM), she was able to impose an alternative system of industrial relations that constrained organized labour's role in contesting workplace struggles (see Winterton and Winterton, 1989). In recent years, states have also provided regulations to help special interest groups and meet more general quality-of-life demands; in addition, it has expressed, in varying degrees, a concern for human rights.

Because of the high cost of this welfare function, together with growing questions regarding its overall appropriateness and effectiveness in a market economy, states have been under great pressure in recent years to scale back and, where possible, privatize many of these activities. For many, this has been made possible by the economic growth of the 1990s and a decline in unemployment rates. However, the demographics of advanced industrial nations suggest that a rapidly growing ageing population will continue to put pressure on state pension provisions, especially since the ratio of working people to those who are retired has fallen in recent decades.

Taxation

Whenever states need money, whether for wars or welfare provisions, taxation is the preferred means of raising the necessary capital. Aside from organized crime groups, states have a monopoly on taxation. Either through progressive income taxes or sales taxes, states rely heavily upon the income generated from these sources to fund the burgeoning bureaucracies of the twentieth century. Without this source of income, much of the state's activities would grind to a halt and its governance rendered ineffective. One only has to look at infrastructural decline and rising poverty in Russia, where tax avoidance has become virtually institutionalized in certain sectors, to understand the consequences of such problems. But taxes have always been controversial, not only because individuals typically dislike losing income to the government, but also because of a longstanding distrust of where that income goes. Clearly, part of any state's legitimacy rests upon its ability to convince the vast majority of its population, both the general public as well as businesses, to pay the requisite taxes. Without this income stream, other state provisions dry up and this further undermines the stability in society.

Infrastructure support

Part of the income from taxes, especially user ones, goes to the building of an infrastructure (roads, airports and so on), which provides the basis for continued market activities. In the early nineteenth century, canal building was a major public project for many industrializing societies; this was followed by railroads from the mid-nineteenth century onwards, then highways and, more recently, aviation operational coordination. Such physical infrastructure can be privatized but, generally, the state takes the early initiatives, either directly or indirectly.

States also have a responsibility for the provision of public goods, such as education and the framework for and maintenance of a legal system. The latter confers continued predictability for economic transactions and guarantees property rights; the former provides a broad level of training so that citizens have the requisite basic skills sets, such as literacy and numeracy, to function effectively in society. This training also provides employers with workers who possess basic skills and who can more easily manage the transition into work process.

Challenges to state authority

It is clear from the above that states have acquired a wide range of responsibilities that are crucial for the smooth functioning of market economies. In many respects, states underwrite the rules of the game and provide essential levels of stability, without which market transactions would be plagued with even greater uncertainty. Yet, in recent decades, it has become clear that economic globalization and an expanding web of transnational regulatory institutions (Holton, 1998; Dicken, 1998) have challenged many of the aforementioned functions of the state. In Europe, the growth of the European Union constitutes a significant supranational regulatory body that has been successful in developing a broader constituency of interests. Exactly how much state sovereignty has suffered is open to extensive debate. It does appear that some regulatory governance has been effectively ceded to this body, especially in the area of monetary and industrial policy. However, individual states retain more than notional control over their territories and their capacity for unilateral action remains largely unfettered.

Whilst larger states clearly retain greater power over their activities than smaller ones, a reduction in state capacity does appear more evident in economic areas. Regionalization, in the form of trade agreements, and transworld governance through agencies such as the World Bank, International Monetary Fund and International Labour Office provide a broad framework for what is often a multi-layered regulatory pattern within which globalized economic activity thrives. But it is the driving force of multinational corporations (MNCs) and technological innovation that has transformed the dynamics of the market economy.

The technological revolution in microelectronics has dramatically increased the speed with which information can be communicated and, together with an increased globalization of media activities, permits information to be exchanged at a rapid rate. It has also made possible the massive flows of capital across political boundaries and helped to build integrated financial markets that have become increasingly transnational in character. MNCs continue to expand in size and power and their global presence has become a feature of the twenty-first-century landscape. They have become effective agents in technology transfer and use their economic clout to negotiate favourable tax rates as well as subsidies from governments. Together, these represent formidable forces for change. As Holton (1998: 80) presciently states:

> flows of investment, technology, communications and profit across national boundaries are often seen as the most striking symptom of global challenge to the nation state.

However, since globalized economic activities have been with us for a long time, why have these particular processes associated with it now assumed such dire consequences for states? The answer to this question lies in the interdependent nature of the changes in technology, trade and MNCs and the ways in which the resulting processes delimit some aspects of state authority whilst, somewhat ironically, depending upon other aspects for their continued development.

Technology, trade and the new global oligopolies

Throughout history, technological innovation has played an important role in reshaping economic activity. Its impact varies according to contextual factors and it is here that the relationship with the state is important. If we examine the rise of commercial activity during the Renaissance in Southern Europe and then the growth of industrialism in Northern Europe in the eighteenth century, we see centralized political entities providing institutional frameworks in which technological innovation can flourish.

Technology's impact varies greatly with the extent of change involved and the context in which it occurs. According to Freeman and Perez (1988), there are four broad types of technological change. Small-scale innovations and incremental changes occur on a fairly regular basis in most societies but in many cases they go unnoticed. More radical innovations can have a greater impact, but typically only when they occur in a cluster. For example, many of the incremental technological innovations associated with the mechanization of agriculture only became evident in the twentieth century when together they were seen as responsible for the displacement of the bulk of the agricultural population in western societies. Thirdly, changes in technology systems generally have wide-ranging consequences inasmuch as they transform economic activity and result in dramatically new ways of doing things. Events associated with the development of interchangeable parts in the mid-nineteenth century would be an example of such a change that had far-reaching organizational consequences. Finally, there are large-scale revolutionary changes, such as the change associated with the introduction of the steam engine, which result in a paradigmatic shift in the style of production and in the emergence of new products and a different way of conceiving economic activity.

Such a paradigmatic shift has occurred in the last few decades as innovations in microelectronics and communications technology have converged and created a powerful enabling force for the growth of international economic activity (Dicken, 1998). Initially separate developments, these two areas of innovation have become a complex organizational entity that we now refer to as information technology. It is this that enables goods to be easily and quickly transported and monitored; ideas and large amounts of information can now be transmitted globally and in an instantaneous fashion. This has led to a shrinking of space and encouraged all sorts of innovations in production systems such as just-in-time, flexibility, network clusters and so on, as well as a potentially new techno economic paradigm of post-Fordism (Vallas, 1999). Because such changes facilitate the internationalization of economic activity and the subsequent growth of MNCs, they are also seen as arbiters of standardization.

The western origin of much of this change has given a westernizing flavour to the process. Whether this further reinforces the notion of convergence, implicit in industrial capitalism, remains debatable. Although imitation and adaptation of technology has proven to be an effective path to industrial greatness, as demonstrated by Japan and, to some extent, the Asian tigers since the 1960s, factor endowments of the sort associated with institution building should not be dismissed. The failure of Argentina and Chile to sustain their late nineteenth-century economic growth, when the technological means for doing so were available, indicates that state policies do matter and there is no logic of technological inevitability. In fact, the path-dependent nature of technological change and its occurrence in areas where state governance capacity has been strongest (Dicken, 1998: 175) suggest that institutional forces continue to be important.

While trading organizations that facilitate the international exchange and shipment of goods have a long and often chequered history (Keay, 1991; Landes, 1998; Milton, 1999), the development of MNCs occurred in the late nineteenth century when they established foreign plants and engaged in FDI (Corley, 1989; Dunning, 1993). The growth of information technology has dramatically enhanced the capacity of MNCs to operate across borders (Castells, 1993; Holton, 1998). It is this transnational activity, and the apparent power that MNCs now have in seeking new locations for production whilst abandoning old ones, that leaves states at the mercy of such enterprises. The fact that many MNCs actively and successfully bargain with states over the provision of resources, such as relocation development grants, infrastructural support and reduced tax liabilities, lends credibility to arguments about increased state dependence upon MNCs for generating employment (and hopefully tax revenues). One only has to look at the various stimulus packages offered to Japanese car manufacturers to locate in the depressed region of northeast England in the late 1980s to understand how much leverage MNC are able to exercise in this project.

Despite the cross-border operational trends of MNCs, the concurrent growth of global cities has resulted in the concentration of much of this economic activity (Sassen, 1991). This process not only gives 'roots' to otherwise placeless MNCs but also reinforces the importance of core activities taking place in strategically important business centres that also happen to be major capitalist states. Much of the value-added activities of MNCs remain in the 'home' country and senior executives' preference for certain 'big city' locations help to cement their immobility.

Undoubtedly, what MNCs have furthered is international trade. Goods have been sold and traded across nascent political boundaries for thousands of years, suggesting that international economic activity is not a new phenomenon. Arguably, the commercial and capitalist revolutions in Europe from the fourteenth century onwards were predicated upon commodity exchanges that generated sufficient amounts of capital for subsequent reinvestment. Yet this type of international economic activity is different from the current transnational economy. The former is characterized by trade between national economies and can include capital flows and international migration; the latter builds upon this by adding transnational processes and institutions that permit far greater integration and standardization of activities (Holton, 1998). While global marketing has spawned a form of cultural universalism, the dramatic increase in transnational financial flows, in part made possible by the deregulation of financial markets in core economies and the privatization of former public monopolies, has increased the dependence of states on trade and investment from outside (Holton, 1998). Furthermore, much of this economic activity occurs within trans-border corporate networks and itself is a product of transnational mergers and acquisitions and the rise of global oligopolies (Scholte, 2000).

While it appears that the above forces have led to structural changes in competition, it is more difficult to determine how much states are subject to the constraints and discipline of capital. If investment decisions and strategic plans that are made in corporate headquarters in the financial capitals can significantly undermine local state initiatives, does this lead to weakened democratic control over economic policy? In the case of McDonald's discussed by Tony Royle in this volume, the company has been quite adept at subtly and overtly undermining local employment practices. Other US-based MNCs have embarked upon similar projects in their overseas expansion. This type of domestic governance crisis would seem a logical consequence of the sort of spatial reorganization that capitalism is currently undergoing.

Despite these trends, if one considers that the bulk of FDI in the last decade has gone to the major capitalist economies, economic and political stability typically trump risk when guaranteed returns appear probable. One only has to look at the MNCs that lost money in embryonic Russian markets during the 1990s to appreciate the benefits of institutional supports that underwrite market legitimacy. The fact that Russia has yet to stabilize its accounting system to offer transparency to future investors is indicative of the need of a regulatory environment, the benefits of which become conspicuous when it is absent. MNCs might appear arrogant in their presumptions about the irrelevance of local practices in some country settings but they nevertheless seek out institutional arrangements in which the replication of their practices is not too difficult.

The interdependent nature of the above changes has transformed global economic activities but such changes also need to be seen in the context of the growth of regional trading blocs and regional regulatory schemes. Trade has been regulated under GATT and now the World Trade Organization (WTO) with numerous initiatives designed to both support trade as well as protect markets in advanced industrial societies. Likewise, NAFTA, trade agreements within Latin America, the European Union and the Asia Pacific Economic Cooperation (APEC) have all promoted trans-border production and created institutions and trans-state laws to regulate economic activities. Furthermore, the growth of the IMF and the World Bank has provided an additional measure of fiscal regulation, albeit one that appears to have had a greater impact on developing countries than on the advanced industrial economies. Nonetheless, these agencies are part of the post-war global regulatory framework whose structures might be loose but whose influence on exchange rates, monetary policy and development capital remain considerable (Holton, 1998).

Whilst states remain crucial as instigators of such regionalization, and western states retain a powerful influence over this process, many of the institutional bodies that have emerged to provide administrative oversight of these entities have acquired a degree of autonomy from the respective states. Furthermore, since regional markets provide certain economies of scale for the distribution and sale of products, large MNCs have typically been a major beneficiary of such actions. The growth of regional consumption patterns, the commodification of a global culture and the emergence of what Scholte (2000: 147) refers to as 'transborder consciousness' have enabled product standardization to emerge, which in turn further benefits the large international firms.

One of the intriguing questions of recent decades, and the subtheme of this book, is how the actions of MNCs, together with the consequences of rapid technological change and this embryonic regionalization, have affected states with different types of capitalist regulation. Both Becker-Ritterspach et al. and Geppert et al. in this volume discuss the ways in which European MNCs are converging in key strategic practices whilst retaining a certain operational distinctiveness. Whether there is a universal recipe for effective corporate organization, and thus some principled form of convergence, is the subject of Mayer and Whittington's contribution. In these and other notable studies on the convergence of capitalist systems, much emphasis is given to discussing whether MNCs from different European, Japanese and North American bases exhibit a gradual homogenizing process in their principal activities and forms. For example, are Shell and BP indistinguishable from Exxon-Mobil and Chevron in their commitment to shareholder value and asset utilization?

Critics of this convergence approach argue the case for the resiliency of divergent capitalisms, especially with the growth of Eastern European and East Asian markets, where different societal institutions and agencies create distinctive business systems (Whitley, 1999). But another, albeit more general approach might be to look at the extent to which certain institutional settings facilitate the type of global economic activity that we are witnessing. This transfers the focus of MNC agency to the specific environment in which they operate. For example, nominally deregulated societies such as the USA and UK might find that their experience of a global economy, which is built around speed of reaction, faster product flows and a strong pressure on cost containment, is less challenging to their domestic institutional structure than in other countries. Conversely, the consensual capitalism of Germany and Scandinavia, where the emphasis is on regulated labour markets and corporatist institutional arrangements, might find itself on the defensive in the finance-driven capitalism that now prevails (Crouch and Streeck, 1997). Perhaps the less directive and less developmentalist Anglo-Saxon states remain more immune to the consequences of such changes precisely because of their lower level of involvement in the economy. On the other hand, the autonomy of developmentalist states has conceivably been eroded and their governance capacity put on the defensive by the changes. This does not necessarily mean that MNCs based in the latter countries will experience difficulties in this new global marketplace, as the evidence of their many successes testify. However, if one considers the impending organizational changes at Deutsche Bank, in which consensual decision-making at management board level is being replaced by a streamlined Anglo-Saxon managerial hierarchy and operational culture designed to foster speedier decision-making (*Wall Street Journal*, 14.02.2002), this suggests that firms operating under these auspices are cognizant of the imperatives of change in the new globalized finance system. Will such change diminish the notion of 'divergent capitalisms' that Whitley (1999) and others argue are caused by distinctive institutional regimes? This brings us back to the final issue that I wish to discuss – how much power do states currently have?

States as the master of markets

Much of the previous section focused upon events and processes that have combined to restrict the governance capacity of states. While it would be implausible to argue that the state has lost its capacity for independent action, it does appear that *some* states are more likely to have been victims of such an erosion of power and that *most* states must now function as part of broader regulatory frameworks. This is despite the fact that such frameworks have been created to sustain the market system that ultimately gives resilience to states. If we add to this the trend in recent years for states to downsize in response to budget crises and a rethinking of their welfare state obligations, it is easy to see a reduced functional capacity for the state. This is especially the case in those states where attempts to shield the domestic population from excessive market risks have led to large welfare state budgets and a high tax rate, which have ultimately constrained competitiveness (Rodrik, 1997). Because states find it increasingly difficult to provide this social insurance, they have scaled back their programmes but, in doing so, they expose themselves, and their population, to precisely the sort of risks that these earlier policies were designed to temper.

Yet, despite the above scenario of crumbling state authority, globalization has yet to delegitimize state institutions. The fact that MNCs continue to expend vast amounts of money to influence state policy makers is a testament to state resiliency. For, as Gray (1998: 71) argues, 'In most parts of the world, state institutions are a strategically decisive territory on which competition between corporations is waged'. Take away the territory and you undermine the ability to compete. This suggests that markets need states perhaps as much if not more than states need markets to flourish. The areas where this dependence on the state is most vital are in the institutional arrangements, infrastructure supports and the more general provision of stability.

It might seem of minor importance to the average consumer who likes to shop for bargains, but firms continue to expend vast amounts of money tracking down and prosecuting the copyright infringements that sometimes generate such bargains. Whether such infringements are in the form of 'knock-offs' that are manufactured cheaply (and illegally) in China or quotas from licensing arrangements that are routinely exceeded (and not reported), firms are forced to rely upon legal systems to enforce correct business practices. In other words, the state remains the final guarantor of stable property rights through patents and codes of behaviour, without which firms lose much of their ability to trade across borders. The rise of globalized economic activity by MNCs continues to be dependent upon accepted regulatory codes that are, however, ultimately enforced in a particular state's courts. China's recent admission into the WTO was contingent upon the country behaving more responsibly in the areas of copyright law. Should infringements persist and China prove unable or unwilling to enforce such rules, FDI could conceivably diminish.

The property rights referred to above are part of a broader set of institutional arrangements discussed earlier that ultimately promote predictability and consistency in the marketplace. Since states maintain such institutional arrangements, their importance is often not recognized until they malfunction. A market economy continues to struggle in Russia because of inadequate institutional arrangements, as well as the incomplete privatization of state assets. The former continues to be haunted by the Soviet legacy where the disregard of regulations was normative (Gray, 1998) and without this economic activity would probably have floundered. FDI in Russia has been stymied in recent years because earlier investors, such as BP in their failed oil and gas venture, saw their investments diminish, if not disappear, in a veritable smokescreen of quasi-institutional prevarication. Similarly, Indonesia after Suharto suffered a breakdown of authority which gave free rein to the more cavalier forms of free enterprise including an increase in piracy in Indonesian waters, but which saw FDI drop from an annual average of 5 billion dollars between 1995 and 1997 to negative annual outflows that reached almost 4 billion dollars in 2000 (*The Economist,* 17.02.2001).

What these examples suggest is that certain institutional provisions need to exist before a market economy can function properly. All, or most, states contain distinctive political and economic processes and institutions that influence and regulate economic activity. But not all such norms are conducive to the support of a market economy. What is crucial in western states is an institutional system that is part of a broader culture in which key features of capitalism (property rights, free sale of labour, individual responsibility and strong work ethic, and laissez-faire) are strongly embedded and function, as Dicken (1998: 82) argues, 'as a container of distinctive business practices'. Since such practices are embedded in this culture that is given resonance by the state, the state continues to play an important facilitative role. Its central role in institution building enables people to develop confidence in state structures and the behavioural guarantees and routines that are implicit in them. It is for such reasons that Hungary has made such strenuous efforts to replicate European Union legal, accounting and tax practices in order to demonstrate its commitment to, and support for, western business practices.

It is also important to recognize that what made firms successful in a particular geographical location probably had something to do with that area. Silicon Valley is not the centre of the software industry in the United States just because it happens to have a nice climate or people like living close to San Francisco; it is because of a unique confluence of factors such as density of research universities, skilled labour and venture capital markets that combine to bring entrepreneurial talent together and create clusters and self-perpetuating networks of microelectronic firms (Saxenian, 1994). Similar arguments could be made for the 'Third Italy' and Baden-Wurttemburg in southwestern Germany, where distinctive groupings have resulted in dynamic clusters of economic activity (Best, 1990). But, once these firms have become established, they are not as mobile as many might fear. Not only are sunk costs difficult to recover when firms move on; the factor conditions that made the place attractive in the first place continue to be a powerful magnet. Some firms threaten to relocate in order to extract concessions from states and local governments. Some actually do move but most prefer to stay. It is the recognition of just this immobility that has led states in recent years to score some remarkable victories over MNCs.

By invoking anti-trust legislation, Joel Kline, the head of the United States Justice Department anti-trust division, has been able to do things to Microsoft that none of its competitors could ever do. Forced to give hours of embarrassing testimony and defend what are essentially future scenarios for the computer industry, Bill Gates came away from this experience with the prospect of his company being broken up. Furthermore, this example shows how immobile companies actually are when faced with this sort of pressure. For, as Micklethwait and Wooldridge (2000: 150) argue:

> ...one reason the federal government can harass Microsoft is because it knows that the computer company will not move elsewhere... its fixed assets may be modest and its workforce small, but it cannot afford to divorce itself from American universities and other American computer companies. Removing itself from America's high-tech cluster would be suicidal.

Along similar lines, it appears that even the most strident anti-big tax firms in Europe are ultimately quite reluctant to move to another country because doing so would be too costly, at least in the short run. States know this and it permits them a certain leverage over firms when it comes to policies such as tax increases.

Related to the above is the growing importance of states in the area of human resource development. As economies have shifted from manufacturing to service industries, the increased importance of knowledge workers has placed a premium on educational institutions. Since states are the provider of the bulk of education, their role and importance inevitably increase as the skill demands rise. Even though company expenditure on training continues to be high, the costs of not only basic, but increasingly higher, education are inevitably borne by states. In the early twentieth century, basic literacy and numeracy were all that was needed for most workers to function in the embryonic mass production industries. Now, despite a proliferation of low-skilled jobs in the burgeoning service sector, some form of college or technical education is a prerequisite for the high value-added jobs cherished by western societies.

The countries that consistently provide large numbers of educated workers are typically those where market activity flourishes. Take away the educational infrastructure and worker training costs can no longer be externalized by firms. Firms might, and frequently do, complain about poor quality workers whose analytical skills are merely rudimentary, but it could be far worse if the state lacked the capacity to provide extensive education.

It is ironic that many politicians complained about extending educational provisions in the nineteenth century for fear of encouraging radicalism. The latter did not occur, at least not often. Neither did the provision of universal suffrage unleash social instability as its detractors had claimed. Nonetheless, states continue to be concerned about social instability and do their utmost to maintain order. The maintenance of order is desirable for obvious reasons, hence the allocation of considerable state resources and efforts in this area. From informal sanctions to punitive measures, states have historically sought to contain unrest amongst their populations. But they have also been proactive and introduced less draconian measures of social control to deal with the social effects of economic instability. Since economic downturns typically increase unemployment, states have seen fit to intervene to provide a cushion for those who are unwitting victims of the market. In part motivated by fear of the social consequences of having large numbers of (male) unemployed roaming the streets, and in part by attempts to introduce Keynesian microeconomic management, such activity has become an important feature of western societies.

Until the collapse of the Soviet Union, the spectre of communism lurked as a reminder for capitalist states of what might happen if working-class concerns were consistently unmet or ignored. Fortunately, the demise of socialism in Eastern Europe in the late 1980s coincided with strong economic growth in the west, reducing much of the 'social dislocation' potential facing western societies. During the peak of the Cold War ideological struggles, the maintenance of social stability in the West continued to make that area attractive and safe for capitalist enterprise. Whilst many policies were designed to offset problems of market instability in the social realm, their effect was also to bolster markets and make such states desirable places in which to do business. In other words, take away social stability and firms will find it difficult to function in the chaos that ensues.

States still matter

Writing this in the aftermath of the terrorist attacks in the United States, it is difficult to continue to consign states to a peripheral or residual role in world affairs. The planes that bombed Afghanistan did not carry the markings of Merrill Lynch, Microsoft or any one of the other big MNCs that have been the key players in global capitalism.

Instead, these actions are unambiguously the projection of one state's, the United States', enormous power in an international arena where markets matter but, ultimately, states still have the upper hand. That is not to say that globalization should be downplayed, it should not, and it is clear that certain aspects of it, such as financial flows, will continue to chip away at the ability of states to control their domestic economic activities. But one of the telling things about developments in Afghanistan is the amount of effort now being put into building precisely the sort of state apparatus and institutions that will give that society a semblance of stability. This suggests two important things.

Firstly, that nation states have become almost indispensable for development to occur at all. Albeit a western construct, the nation state is inseparable from capitalist development and has become the norm for the types of infrastructure that permit markets to flourish. Furthermore, nation states permit a level of 'civility' (Mann, 1977), which appears to underwrite the consensus building and predictability that are cornerstones of the democratic and quasi-democratic societies where capitalism thrives. Rather than undermine the nation state, globalization appears to require reasonably stable states in order to function most effectively.

Secondly, this leads us to recognize the symbiotic nature of globalization and the nation state. As Mann (1997) has argued, the rise of transnational capitalism occurred alongside the growth and consolidation of the nation state, first in the West (and North) and, more recently, in Asia and Latin America. Each would appear to draw strength from the other in a fairly complex interdependency. In some instances, state autonomy is eroded but in others it is clear that transnational capitalism is reined in by states. States constitute many of the rules by which market activity flourishes but are then often constrained by the results of just those market activities. Perhaps one of the most underinvestigated features of globalization is the extent to which it serves to integrate states more tightly, forcing upon them a transnational coordination role that ultimately plays to their own domestic economic strengths. Rather than weaken states, such a complex integration can actually embolden them since it reinforces their own sense of identity.

In the arguments that I have presented above, an attempt has been made to move away from the caricatures of globalization that all too often distort any discussion of its extent and impact. Rather than assume a priori that an increase in transnational economic activity will inevitably erode state capacity for independent action, I have argued for a more nuanced view of the intricate balance between the two. States made capitalism possible and continue to constitute the conditions for its reproduction. Globalized market activities sustain state development in complex, but often essential, ways and permit levels of growth that, in turn, build upon state governance capacity. Instead of seeking a simplistic causality that will always be conceptually problematic, this interdependent approach would appear to offer a more realistic assessment of events. It also enables us to focus upon different levels of integration into the world economy of states as well as different types of state governance, such as levels of welfare state functions and corporatist inclinations. In turn, this will then provide a richer, but more complex, backdrop against which to assess the transnational capital and industrial activity that are central to current discussions of globalization.

Acknowledgements

I would like to thank the following for their useful comments on an earlier draft of this chapter: David Coates, Mike Geppert, Cindy Kelly and Dirk Matten.

References

Berger, S. and Dore, R. (1996) *National Diversity and Global Capitalism*, Ithaca: Cornell University Press.
Best, M. (1990) *The New Competition*, Boston: Harvard University Press.
Castells, M. (1993) 'The information economy and the new international economic order' in Carnoy, M., Castells, M. and Cohen, S. S. (eds) *The Global Economy in the Information Age*, University Park, PA: Pennsylvania State University Press.
Coates, D. (2000) *Models of Capitalism*, Cambridge: Polity Press.
Corley, T. A. B. (1989) 'The nature of multinationals', in Teichova, A. et al. (eds) *Historical Studies in International Corporate Business*, Cambridge: Cambridge University Press, pp. 43–56.
Crosby, A. W. (1997) *The Measure of Reality*, Cambridge: Cambridge University Press.
Crouch, C. and Streeck, W. (1997) *Political Economy of Modern Capitalism*, Thousand Oaks: Sage.
Dicken, P. (1998) *Global Shift*, New York: Guilford Press.
Dunning, J. H. (1993) *Multinational Enterprises and the Global Economy* Reading, MA: Addison Wesley.
Freeman, C. and Perez, C. (1988) 'Structural crises of adjustment, business cycles and investment behaviour', in Dosi, G., Freeman, C., Nelson, R., Silverburg, G. and Soete, L. (eds) *Technical Change and Economic Theory*, London, Pinter, Ch. 3.

Gray, J. (1998) *False Dawn: The Delusions of Global Capitalism*, London: Granta Books.

Held, D., McGrew, A., Goldblatt, D. and Perraton, J. (1999) *Global Transformations*, Stanford: Stanford University Press.

Hirst, P. and Thompson, G. (1996) *Globalization in Question*, Cambridge: Polity Press.

Holton, R. J. (1998) *Globalization and the Nation-State*, Basingstoke: Macmillan.

Hutton, W. and Giddens, A. (eds) (2000) *Global Capitalism*, New York: New Press.

Keay, J. (1991) *The Honourable Company*, New York: Macmillan.

Kuttner, R. (2000) 'The role of governments in the global economy', in Hutton, W. and Giddens, A., op. cit., pp. 147–63.

Landes, D. S. (1998) *The Wealth and Poverty of Nations*, New York: Norton.

Mann, M. (1997) 'Has globalization ended the rise and rise of the nation-state?', *Review of International Political Economy*, 4/3, pp. 472–96.

Micklethwait, J. and Wooldridge, A. (2000) *A Future Perfect*, New York: Crown.

Milton, G. (1999) *Nathaniel's Nutmeg*, London: Sceptre.

Mittelman, J. H. (2000) *The Globalization Syndrome*, Princeton: Princeton University Press.

Ohmea, K. (1990) *The Borderless World: Power and Strategy in the International Economy*, London: Fontana.

Rodrik, D. (1997) *Has Globalization Gone Too Far?*, Washington: Institute for International Economics.

Sassen, S. (1991) *The Global City: New York, London, Tokyo*, Princeton: Princeton University Press.

Saxenian, A. (1994) *Regional Advantage: Culture and Competition in Silicon Valley and Route 128*, Cambridge, MA: Harvard University Press.

Scholte, J. A. (2000) *Globalization: A Critical Introduction*, Basingstoke, Palgrave.

Strange, S. (1996) *The Retreat of the State*, Cambridge: Cambridge University Press.

Vallas, S. (1999) 'Rethinking post-Fordism: The meaning of workplace flexibility' *Sociological Theory*, 17/1, pp. 68–101.

Weiss, L. (1998) *The Myth of the Powerless State*, Ithaca: Cornell University Press.

Whitley, R. (1999) *Divergent Capitalisms*, Oxford: Oxford University Press.

Winterton, J. and Winterton, R. (1989) *Coal, Crisis and Conflict: The 1984–85 Miners' Strike in Yorkshire*, Manchester: Manchester University Press.

11
Globalization and the Effects of Diversity and National Identity – with Illustrations from Three British Companies

Anna Lorbiecki

Both 'globalization' and 'managing diversity' have become central themes in academic and popular business discourses. Of the two, globalization is the older concept and is signified by such terms as 'the global village' (McCraken, 1988), 'the global market place' (Paliwoda, 1993) and 'the global economy' (Hirst and Thompson, 1994). It presents a view of the world and its people, whether as organizational managers, employees or customers, as being increasingly 'connected'. More recently, globalization has been coupled with the younger concept of diversity management, which originated in the US and, as Litvin (1997) observes, has been quickly leapt upon by scholars and practitioners as an important tool in harnessing the energies of organizations in the global battle for economic success. While there are many different interpretations and understandings of diversity management (see Kirton and Greene, 2000; Lorbiecki and Jack, 1999 for overviews of the literature), it is underpinned by the central belief that organizations with highly diverse workforces – in terms of gender, age, ethnicity, able-bodiedness, religion, sexual orientation and other differences – perform better in today's 'global' economy than corporations that are monocultural or homogeneous. It is argued by leading advocates, such as Thomas and Ely (1996) and Dass and Parker (1999), that it makes good business sense to increase the number of different affinity groups on corporate payrolls, because their members are more in tune with the varied needs and tastes of people within our increasingly diverse and multicultural societies.

The recognition that consumers, workforces or societies are not homogeneous, but made up of people who 'are not like you' and, more importantly, 'do not wish to become like you' (Kandola and Fullerton, 1998: 12), focuses attention on a need for plurality and differentiation. An emphasis on diverging, multiple perspectives, however, does not fit easily with the standardizing rhetoric of globalization discourses and the trend towards homogenization or 'McDonaldization' (Ritzer, 1993). Although international firms and their managers are advised 'to think globally and act locally', it is difficult, in practice, to achieve global thought and local action because the universalistic principles, often assumed in globalization discourses, are diametrically opposed to the ethnographic concepts required to encourage local action and plural meanings. Furthermore, when this instantiation of globalization relates more to managing worldwide, or those 'over there', organizations tend to overlook the whole range of internal differences (gender, age, able-bodiedness, sexual orientation and so forth), with their attention being focused instead on race or ethnicity, under the guise of comparing national cultures.

The heightened realization that 'difference', whether cross-national or intra-national, is an integral part of organizational life makes work-places not only more exciting but also more complex. As Friedman (1995) explains, the phenomenon currently referred to as 'globalization' transmits difference everywhere and simultaneously makes it more problematic. While mergers, joint ventures, (relatively) cheap travel and new technologies bring diverse groups increasingly in contact with one another, we are also experiencing, according to Friedman, the paradox of *compression* – diminished distance between different cultures – and *implosion* – increased consciousness of one's own identity. While questions of identity are always exceedingly complex, as they involve intersections of race, gender and class (McClintock, 1995), for British organizations there is the added twist of the *consequences* of Britain's imperial past. As Mishra and Hodge (1991) explain, the effects of British colonialism did not cease with the end of colonial rule, but continue into the present and are most sharply felt by women and men with ancestral roots in Britain's former colonies. Not only have such people borne the brunt of racism and discrimination, but they have also been made to feel 'out of place' in the Englishness of Britain's empire, with its associated notions of superiority and inferiority, as described by Baucom (1999) in his book of that title. The consequences of imperialism are not, however, just felt at home. Questions of Britishness and what it stands for in the minds of employees, consumers and customers also tax British organizations as they attempt to present a more cosmopolitan image of themselves.

For example, during my Leverhulme-funded research on '*Diversity Management and Being "British"*' in three leading British organizations – British Aerospace (now known as BAE Systems and referred to as BAES), the British Broadcasting Corporation (BBC) and British Telecom (BT) – I was struck by the importance managers placed on issues of national identity, diversity and imperialism in relation to organizational quests for globalization. In addition to managing the cultural exigencies of doing business abroad, these managers also have to respond to local demands for recognition and inclusion from members of different identity groups, who, because of their identity (whether as women, British Asians or black Britains), have hitherto been excluded. Although such exclusion is being partly addressed by diversity initiatives, here I argue that adopting ideas from post-colonial inquiry (see Said, 1978; Spivak, 1993; Jaya, 2001; Trowler, 2001) can help organizations to become even more inclusive. Post-colonial inquiry is helpful because it exposes the limitations of managing only from a western/US point of view and the subsequent wastage of non-traditional ways of knowing, particularly within white, male-dominated organizations, such as BAES and BT.

Using findings from my research, this chapter examines the relationships between globalization, diversity and national identity through a post-colonial lens. Structurally, there are three sections. The first section begins with a discussion of the tensions that arise between globalization and diversity management when British organizations expand over a wider geographical area. I then examine, in the second section, diverse interpretations of Britishness given by respondents and how their meanings differed when related to globalization compared to when they were more local. The section also looks at the continuity of Britain's imperial past into the present and the consequences of colonialism on contemporary gender and race relations in British organizations. The third section links national identity, globalization and post-colonial inquiry as a means of legitimating the important, and alternative, understanding that emerges from an *outsider-within* status (Collins, 1986) held by women and men not normally given the insider power accorded to white, male executives. Although being an outsider-within can be extremely stressful, it can also be an energizing force for greater social inclusion, as the men and women who occupy this status often have the passion and courage to speak out against racism and other forms of discrimination. Their voices need, however, to be supported to a much greater extent by powerful insiders, if British organizations are to become fully inclusive, both at home and abroad.

Globalization and diversity

This section examines the tensions that arise for organizations when they expand over a wider geographical area, illustrated by data from BAES, the BBC and BT. Driven by the saturation of domestic markets, the intensification of competition between nations and firms and the desire for sustained business performance, organizations have searched for new markets further and further afield from their original, domestic bases. Acquisitions, mergers and joint ventures, particularly with companies abroad, have emerged as favoured vehicles for international expansion because they offer lower production costs and provide wider access to the resources, knowledge and skills required for commercial growth. For instance, within the three British organizations studied, BAES has a number of joint ventures with other European aviation companies, which together formed the Airbus Industrie, and it also runs the multi-billion pound Al Yamamah project with the Saudi Arabian government, one of its biggest customers. BT has been involved in a series of joint ventures since 1988 and its earliest creations were in Spain and Belgium, where BT Tel and BT Belgium were created. In 1995, BT travelled further afield and established joint ventures: in Germany to form Viag Interkom; in Italy to form Albacom and in Sweden to form Telenordia. Between 1996 and 2001, more joint ventures led to the creation of Telefort in the Netherlands, Cegetel in France, Sunrise in Switzerland, Ocean in Ireland, BT Ceska and BT Slovakia in Eastern Europe and BT Hungaria, although it subsequently sold its stake in Sunrise in 2000.

While the BBC does not appear to be involved in joint ventures, it sees itself, through its World Service radio broadcasts and the sale of its television programmes abroad, as a British organization with 'the power to bring the world together'. Recently, however, its senior management has become anxious about its middle-class, middle-England 'image', as the BBC has taken a beating from other satellite, terrestrial and cable broadcasters, whose programmes are seen to be more attractive to minority ethnic viewers at home and to the huge Asian populations overseas. As a BBC respondent explained:

There is a lot of ignorance and prejudice regarding 'minorities' because there is still this arrogance in the mainstream broadcasting industry that the rest of the world doesn't know anything about the media. Now that was fine ten years ago when countries like India or Pakistan or whatever, were not that technologically advanced or weren't in broadcasting. But it's all changed now. India does more, has more amazing IT output than the UK. And suddenly organizations like the BBC have to think on a global scale and they are worried because why should minorities now pay a license fee when they do not provide what they want, and they can go to 15 digital channels, if they want to.

As part of its strategy for global success, BBC1 replaced its old blue and black globe with a brightly coloured orange and yellow balloon to signal its intention of producing television programmes that bring the 'whole country and the world together' (Ahmed, 1997). This revamping of corporate imagery as a way of appearing more attractive to a wider range of national, and international, consumers is also exemplified in British Airways' contentious decision to remove the red, white and blue of the Union Jack from the tailfins of its aircraft and replace them with 'world images' from Africa, Poland and China to convey the message that 60 per cent of its customers are from outside Britain. Curiously, part of these attempts to appear more global also included name changes that erased British national identity from corporate titles. What used to be British Telecom is now know in Britain as BT, but when it is involved in joint ventures overseas it changes its name to Concert in the US, or to others, as outlined above. Similarly, British Aerospace used its merger with Marconi Electronic Systems in 1999 to drop its British identity and is now called BAE Systems instead.

The expansion of organizations into a global or international arena is accompanied, however, by a new set of management problems, as they now have to manage the complexity of uniting their various companies in different countries, often under a single corporate banner. A popular management solution, as mentioned above, is 'to think globally and act locally', but, in order to do this, organizations have to consider whether there are any real differences between global, international and domestic management processes and practices. The extent to which they are considered to be different is the subject of much debate, which has, as Ralston et al. (1993) noted, polarized between two opposing views: convergence or divergence. The *convergence* position presents a view of the world, notably Levitt's (1983), of converging consumer tastes and preferences, serviceable through standardized products manufactured within a framework of increasingly universal managerial philosophies and practices, deploying the 'one best way'. From this perspective, it is assumed that national borders and cultural differences represent a diminishing impediment to business and that managers in industrialized nations will increasingly embrace the attitudes and behaviours common to managers in other industrialized nations, despite their cultural differences. In contrast, the *divergence* position, such as Guirdham's (2000), suggests that, for whatever reasons (which might be different stages of economic development, different systems of government, issues of sovereignty or even the extent to which a country had been invaded), workforces contain individuals who retain diverse, culturally based values, despite any economic or social similarities between nations. These points are echoed in Taplin's chapter in this volume, which investigates and offers a critique of the presumed power of globalization over state–business relationships.

At this point in time, both the customers and employees within BT's European orbit are confused. From their various locations, for instance France, Hungary or Ireland, their loyalties are to their national companies, each of which has a distinct identity or national culture from all the others and from BT head offices in London. Although BT wishes to transform itself into 'one company in many countries', it faces the dilemma of choosing either a divergent or convergent strategy, or a mix of the two. In their analysis of the strategies that companies use to overcome the liability of doing business abroad, Sjörgen and Jansen (1994) noted that they can be split into two broad types. The first type of strategy is based on *integration* and attempts to reduce the liability of foreignness by standardizing structures, systems and processes across the organization as a means of suppressing deviation from centralized, global ambitions. Under this scenario, an organization needs to select individuals prepared to accept centralized control and then socialize them by instilling a transnational culture that aims to create a uniform workforce, all moving towards common goals, beliefs and values, regardless of whichever place in the world they may work. Following this homogenizing tactic could, however, be risky, as it might obliterate the very diverse and distinct French, Hungarian and Irish attributes that attracted BT to buy into the companies in the first place.

To avoid these problems, BT could decide upon a *differentiation* strategy instead, which, according to Sjörgen and Jansen, attempts to reduce the liability of foreignness by accepting variations in managerial activities deemed necessary for preserving local identity, interests and responsiveness. Under a differentiation approach, the implications for BT are quite different from those under the integration scenario. The accent is more on recruiting a diverse workforce and creating developmental processes that help individuals to learn to manage the differences and beliefs arising from such diversity. At which point, organizations have to then try and understand what the term 'diversity' actually means. Understanding diversity, however, is highly problematic, as questions of diversity or difference are addressed primarily through two distinct, and separate, managerial discourses (Tung, 1995): *cross-national diversity*, which refers to managing the interface between peoples of two countries, and *intra-national diversity*, which refers to coping with the realities of an increasingly diverse workforce, both ethnically and in terms of gender, in a given country

The literature on cross-national diversity is vast. It includes ideas and advice on: expatriate adjustment (Black et al., 1991); notions of international or global managers (Bartlett and Ghoshal, 1989); selection procedures for overseas assignments (Tung, 1981); comparative and cross-cultural management studies (Hofstede, 1980, 1991; Hampden-Turner and Trompenaars, 1993) and cross-cultural teamwork (Smith and Berg, 1997). Together, they form powerful discourses on the cultural exigencies of doing business over a wider geographical area and serve to highlight the ever-complex ways in which we are all 'culturally' different. The relativism underpinning most cross-cultural studies has, however, been severely criticized (see McSweeney, 2002) because their definition of culture assumes that values and beliefs are 'shared' or held in 'common'. Barth (1989) provides a critique of relativist models of culture, such as Hofstede's, by arguing that views of what is normally called 'culture' often fall into the trap of misconstruing description for explanation. Culture, he argues, is not a hidden code to be deciphered, but rather a relatively unstable product of the way people create meaning. Hence, cultural meanings are not the same for all members of a population, they depend on gender, race and place, the positions of individual actors in society and their distinct experiences, knowledge and orientations. This is a point supported by contemporary debates on diversity management, which emphasize the ways in which we are all 'different'.

Within the literature on intra-national diversity – more commonly known as 'diversity management' – much emphasis is placed on acknowledging, accepting and celebrating a huge array of 'differences' ascribed to race, culture, ethnicity, age, able-bodiedness, gender, values, experiences, class and ways of working (Thomas and Ely, 1996; Dass and Parker, 1999). Instead of fearing differences, organizations are called upon to see them as an 'asset', vital to commercial success. The recognition, however superficial, by many organizations that employees are not a homogenized mass does not mean that all 'differences' are, as Hardy (2001) points out, of equal worth. Neither societies nor organizations are neutral when it comes to questions of difference and, in seeking to 'manage' diversity, organizations have to recognize and tackle the deeply embedded processes and practices that play an integral part in structuring discriminatory experiences at work. Within Britain, discriminatory practices have been identified in the Metropolitan Police, which has had to respond to the charges of *institutional racism* levied against it by the 1999 McPherson Report, which heavily criticized its inadequate investigation of the murder of the black schoolboy, Stephen Lawrence. Discrimination is also endemic within British universities as identified by the 1999 Bett Report, which reported on the unequal pay and status of women and minority academics.

At government level, there are grave concerns that the opportunities offered by Britain's rich diversity are being squandered through racism and discrimination, thus damaging the nation's position in world markets. As part of its efforts to combat social exclusion, the Labour government commissioned the Runneymede Trust to produce a report on *The Future of Multi-Ethnic Britain*, published in October 2000. Even though the findings of that Report proved controversial, due to their distortion and trivialization by the media, it aimed to take 'a calm and long-term view of the current state of our multi-ethnic nation and suggest ways of countering racial discrimination and disadvantage' (Parekh, 2000). In particular, the report criticized the southern English-centredness of Britain's *imagined community* and the exclusion of millions of multiple identities – Welsh Europeans, Pakistani Yorkshiremen, Glaswegian Muslims and English Jews – from its traditional images.

Although the BBC's brightly coloured balloon and British Airways' redesigned tailfins can be interpreted as attempts to become more inclusive by better reflecting both the nation's, and other countries', multiculturalism and heterogeneity, the identity of nations is not limited to questions of ethnicity or culture. As demonstrated in the next section, interpretations of British national identity are also linked to history, imperialism, Englishness and gender: factors which British organizations have to take into account when deciding whether to opt for a convergence or divergence approach when managing at home and abroad.

Diversity and national identity

When embarking upon my study of Diversity Management and Being British, my primary aim was to explore the significance of national identity for organizations as they attempted to become both global and local. Asking respondents about Britishness would, I assumed, anchor their accounts firmly within a national context, which had not yet been explored in the literature on diversity management. During my in-depth interviews (36), however, it soon became clear that interpretations of Britishness differed when related to globalization, compared to when its meanings were more local.

Global and local interpretations of Britishness

When respondents in British Telecom were asked why they thought it had changed its name to BT, they related this, in the main, to BT's aspirations of being seen as a global company, with operations and joint ventures all over the world, as illustrated below:

> We are a global company now and that British aspect has really gone and we are worldwide, and we employ people of every race, religion... within every country that we exist. There's no reason to actually consider ourselves to be British, so... the barriers there are being broken down. BT, rather than British Telecom, because I mean, it's recognised now that we are not just a British company; we are not just supporting the turf and infrastructure within the British Isles or the UK. We have joint ventures, global ventures all over the world and we've established links everywhere.

Furthermore, BT no longer wanted to sound as if it was British around the rest of the world, and thus was compelled to remove the British or the explicit Britishness from the name. Not using the term British Telecom meant that it would not be seen as *'a pompous, big British boy trying to create a new Empire or anything like that.'*

British Aerospace, now known as BAE Systems (BAES), used its merger with Marconi Electronic Systems in 1999 as an opportunity to redefine its corporate identity and *'we deliberately dropped the British title because we didn't see ourselves as a British company.'* It, too, saw itself as a 'global player', although its major interests were confined to only nine countries. Mention of imperialism was, however, a feature of more local identities, particularly for those with an Afro-Caribbean or Asian ancestry:

> British... I think I've had this discussion with someone before. I think it's actually quite common with um, I don't know whether it's something I've read or seen somewhere with people from you

know my community, you know, black people. They see themselves as British before they see themselves as English. I don't know, I think it's always a bit too nationalist you know to see yourself as English; it always has to sort of break yourself down that much. Whereas British, I don't know, just has a better feel to me. If you say British to me, it's talking about more cultures, anyway you know because people who came over here in different waves of migration were part of the British Empire, you know and that's different cultures you see. So I think to see yourself as British, you know, you are sort of holding on to lots more cultures than English really.

Viewing Britishness as a separate category from Englishness, in this instance, served to resolve questions of belonging or social exclusion, as here it was being used to bring a number of different cultural identities under a national identity that was seen to be 'culturally inclusive'. Britishness was also held to be important for BAES's expatriates working in Saudi Arabia, as they liked to feel that there was a *comforting hand* to support them during any trials and tribulations. These employees were unhappy with BAES losing its British title as it rocked their sense of security and sense of belonging, back home. Nor did the Saudi Arabian government like the loss of Britishness, as they felt their relationship was with Britain, and not some anonymous multinational. Furthermore, in the US, the BAES acronym was often confused with BA – British Airways.

The comfort engendered by the term 'British' also provided a get-out from using a separate English cultural identity. Englishness was often associated with very racist or negative connotations and conjured up pictures of English hooliganism and xenophobia displayed at international football matches, particularly when played abroad. Englishness, as opposed to Irish, Scottish or Welsh identities, was also proving difficult for the BBC, which had moved to a more regional form of broadcasting. While devolution had played a strong role in helping to make Welsh, Scottish and Irish identities more visible, it was hard for the BBC to know how to portray Englishness. It was, as illustrated by the following quote, difficult for the BBC to know whether to fly the St George's Cross (English flag) over its buildings:

Should we fly the St George's Cross above the BBC in England and you go to Scotland and you go to Northern Ireland, you will see their respective flags flying there. But what's happened is that the St George's Cross has been so closely associated with the kind of political activity that people don't really like, Enoch Powell, for example.

Although it was easy for respondents to say that they were Irish, Scottish, Welsh or even a Yorkshireman and feel *proud of it*, it was less easy to display English patriotism. Part of the reason for this lies with Britain's history of racism, which was at one of its most venomous peaks during the 1960s. On 22 April 1964, Enoch Powell, an influential Conservative MP, delivered a xenophobic speech on English nationhood to the Royal Society of St George. In that speech, he declared that: it was the task of his generation to reclaim their English heritage, to rediscover that earlier generation of Englishmen who had lived before the 'expansion of England' and had been *untainted* by Empire (quoted in Rutherford, 1997: 112, my emphasis). A view repeated, four years later, in his infamous Rivers of Blood speech, in which Powell depicted British 'immigrants' from the West Indies and Asia as 'alien invaders' (Phillips and Phillips, 1998: 77). Powell's calls for a pure (white) English nation demonstrates how this type of racial narrative was used to shape the idea that some races or ethnicities were 'better' than others, as discussed below.

Continuity of Britain's imperial past into the present

As Calas (1992) established in her critical analysis of management studies on other cultures, the frames used in management research to look at difference or diversity are not neutral, but gendered and racial. In her study, Calas noted that management research on how 'other people in the world are *different*' often drew upon an Enlightenment trope of progress, which included notions of superiority and inferiority and declared some races 'better' or more 'advanced' than others. This Enlightenment notion of progress was, McClintock (1992) argues, one of the most tenacious and ugly doctrines of colonialism: it led to an elaborate series of hierarchical binary polarities, which constructed the West as 'superior', white and masculine and the non-West as 'inferior', black/brown/yellow and feminine (Prasad, 1997). Knowing other people through these discursive binary polarities underpinned imperial dominance and, more insidiously, also became the mode of thought by which the colonized were persuaded to know themselves (Ashcroft et al., 1995).

Within post-colonial theory, coined around 1959 (Mishra and Hodge, 1991), the emphasis is on the *consequences* of colonialism, which did not disappear with the formal end of colonial rule, but continue into the present. This colonial experience has had a significant effect on Britain (Kirton and Green, 2000), as it laid the foundations of employment segregation by race and gender. As Anthias and Yuval-Davies (1992) point out, British subjects from its ex-colonies in the Caribbean, India, Pakistan and Bangladesh were actively recruited by British Rail and London Transport (mainly men) and the National Health Service (mainly women) to do the (dirty) work that the indigenous population did not want. The work available to them was mainly in the public sector, with lower wages than private industry, and in industrial work with long hours, shift work and poor conditions. This colonial experience has had a significant effect on gender relations and sexuality in the workplace, as illustrated by Mill's (1998) study of corporate masculinities in British Airways. The occupation of the high status position of airline pilot by mainly white, middle-class men; the mid-status, 'service' role of cabin staff by women, or by men often deemed to be gay or effeminate, and the lower status, behind-the-scenes roles of ground staff and baggage handlers, by working-class men and women, often from ethnic minorities, are, he argues, the products of pervasive, hyper-masculine discourses and practices.

Masculine discourses and practices are very strong in BAES and BT. Their workforces are respectively 97 per cent and 88 per cent male and almost 95 per cent white. Although these figures reflect the predominantly white, male environments traditionally found in the engineering and manufacturing industries, of which they are a part, a sense of what it might be like to work in BAES is provided by the following quotation:

> [BAES] is traditionally engineering, very focused in terms of its manufacturing background in that what we like doing is designing and building futuristic aircraft...You know we're, if you like, the traditional image of British Aerospace as boys with toys (laughs).

This image of BAES as a business of boys with toys or dads and lads, as quoted by another respondent, forms part of a very patriarchal articulation of its culture. A similar picture is also found within BT, which was described by a senior, female HR manager as male-dominated, command and control; a work environment in which it is very difficult to explain to 'control freaks' why it is important to have social diversity, and to get them to start changing the way that they do things. Within BAES, patriarchy is further maintained by the power of its two major customers: the Saudi Arabian government and the Ministry of Defence (MoD), who place gender and nationality restrictions on

BAES's workforce. Under the terms of the Al Yamamah project, women, British or otherwise, are forbidden by the Saudi Arabian government to work in their country. The ban on women working in Saudi Arabia makes it difficult not only to promote a standard of equal work opportunities across their business, but is difficult to challenge, as illustrated below:

> If we want to send a female colleague to Saudi Arabia, they simply will not be admitted, they will not be allowed in and the Saudis would decline to deal with them. And, therefore, I find it very difficult because we're not about to tell them they're wrong because the last thing we want to do is fall out with a major customer. So what we do is, we play along and we find ways around it or we accommodate their preferences...But I am confident that if I said to our chairman or chief executive 'this is wrong and you've got to challenge it', I would be very quickly sat on and told to behave myself.

Women, however, are not the only group to be excluded from prestigious international assignments in BAES. The MoD, another major and highly influential customer, also puts limits on who BAES can employ, but in this case such exclusion is along the lines of nationality and race. The design and manufacture of its military aircraft and aviation systems are highly sensitive and surrounded by national security. All potential employees of BAES have to be vetted by the MoD and work restrictions are placed on non-UK nationals or those from non-NATO partners, such as Ireland, China, India, North Korea, Iran, Iraq, Pakistan and Serbia. Given that Britain has many minority ethnics with ancestral roots in India, Pakistan and China living near BAES's work sites, their identity makes it very difficult for them to gain employment within this organization, as security checks are made not only on them, but also on their parentage. The secrecy surrounding BAES creates immense hurdles for both the organization and the ethnic minority populations on its doorstep. The intensity of its security procedures has, for instance, given Asian parents the view that BAES only wants to recruit white people and, therefore, they do not encourage their children to go into engineering jobs in that organization. The absence of ethnic minorities and the typical masculinity of engineering have left BAES with a very white, male workforce, very comfortable with itself. Although BAES, as part of its Agenda for Change, has recently developed a new, ten-year diversity policy that seeks to open its doors to women and minority ethnics, it is very difficult for them to break into BAES's white, male environment.

The gendering in Britain of engineering as a (primarily) male occupation, coupled with the conflation of minority ethnics as a perceived security risk, makes it difficult to know how social inclusion within BAES can ever be realized. It also raises questions about the exclusivity of other organizations involved in the defence industry or matters of national security. One solution, however, has been offered by BT, which has reconfigured 'engineering' so that it is seen as less scientifically based and more related to computing, design and customer services and, in this way, hopefully, more attractive to women. The ability to reframe occupations so that they appear more open to women and minority ethnics, as well as to men and majority ethnics, offers a practical insight into how doors to diversity can be opened. These doors can, however, be opened further if theoretical ideas from post-colonial theory are also included, as outlined below.

National identity, globalization and post-colonial inquiry

The fact that BAES is now trying to open its doors to women and ethnic minorities means that at one time they were shut. Part of this closure was, as discussed above, due to notions of superiority and inferiority inherent in British colonial rule, which paved the way for acts of racial and sexual discrimination that continue into the present. We are, however, helped in our struggle against discrimination and neo-colonialism by the post-colonial ideas of writers such as Edward Said (1978), Gayatri Spivak (1993), Homi Bhabha (1994) and Arturo Escobar (1995), who have challenged the hegemony of western, Anglo-Saxon views of the world. Although conventional management studies have been largely untouched by post-colonial inquiry, its presence is now being felt in a number of critical debates: for instance, on sustainable development in poorer countries (for example Banerjee, 2000) and in critiques of stereotypical 'Third World' images used by the burgeoning tourist industry (for example Barringer and Flynn, 1998). Here I take up the argument, initiated in Said's (1978) *Orientalism*, that the dynamics of colonialism, empire, power and domination are just as intimately implicated in current discourses on globalization as in nineteenth- and twentieth-century western scholars' cultural productions of the East.

Much of the knowledge used to promote globalization has, Jaya (2001) points out, been from western or North American points of view. Seeing the world through these eyes, Trowler (2001) argued, is extremely limiting as it fixes the ways in which organizations and their workforces see the world that they live in. Furthermore, it perpetuates the 'dreadful secondariness' (Said, 1978) of certain ethnicities as epitomized by the 'evil' rhetoric surrounding the tragic loss of life in the destruction of New York's Twin Towers. Post-colonial unveilings of the homogenizing, colonizing impulses of globalization make the legitimation and inclusion of non-western epistemes a matter of urgency, if the rationales behind such actions are to be better understood. Whilst the ways in which organizations manage their joint ventures or diverse workforces might seem far removed from the events of 11 September 2001, the knowledge used about 'difference' can have far-reaching consequences, as it privileges some views while denigrating others. Contrary to popular images conjured up in international management texts, people from Japan, India, France or Germany are just as diverse as the British people described in this chapter. While different countries have a variety of approaches to 'difference', including historical, legal, social and political perspectives, organizational responses are used here as the central units of analysis. For example, the existence of the Al Yamamah project in BAES brings British employees closer to people in Saudi Arabia, yet at the same time that proximity plays a part in producing an image of Saudi Arabians as *aliens*, all identical to one another. This is illustrated by the following quote from a cross-cultural trainer in BAES, who was trying to overcome negative stereotyping:

> Because a man [Saudi] is working in the eastern region, his roots may well be in the southern region and he's going to react differently to someone who is from there. So you have to get these points across that they react differently to similar situations. It's difficult to get these individual messages across to the guys that there are many variations in Arab cultures.

The institutional temptation to stereotype and demonize other cultures can, however, be difficult to resist in the day-to-day relationships in joint ventures when, for instance, a representative from one nation has to break the news to her in-country team back home that they have to change a product's design:

When I come back and say, 'Sorry guys, but the work of the last three months has to change'. It would be easy for me, and for them, to blame the Spanish guys, thus giving the impression that the Spanish are awkward buggers.

The ability, no matter how tempting, to resist blaming 'the others' because of their 'nationality' becomes even more necessary when gender and ethnicity are interwoven. As both the academic literature and data from my study suggests, it is clear that the rise of international management creates additional hurdles for women. For example, there is the popular belief among organizations that women will jeopardize business dealings with 'the Japanese', because sending a woman would be regarded as a mark of disrespect in a country which is perceived to view women as inferior. Although there were stories of women feeling dismissed or male Japanese managers giving them the honorary title of 'Mr' as a means of granting them equal status, these stereotypes were punctuated by narratives that broke the women can't do business in Japan mould. During a dinner in Japan that had been organized as a social get-together for young British engineers, a woman engineer was asked to join a senior Japanese manager at his table:

He had worked in Europe for a few years so he understood that women were not second-class citizens. And I thought that it was really nice because he broke his tradition [though still a stereotype] by letting me join him and drink beer out of a bottle and have a cigarette.

This gesture of inclusion is the type of activity that needs to be fostered if individuals are to feel that they belong. However, returning to issues of intra-national diversity, invitations to join a meeting do not guarantee the acceptance of 'insiders', as illustrated by the following remarks made by a broadcasting editor in the BBC:

Programme makers, white, male middle-class coming into the BBC or ITV are not used to minorities, or they weren't used to. And it was so difficult for them to judge whether to bring someone in because their values are so different from that person they perceive to be. And you know that person is sitting there, probably doesn't go to the pub or drink to chill out, so that white middle-class male will be thinking, 'Argh, this guy doesn't know how to have fun'. But there are different ways of having fun, aren't there?

Excluding people, simply because they do not know how to have 'fun', illustrates how this type of evaluation can lead to the recruitment of same-minded people – organizational cloning – and the perpetuation of homogeneity. As part of their strategy to reduce this homogenizing propensity, BT and the BBC have adopted a two-pronged strategy for enhancing workplace diversity: an *outward* tactic that involves reaching out into the community and an *inward* tactic that focuses on internal processes, structures and practices. It is hoped that by changing corporate imagery, climate and workplace attitudes, they will create work environments that both attract underrepresented groups into the organization and retain them, as they will be treated with more dignity, respect and egality. Although increasing the number of different affinity groups onto the payroll is, as Dass and Parker (1999) argue, an important step in increasing heterogeneity, an organization then needs to consider what they are going to do with them. Most importantly, organizations are advised not to ghettoize women and men into jobs that limit them to 'knowledge of their own people', but to bring them into the mainstream of corporate life, where they are able to offer ideas of doing 'work'. However, as Spivak (1993) sharply reminds us, bringing the margin into the mainstream is not easy as the 'air is thick with content' and includes marks of racism and discrimination. Furthermore, although women, minority ethnics and members of other marginalized groups have been admitted into organizations, they are rarely, Collins (1986) observed, given the insider power accorded to white, male executives and occupy an outsider-within status instead.

The experience of being tolerated, rather than accepted, can, however, become an energizing force for a greater awareness of racism and sexism in organizations. During the course of my research, I was particularly struck by the identity of those people working on issues of social inclusion or diversity – people who I have called *diversity vanguards* (Lorbiecki, 2001). They were mainly women, often with an Asian or Afro-Caribbean background; also men with this ethnic ancestry or from those labelled 'disabled', and a small number were Irish, Scottish or Welsh. Although many of them were passionate about social inclusion, being involved in organizational equity projects can be extremely stressful and challenging, as it means, as Acker (2000) notes, coping with the gendered and racial contradictions that arise from monitoring and policing those with a higher organizational status than themselves.

The understanding that emerges from not fitting in is, if adequately supported, of great benefit to organizations, as these vanguards of social inclusion help others to understand and engage with embarrass-ing subjects, such as disability, racism, sexism or homophobia, when they usually don't know how to bring these topics up. More import-antly, such people felt that they had learnt, from their outsider experiences, to speak, to a greater or lesser extent, both within and across privileged and disadvantaged communities. The voices and knowledge of these valiant men and women do, however, need to be recognized and more valued. And while they might have to temper their passion for radical social change (Meyerson, 2001), the courageous steps they take help British organizations to move along the hard road towards greater equity at work.

Conclusions

In the above sections, I have tried to illustrate how each of the three domains of globalization, diversity and national identity are inter-related. Globalization strategies often include diversity initiatives, either explicitly or implicitly, in order to reach a wider range of consumers and clients. Within this context, diversity management can involve the recruitment and promotion of employees and managers who are seen to be more representative of a wide range of differences. However, diversity initiatives driven by economic imperatives often focus on dimensions of diversity that are relevant to the specific objectives of globalization, rather than recognizing that it is part of a wider strategy for social inclusion.

The interface between diversity and national identity may be viewed in many ways, with local customs and cultures in different countries either encouraging or constraining a company's ambition for increased workforce diversity and social inclusion. While the expansion over a wider geographical area, plus hostility from employees and con-sumers, have caused organizations to bring 'outsiders' in, the power of major customers and the gendered nature of occupations can limit their intentions. Such limitations were clearly to be seen in the case of BAES, whose efforts to increase the number of women and ethnic minorities were being thwarted by the Saudi Arabian government, the tight security procedures of the MoD and the gendering of engineering as a male occupation.

There is also the dilemma about whether national identity can be used to support globalization or whether it acts as a hindrance. Attempts by British Airways, BAES and BT to hide their national ident-ity seem to have been successful in some contexts but unsuccessful in

others. In the case of British organizations, the notion of national identity is especially complex, because of the overtones of colonialism
linked to the term 'British' in the minds of people at home and abroad.
Post-colonial issues are not, however, exclusive to Britain, as they are
relevant to any country with a history of colonial, or neo-colonial,
ventures.

Overall, it seems that when organizations pursue strategies of globalization, issues of cross-national and intra-national diversity and
national identity are likely to be problematic. No specific solutions to
these dilemmas are offered at the present time, as my purpose here is
to raise awareness of the complications and paradoxes involved.

Acknowledgements

The research mentioned formed part of a two-year study, funded by the
Leverhulme Trust. I would like to thank all the respondents within
BAES, BT and the BBC who gave so freely of their time and opinions
during the study. Special thanks go to Wendy Langford, my research
associate, who spent many hours analysing interview transcriptions to
provide meaningful data.

References

Acker, J. (2000) 'Gendered Contradictions in Organizational Equity Projects',
   Organization, 7(4), pp. 625–32.
Ahmed, K. (1997) 'What's in an Image?', *The Guardian*, 4 October, p. 6.
Anthias, F. and Yuval-Davies, N. (1992) *Racialized Boundaries*, London: Routledge.
Ashcroft, B., Griffiths G. and Tiffin, H. (eds) (1995) *The Postcolonial Studies Reader*,
   London: Routledge, pp. 1–4.
Banerjee, S. B. (2000) 'Whose Land is it Anyway? National Interests, Indigenous
   Stakeholders and Colonial Discourses: The Case of the Jabiluka Uranium
   Mine', *Organization and Environment*, 13(1), pp. 3–38.
Barringer, T. and Flynn, T. (eds) (1998) *Colonialism and the Object: Empire,
   Material Culture and the Museum*, London: Routledge.
Barth, F. (1989) 'The Analysis of Culture in Complex Societies', *Ethnos*, 54,
   pp. 120–42.
Baucom, I. (1999) *Out of Place: Englishness, Empire, and the Locations of Identity*,
   Princeton, NJ: Princeton University Press.
Bartlett, C. and Ghoshal, S. (1989) *Managing Across Borders: The Trans-national
   Solution*, Boston: Harvard Business School Press.
Bhabha, H. K. (1994) *The Location of Culture*, New York: Routledge.
Black, J. S., Mendenhall, M. and Oddou, G. (1991) 'Towards a Comprehensive
   Model of International Adjustment: An Integration of Multiple Theoretical
   Perspectives', *Academy of Management Review*, 16(2), pp. 291–317.

Calas, M. (1992) 'An/Other Silent Voice? Representing "Hispanic Woman" in Organizational Texts'. In A. J. Mills and P. Tancred (eds) *Gendering Organizational Analysis*, London: Sage, pp. 201–21.

Collins, P. H. (1986) 'Learning from the Outsider Within: The Sociological Significance of Black Feminist Thought', *Social Problems*, 33(6), pp. 14–32.

Dass, P. and Parker, B. (1999) 'Strategies for Managing Human Resource Diversity: From Resistance to Learning', *The Academy of Management Executive*, 13(2), pp. 68–80.

Escobar, A. (1995) *Encountering Development: The Making and Unmaking of the Third World*, Princeton, NJ: Princeton University Press.

Friedman, J. (1995) 'Global Systems, Globalization and the Parameters of Modernity'. In M. Featherstone, S. Lash and R. Robertson (eds) *Global Modernities*, London: Sage.

Guirdham, M. (2000) *Communicating Across Cultures*, Basingstoke: Macmillan.

Hampden-Turner, C. and Trompenaars, F. (1993) *The Seven Cultures of Capitalism*, London: Piatkus.

Hardy, S. (2001) *Small Step or Giant Leap? Towards Gender Equality at Work*, Industrial Society: London.

Hirst, P. and Thompson, G. (1994) 'Globalization, Foreign Direct Investment and International Economic Governance', *Organization*, 1(2), pp. 277–303.

Hofstede, G. (1980) *Culture's Consequences*, London: Sage.

Hofstede, G. (1991) Cultures and Organizations: Software of the Mind, London: McGraw-Hill.

Jaya, P. S. (2001) 'Do We Really "Know" and "Profess"? Decolonizing Management Knowledge', *Organization*, 8(2), pp. 227–33.

Kandola, R. and Fullerton, J. (1998) *Diversity in Action: Managing the Mosaic*, 2nd edn, London: Institute of People Development.

Kirton, G. and Green, A. (2000) *The Dynamics of Managing Diversity: A Critical Approach*, Oxford: Butterworth-Heinemann.

Levitt, T. (1983) 'The Globalization of Markets', *Harvard Business Review*, May–June, pp. 92–102.

Litvin, D. R. (1997) 'The Discourse of Diversity: From Biology to Management', *Organization*, 4(2), pp. 187–210.

Lorbiecki, A. (2001) 'The Openings and Burdens for Women and Minority Ethnics Being Vanguards of Diversity Management', Presented at the Rethinking Gender, Work and Organization Conference, June, Keele University, UK.

Lorbiecki, A. and Jack, G. (2000) 'Critical Turns in the Evolution of Diversity Management', *British Journal of Management*, Special Issue, ss. 17–31.

McClintock, A. (1992), 'The Angels of Progress: Pitfalls of the Term "Postcolonialism"', *Social Text*, Spring, pp. 1–5.

McClintock, A. (1995) *Imperial Leather*, London: Routledge.

McCracken, G. (1988) *Culture and Consumption*, Bloomington: Indiana University Press.

McSweeney, B. (2002) 'Hofstede's Model of National Cultural Difference and their Consequences: A Triumph of Faith – A Failure of Analysis', *Human Relations*, 55(1), pp. 5–34.

Meyerson, D. E. (2001) *Tempered Radicals*, Boston, MA: Harvard Business School Press.

Mills, A. J. (1998) 'Cockpits, Hangars, Boys and Galleys: Corporate Masculinities and the Development of British Airways', *Gender, Work and Organization*, 5(3), pp. 172–188.

Mishra, V. and Hodge, B. (1991) 'What is Post(-)Colonialism?', *Textual Practice*, 5(3), pp. 399–415.

Paliwoda, S. (1993) *International Marketing*, 2nd edn, Oxford: Butterworth-Heinemann.

Parekh, B. (2000) *The Future of Multi-Ethnic Britain*: The Parekh Report (chair–Parekh), London: Profile Books.

Phillips, M. and Phillips, T. (1998) *Windrush: The Irresistible Rise of Multi-Racial Britain*, London: Harper & Collins.

Prasad, A. (1997) 'The Colonizing Consciousness and Representations of the Other: A Postcolonial Critique of the Discourses of Oil'. In P. Prasad, A. J. Mills, M. Elmes and A. Prasad (eds) *Managing the Organizational Melting Pot: Dilemmas of Workplace Diversity*, London: Sage, pp. 285–311.

Ralston, D. A., Gustafon, D. J., Cheung, F. M. and Terpestra, R. H. (1993) 'Differences in Managerial Values: A Study of US, Hong Kong and PRC Managers', *Journal of International Business Studies*, second quarter, pp. 250–75.

Ritzer, G. (1993) *The McDonaldization of Society*, London: Pine Forge.

Rutherford, J. (1997) *Forever England – Reflections on Masculinity and Empire*, London: Lawrence & Wishart.

Said, E. W. (1978) *Orientalism*, London: Penguin.

Sjögren, A. and Janson, L. (eds) (1994) *Culture and Management (2)*, The Multicultural Centre, Botkyrka and The Institute of International Business, Stockholm, Sweden.

Smith, K. and Berg, D. (1997) 'Cross-cultural Groups at Work', *European Management Journal*, 15(1), pp. 8–15.

Spivak, G. C. (1993) *Outside in the Teaching Machine*, New York: Routledge.

Thomas, D. A. and Ely, R. J. (1996) 'Making Differences Matter: A New Paradigm for Diversity Management', *Harvard Business Review*, Sept.–Oct., pp. 79–90.

Trowler, P. (2001) 'Captured by the Discourse? The Socially Constitutive Power of New Higher Education Discourse in the UK', *Organization*, 8(2), pp. 183–201.

Tung, R. (1981) 'Selection and Training of Personnel for Overseas Assignments', *Columbia Journal of World Business*, 19, pp. 482–94.

Tung, R. (1995) 'Strategic Human Resource Management Challenge: Managing Diversity', *The International Journal of Human Resource Management*, 6(3), pp. 482–94.

12

German Management Facing Globalization: The 'German Model' on Trial

Gert Schmidt in collaboration with Karen Williams

Introduction

This paper investigates the particular challenges facing German management as they seek to adjust to the global economy by increasingly internationalizing their business operations. Although globalization is a challenge to all national economies, the German economy, as an example of what Taplin describes in this volume as 'consensual capitalism' based on an activist state, is finding the adjustments especially difficult as they question the fundamental structure and characteristics of the national business system. In this paper, we focus on the ongoing debate about whether the 'German model', previously seen by many, not only in Germany, as a highly successful social welfare state, is now a liability in terms of Germany's attractiveness as a location for business investment. We investigate German managers' views on the issue, which are ambiguous since they want to retain what they see as the advantages of the model whilst introducing some Anglo-Saxon-style reforms. It is an open question whether they will be able to 'have their cake and eat it'. No one knows as yet what the next phase of the German model will look like, although this paper makes some tentative suggestions about this. In conclusion, we question the longstanding attachment to national models as champions in management thinking. In the complex reality of globalization, it seems foolhardy to major on the 'one best way'.

The general scenario

At the end of the twentieth century, the classical model of industrial society, conceptualized by economists, historians and the first generation of sociologists in the late nineteenth century, has been called into question. What is currently on the agenda of the political and social science discourse is, firstly, the future of the so-called 'Taylor – Ford regulation model', which has essentially characterized the process of industrialization for the last 60 years or so, and, secondly, the future of European models of 'social welfare societies', which were also established in the post-war period.

Along with the push towards globalization and internationalization, outlined in earlier chapters, such as those by Becker-Ritterspach et al. and Geppert et al., business enterprises are increasingly experiencing strong pressures towards mobility of capital investment, flexibility of labour use, and decentralization of production and research and development activities in order to reduce costs and promote market positions to increase productivity. Some of the key formulae being used are those of lean management, just-in-time production, global sourcing, global marketing and global production. National systems are seen to be losing some of their earlier regulative importance (for general orientation, see Porter, 1990; Castells and Hall, 1994; Hirst and Thompson, 1996; Sassen, 1996; Thurow, 1996; Albrow, 1997; Schmidt and Trinczek, 1999). As the work by Taplin in this volume shows, globalization is having more of an impact on activist states with consensual capitalism, as the state loses its capacity to direct economic activity within its borders and is on the defensive against the Anglo-Saxon style of finance-driven capitalism.

The particular challenges for management in Germany

Whilst globalization and decentralization are challenging management's strategies in all industrial societies, the German scenario is marked by a number of specific characteristics that are based on the structure of the economy, the history of industrial policy, the peculiarities of the institutional setting of industrial conflict and the tradition of vocational training, among other factors (see, among others, Markovits, 1982; Streeck, 1995; Jürgens et al., 2000; O'Sullivan, 2000; Upchurch, 2000).

Several papers in this volume illustrate the particular societal pattern of German industrialization including Brussig and Gerlach on the relationship between the large German manufacturers and small and medium-sized enterprises and Mayer and Whittington on the Rhenish capitalism model of long termist, consensual management and close relations between the companies and the banks, also alluded to in Becker-Ritterspach et al., where the different ownership structures of the German, Finnish and American multinational companies invest-igated have influenced their internationalization strategies. These peculiarly German characteristics are, however, being increasingly challenged by neo-liberalist theories of efficient economic develop-ment, both within the European Union and globally.

However, this has not always been the case. In the 1960s and 1970s, there was a lot of hype about the 'German Model', which was seen as successfully combining capitalistic dynamics and social stability with a broad consensus. It was seen by many as representing the ideal of the modern social welfare state. Indeed, a well-known German chancellor travelled from conference to conference, telling his political friends from Britain, the US and France what they should be doing to achieve the goals of currency stability, comfortable growth rates, an export surplus and low unemployment rates. They were told to follow the German model to achieve the golden path of economic and social progress. However, pride often comes before a fall and current German economic indicators on the GDP, economic growth and unemployment give no room for boasting, Germany having only narrowly missed a warning from the European Central Bank for its lack of financial discipline!

There is no doubt that the German economy has been in a critical condition since the beginning of the 1990s, with over 4 million unemployed, reduced profit margins in many branches and the slowing down of investment in new technologies and new products and so on. This was the scenario up to the mid-1990s and the situation has not improved much since then. The problem of the reunification of the two Germanies, with its massive impact on the state budget and the processes of deindustrialization in many areas of East Germany, is only one factor in trying to understand this reversal of fortune. Other factors have been heavily debated in the German economic press and among academics too.

The fact that the German economy is still very much oriented towards heavy industry and engineering and remains relatively underdeveloped in industries associated with the post-industrial economy are seen by some as an important weakness. More than one-third of the working population is still engaged in the so-called industrial sector in Germany as against only about one-quarter in the US. Despite the fact that there are some problems of statistical equivalencies, there is no doubt that the German economy, with its strong position in automobile production and the machine-tool industry, is still more 'industry-oriented' than other developed economies. Harzing et al. have investigated the continuing German 'production template' in its multinational companies earlier in this volume as evidence of the importance of a country of origin effect even in the age of globalization.

In addition to this, flexibility of labour is progressing only very slowly in Germany, in contrast to the United States and Japan, and also, for example, the Netherlands. The institutional and cultural supports for traditional work patterns such as the 'normal working day' and long-term work contracts are still strong. Labour costs are also at the highest level compared to other nations, whilst the comparative advantage of a high-quality labour force is diminishing with the expansion of lean production methods. Overall, the German labour market is rather resistant to the introduction of new types of low income work with flexible working arrangements and new income configurations to reintegrate the long-term unemployed.

Political and bureaucratic rigidities are also seen as creating barriers to product and process innovation as well as risky future-oriented research investments (for example, nuclear energy and biogenetics). Last, but not least, the German system of industrial relations is said by many commentators to give too much power to the unions and this hinders the adaptation of business to the new challenges of the globalized economy.

The debate on the German model

Against this background in Germany, there has been an ongoing debate over the last few years about *Standort Deutschland* (Germany's position as an attractive location for investment) versus *Modell Deutschland* (the German model). Recent government rhetoric, a wide range of economic literature and, in particular, strategic arguments made by entrepreneurs have been aimed at remodelling the German model. Entrepreneurs' arguments have focused on issues such as the need to resolve the problems of sick payment and obstacles to part-time working and, particularly, the introduction of better options for the creation of low-salary jobs. This discussion is basically moving in the direction of weakening traditional working arrangements based on a social democratic consensus model in favour of neo-liberal options for bargaining and power-play on the labour market. As in other western nations, neo-liberalism has been gaining the upper hand in the ideological arena in Germany too – almost to the extent that one might say: the ideology of the market has cleared the market of ideologies.

Looking closer at the changing industrial relations scenario in Germany, there is no doubt that the unions nowadays are on the defensive regarding the modernization of the German economy. During the last 10 to 15 years there has scarcely been a single topic on employment policy that the unions could feed into the debate as an indicator of a progressive, forward-looking approach.

Management, on the other hand, is clearly on the offensive and is supported in this by most of the economic 'wisdom' being generated by leading newspapers and journals. Most managers, however, have no wish to overthrow the strategic pillars of the traditional German model. There is, of course, a lot of aggressive public rhetoric on the necessities of radical change in the face of globalization and new technologies. However, if you take the time to analyse the more serious statements of leading managers, you will come across two truisms: 'You don't throw the baby out with the bath water' and 'You don't kill the goose that lays the golden eggs!'

The issue of management attitudes to the German model was dealt with in a graduate seminar at the Institute for Sociology in the University of Erlangen-Nuremberg in 1994, where a number of key management journals such as *Manager-Magazin, Capital* and *Wirtschaftswoche* were systematically investigated and several dozens of interviews with prominent industrial leaders and managers during the early 90s were analysed. This revealed not only clear support for cost cutting by the introduction of lean management methods, together with the need to cut back on labour costs by downsizing the welfare state, as well as the call for more 'friendly' state legislation on issues such as tax regulation and risk investments, but also a clear commitment of management to the pillars of the German model. These pillars include a high-quality and motivated workforce, stable, calculable industrial relations based on the existence of strong, reliable unions and a system of social security that guarantees general living conditions for all citizens in order to avoid social unrest and political radicalism.

A major characteristic of the history of industrial relations and industrial conflict in Germany since the end of the Second World War has been the premise that there should be 'No winners – no losers'. Even major industrial conflicts in the post-war period have not led to a crackdown on one of the conflict parties. A survey of major strikes in the metalworking and chemical industry in the 1960s and 1970s, as well as the latest conflicts over, for example, the Volkswagen '5000 × 5000' model, reveals how this pattern of avoiding total victory or total defeat of one of the parties involved has proved itself in practice. The 5000 × 5000 model describes Volkswagen's approach to manufacturing in a high-wage country increasingly under pressure from locations (most notably from within the multinational group) in Eastern and Southern Europe. The model aims at securing employment for 5000 workers in Volkswagen's north German plants by freezing their income at the level of DM 5000 (Sauga, 2001). The model has been praised for its compromise between global pressures on the cost structure of an MNC, on the one hand, and an employer's social responsibility for a region on the other, since Volkswagen is the major employer in large parts of the German federal state of Lower Saxony.

German managers' reactions to the Anglo-Saxon model characterized by Thatcherism and Reaganism have been ambivalent and paradoxical. They would like to enjoy some of the advantages of Anglo-Saxon pro-enterprise and pro-capital public opinion and state policy, but they are also aware of the negative aspects of the Anglo-Saxon model, such as low motivation of the workforce, low skills profiles of industrial workers and unstable social environments with respect to crime levels and so on. Boggis's paper in this volume on manufacturing in Wales illustrates some of the disadvantages of a competitive approach based on low labour costs, low social provision and a weak institutional framework to safeguard labour. It appears in Wales to be heralding the end of manufacturing operations as work is transferred abroad to countries with even lower labour costs and social provision. This demise is marked by extreme workforce insecurity and hostility to any cooperation between unions and management. Similarly, Tempel's study of British and German multinationals and their subsidiaries also gives examples of how a weak institutional framework of industrial relations in the UK tends to lead to job cuts, even where UK operations are judged more efficient compared to German plants, as in the case of the two research and development units. The UK model of Anglo-Saxon capitalism appears to lead to the deterioration of many of the basic requirements for high-skill manufacturing operations, such as high levels of cooperation in the workplace, high skills and quality, high-tech operations and high levels of productivity. As Geppert et al.'s study points out, the shift in two British subsidiaries of the investigated MNCs to pure service operations is seen as the only way out of a vicious circle of low level manufacturing performance.

Faced with a more competitive world market situation, German managers realize that the so-called German model has to change in some areas, but that the basic model needs to be kept alive as a resource for the future of *Standort Deutschland* (Germany's position as an attractive investment location). This is also the conclusion reached by Morgan et al. in their study of German multinational companies, who want to keep their position in the German system with all its advantages but have the flexibility to incorporate aspects from other systems with other advantages (Morgan et al., 2001). Most of German foreign direct investment is high tech and looks for new ideas and practices in its so-called 'vanguard subsidiaries' (Ferner and Varul, 2000). Taplin, in this volume, emphasizes some of the advantages for multinational companies in countries where the state plays a strong regulatory role, such as the possibility of externalizing training costs of workers and the maintenance of order and social peace. All capitalist development, and this includes the current globalization developments, requires stable national state systems. German companies have had their first successes in the German system and enjoy certain advantages as a result of the institutional and regulatory framework. Thus, whilst the public discourse on Germany's competitive position generally focuses on *Modell Deutschland* versus *Standort Deutschland*, that is, the German model being seen as threatening Germany's attractiveness to investors, a more subtle approach based on actual German management opinions shows the need for a combination of both *Standort Deutschland* and *Modell Deutschland*. The issue is one of how to modernize the German model and how to control for the unintended consequences of a partial modification of the model (see Schmidt, 1999; Baums et al., 1996).

New management orientations in Germany to the German model

A study conducted by the Akademie für Technikfolgenabschätzung des Landes Baden-Württemberg (see Abel et al., 1998) covering a broad range of German enterprises has shown that there are three types of management orientation on the *Standort Deutschland* versus *Modell Deutschland* issue. The first is found in many blue-collar-based industries, which keep firmly to the traditional highly regulated and consensus-oriented model. This orientation is clearly shown by management in firms such as Daimler Benz and Bosch, for example, and can be termed a *strategy of conservative remodelling*. Secondly, many white-collar-based industries are trying to replace essential elements of the 'old' model by new structures of control. Good examples of firms in this field are ABB and IBM. This position is described as a *strategy of aggressive remodelling*. Finally, some new 'knowledge-based' firms are trying to get rid of the old model more or less altogether and are looking for totally new structures of social integration and worker commitment. The software producer SAP is a prominent example of this approach, which may be described as a *strategy of radical remodelling*. Thus, the study reveals a clear differentiation of management positioning within Germany.

Other studies on developments in the German industrial relations system support the finding that the traditional system continues to operate in large manufacturing companies but is being undermined in the service sector, smaller companies and in the former East Germany (Hassel, 1999). Royle's study in this volume of McDonald's operations in Germany, on the other hand, shows a serious attempt being made by a foreign-owned company to avoid the German institutional framework altogether. US-based companies appear to be attacking national institutional frameworks in Germany, and in Europe as a whole, at both ends of the spectrum – in the low-skill, service-based sectors as well as in the high-skill, knowledge-based sector. Similarly, Tempel's study in this volume shows the frustration of UK-based multinationals with the German works council system due to its power to block changes to work organization and payment systems and the enforcement of a 'semi-perpetual bargaining relationship' between the works council and local management. This relationship is graphically illustrated in Geppert et al.'s work earlier in this book on a Finnish multinational in Germany, which is seeking to impose a standardized lean production model in a formerly German-owned escalator company. The Finnish management's battle with the works council is still ongoing. Thus, the advantages of the German model often seem to be less apparent to foreign investors in Germany and Tempel, in her contribution, provides evidence of foreign multinationals shifting investment to countries such as the Netherlands, where there is greater flexibility.

The social embeddedness of management in Germany

Studies of German top management have shown, as we have seen earlier, a differentiation in management positioning based on industry sector with regards to the viability of the German model. Ganter and Walgenbach in this volume point to a further differentiation between senior and middle management in Germany. Senior management are becoming increasingly more international in their training and experience and are therefore more likely to question the German model and recommend innovations culled from their international contacts. Middle management, on the other hand, are more national in their focus as they have close interaction with the German workforce and are part of the same dual training system for manufacturing with its highly technical focus. Tempel, in her paper, gives examples of German subsidiary-level management using German labour law to resist the implementation of British parent company policies on outsourcing in Germany. Geppert et al. also found this type of behaviour in the German subsidiary of the Finnish multinational, where subsidiary management worked together with the works council to resist the parent company's plans and had ultimately to be replaced by Finnish managers before any changes could be introduced.

Generally, German management is seen as being far more embedded in their national system than British management and German multinationals tend to be described as national companies with international operations (see Becker-Ritterspach et al., Geppert et al., Harzing et al., and Tempel in this volume). They do not fit the 'stateless' model of MNCs envisaged by many of the globalization theories; the stateless model is more applicable to the increasingly 'denationalized' UK MNCs (see Tempel). Instead, German MNCs appear to be rooted in industrial complexes within Germany and, at least in manufacturing, seek to replicate the production template they have found so successful at home in their subsidiaries abroad (see Harzing et al.'s paper). Lane, however, argues in a recent paper (Lane, 2000) that this attitude is changing as they go further down the path of internationalization. In her view, they will become less 'embedded' in the German national system and consequently more denationalized in their operations over time. As Harzing et al. indicate in their paper, however, Lane's study is based on the views of senior management and these views need to be verified by empirical investigation of what is actually happening in practice.

For the time being, the results of existing studies on the orientations of German management show evidence that many managers still take the German model seriously: the so-called German model has its advantages and losing them would be rather risky!

There are signs, though, that management is using the actual crisis situation in the German economy to try to loosen the grip of the old German model of regulation and consensus culture. Their 'ideal' would comprise being able to take for granted the positive qualities of the German model on the one hand, whilst incorporating new neo-liberal, Anglo-Saxon elements into the German economy in general and into the industrial relations arena in particular. Elements of this paradigm would include global information orientation and exploitation of foreign investment, local commitment by private enterprises on an economic, political, and cultural level, engagement in networking and alliances, both intra-sectoral and inter-sectoral in nature, the enlargement of economic activities and a deepening 'economism' or profit orientation within the organization and, finally, the avoidance of strategic 'lock-ins', for example regarding in-sourcing versus outsourcing (see Grabher, 1993).

Challenges to German management's 'sensible pragmatism'

This picture of a 'sensible pragmatism' of German management, revealed in the studies undertaken in the 1980s and the 1990s, indicates, we have argued, a deterioration in the success of the post war German model of industrial relations, on the one hand, but represents a new phase of exactly this same model on the other hand.

The debate and the bargaining processes associated with the famous working time model at Volkswagen in the mid-1990s, which was outlined earlier, can be seen as a particular milestone in the recent history of German industrial relations. Once again, at the start of the twenty-first century, it is another Volkswagen-based discussion on the new frontiers of employment policy that may become a further milestone in German industrial history. The political process and the final arrangements associated with the so-called Volkswagen 5000×5000 concept are clearly directed towards the new issues facing employment policy in the next decade. For example, how to integrate low salary payment with high qualification strategies and the necessities of flexible workforce use? How to keep and stabilize the central achievements of post-war employment policy in Germany and how to balance these against the need for adaptation to new globally and nationally produced problems?

Regardless of how we evaluate these milestones and other precarious arrangements in German industrial relations, the sensible pragmatism approach of German management developed in the 1990s is being further challenged as the new century begins. Along with ongoing technological progress and globalization, the socioeconomic impact of what could be termed 'shareholderization' has been dramatically destabilizing economic strategies and social interest consensus in Germany during the last few years. Although Mayer and Whittington have argued in this volume that the German business system is less amenable to finance-driven control of companies and shareholder value has not been uppermost in management's thinking in the past, pressure from the new internationalization strategies of German MNCs is leading to the increasing importance of these Anglo-Saxon business characteristics. Taplin, for example, in his contribution, points to the increasing 'Anglo-Saxonization' of the Deutsche Bank in recent months in the changes being made to the dual board system of corporate governance. This will impact on German companies, who traditionally rely on the long-term support of the German banks in terms of finance and also their representation on the companies' supervisory boards. The economic turbulence during the last decade in the Far East and South America and the end of the long boom in the US economy are also creating qualitatively new challenges for management in Germany that is, in all probability, going to be less and less German (see Jürgens and Rupp, 2002).

Conclusion

In conclusion, management activity and orientation is, by its very nature, historically 'embedded'. At the end of the twentieth century and at the beginning of the twenty-first century, economic and social policy in all the developed countries is faced with the triangular problem configuration of how to guarantee reproduction of a high-quality and highly motivated workforce whilst promoting innovative business activities in an environment where there is a high level of social welfare and a general perception of 'fair deals' in society as the basis for social peace.

Obviously, globalization and internationalization will force management into new frameworks of reasoning and action. National management cultures will erode in many branches and sectors of the economy. Companies such as Siemens, Bull, Olivetti, Sony, Philips and General Electrics are going to be less and less national in many respects. On the other hand, even multinational firms and so-called 'global players' have to work with regions and localities since 'the local is becoming a global resource'. This will most probably lead to a multitude of pragmatic economic and business strategies, not to so-called 'best ways' in terms of business recipes! Lorbiecki in her paper has looked at this complex process of combining globalization with diversity, both in terms of the workforce and the different societies that multinationals will be operating in, together with the management of national identity, whilst Becker-Ritterspach et al. and Geppert et al. provide evidence of the very different strategies for globalization which are emerging even within the same industry branch.

It seems likely that the era of 'national models' has ended. After the Second World War, we had the American model of success, then there was a German model in the 1960s and 1970s; for a short period of time an Italian and a Swedish model received some attention and in the 1980s we looked to the Japanese model to bring superior economic performance. Nowadays, the new Anglo-American model seems to fascinate many. But we should be cautious: all models have proven to be short-lived. It is probably high time to abandon a simplistic mode of model-based thinking altogether, as it has, all too often, acted as a break on creative thinking.

Globalization is, as stated earlier, forcing management to reason and act in new ways in all the developed economies to minimize the costs and maximize the benefits of operating in different local, national and regional environments. The studies in this volume have shown the very different approaches of MNCs to the challenges in terms of reorganizations and organizational change.

This volume has explored some of the idiosyncratic features of the British and German national business systems which do not appear to be made obsolete by globalization but may even be enhanced, as MNCs seek to exploit regional and national advantages and play to the strengths of particular business systems in their global operations. Adept local managers in the MNCs' subsidiaries will also seek to uphold the virtues of their own particular systems. It is, however, unlikely that a particular national business model can be heralded as a global solution for all businesses. This would, anyway, reflect a conservative perspective in a constantly changing international environment. Indeed, national business systems are themselves not static but are continually shifting and changing as they respond to new environmental challenges.

Note

This paper is based on a presentation made by Gert Schmidt at a research conference in 2001 entitled 'Management of Change in Multinational Companies: Global Challenges and National Effects', which was organized by Karin Lohr and colleagues in Humboldt University, Berlin and the Globe Research Group in Swansea. Karen Williams helped to expand the paper to include insights from this volume and elsewhere and contributed on language and style issues.

References

Abel, J., Braczyk, H.-J., Renns, C. and Töpsch, K. (1998) *Wandel der Arbeitsregulation*, Stuttgart.
Albrow, M. (1997) *The Global Age*, Stanford.

Baums, T. and Frick, B. (1996) *Co-determination in Germany: The Impact on the Market Value of the Firm*, Osnabrück.

Castells, M. and Hall, P. (1994) *Techno Poles of the World: The Making of the 21st Century's Industrial Complexes*, London/New York.

Ferner, A. and Varul, M. (2000) 'Vanguard' Subsidiaries and the Diffusion of New Practices, *British Journal of Industrial Relations*, March, pp. 115–40.

Grabher, G. (1993) The Weakness of Strong Ties: the lock-in of regional development in the Ruhr area" in Grabher, G. (ed) *The Embedded Firm. On the Socioeconomics of Industrial Networks*, pp. 255–77.

Hassel, A. (1999) The Erosion of the German System of Industrial Relations, *British Journal of Industrial Relations*, 37, 3: 483–505.

Hirst, P. and Thompson, G. (1996) *Globalization in Question. The International Economy and the Possibilities of Governance*, Cambridge.

Jürgens, U., Naumann, K. and Rupp, J. (2000) Shareholder Value in an Adverse Environment: The German Case, *Economy and Society*, Vol. 29.

Jürgens, U. and Rupp, J. (2002) *The German System of Corporate Governance – Characteristics and Changes*, Berlin (WZB discussion papers).

Lane, C. (2000) 'Understanding the globalization strategies of German and British multinational companies', in Maurice, M. and Sorge, A. (eds), *Embedding Organizations: Societal Analysis of Actors, Organizations, and Socioeconomic Content*, Amsterdam/Philadelphia: John Benjamins, pp. 188–208.

Markovits, A. (1982) *Political Economy of West Germany: The Model of Deutschland*, New York.

Morgan, G., Kelly, B., Sharpe, D. and Whitley, R. (2001) 'Multinationals as organisations', *ESRC Transnational Communities Programme Conference*, Warwick.

O'Sullivan, M. (2000) *Contests for Corporate Control: Corporate Governance and Economic Performance in the United States and Germany*, Oxford.

Porter, M. E. (1990) *The Competitive Advantage of Nations*, New York.

Sassen, S. (1996) *Losing Control – Sovereignty in an Age of Globalization*, New York.

Sauga, M. (2001) Taugt VW als Modell? *Der Spiegel*, 36, 3 September 2001.

Schmidt, G. (1999) Ajerca del futuro de los sindicatos en las avanzadas sociedades industriales europeas al final del sidlo XX., in Pries, L. and de la Garza, E. (eds) *Globalisación i cambios en las relationes industriales*, México.

Schmidt, G. and Trinczek, R. (eds) (1999) *Globalisierung – Ökonomische und soziale Herausforderungen am Ende des 20. Jahrhunderts*, Baden-Baden.

Streeck, W. (ed.) (1995) *Works Councils, Consultation, Representation and Cooperation in Industrial Relations*, Chicago.

Thurow, L. (1996) *The Future of Capitalism*, London.

Upchurch, M. (2000) The Crisis of Labor Relations in Germany, *Capital and Class*, 70.

Index